Values-Based LEADERSHIP

Susan Smith Kuczmarski
& Thomas D. Kuczmarski

PRENTICE HALL
Englewood Cliffs, New Jersey 07632

Prentice Hall International (UK) Limited, *London*
Prentice Hall of Australia Pty. Limited, *Sydney*
Prentice Hall Canada, Inc., *Toronto*
Prentice Hall Hispanoamericana, *S.A., Mexico*
Prentice Hall of India Private Limited, *New Delhi*
Prentice Hall of Japan, Inc., *Tokyo*
Simon & Schuster Asia Pte. Ltd., *Singapore*
Editora Prentice Hall do Brasil, Ltda., *Rio de Janeiro*

10 9 8 7 6 5 4 3 2

Library of Congress Cataloging-in-Publication Data

Kuczmarski, Susan Smith.
    Values-based leadership : rebuilding employee commitment,
performance, and productivity / Susan Smith Kuczmarski and Thomas D.
Kuczmarski.
        p.   cm.
    Includes index.
    ISBN 0-13-121856-5
    1. Leadership. 2. Corporate culture. 3. Employee motivation.
4. Employee empowerment. 5. Commitment (Psychology)
I. Kuczmarski, Thomas. II. Title.
HD57.7.K83 1994
658.4'092--dc20   94-35330
                                                         CIP

ISBN 0-13-121856-5

Prentice Hall
Career & Personal Development
Englewood Cliffs, NJ 07632
Simon & Schuster, A Paramount Communications Company

Printed in the United States of America

Dedication

To John, James, and Thomas

About the Authors

Dr. Susan Smith Kuczmarski is an educator, teacher trainer, group facilitator, and leadership trainer. She serves as executive vice president of Kuczmarski & Associates. She holds a doctorate and two masters degrees in sociology and education from Columbia University and an undergraduate degree from the Colorado College. Dr. Kuczmarski has taught at Columbia, Northwestern, University of Illinois, National-Louis University, and several small colleges. She was named an International Fellow of Columbia University, and is listed in *Who's Who in the World*. Seeing the need for norms and values within an international community, she trained new delegates from member countries at the United Nations. Her areas of expertise include innovation teaching methods, group processes and interaction, and shared leadership. She has developed and conducted leadership training programs for a variety of corporate and noncorporate groups.

Thomas Kuczmarski is president and founder (in 1983) of the mid-sized, Chicago-based consulting firm, Kuczmarski & Associates, recently named one of North America's "100 Leading Management Consulting Firms" by *Consultants New*. He is one of the country's top experts on innovation, management, growth strategies, and new-product development. He is regularly quoted and published in leading magazines and newspapers including *The Wall Street Journal, Fortune, Newsweek,* and *U.S.A. Today*. Before starting his own highly successful firm, Mr. Kuczmarski was a brand manager at Quaker Oats and then a principal at Booz • Allen & Hamilton. He holds two masters degrees in business and international affairs from Columbia University, where he was named an International Fellow, and a B.A. from the College of the Holy Cross. He has been a professor at Northwestern University's Kellogg Graduate School of Management and a lecturer at Columbia University's Executive Management Program. Mr. Kuczmarski is also the author of *Managing New Products: The Power of Innovation* (Prentice Hall), now in its second edition.

The Kuczmarskis live in Chicago with their three sons, John, James, and Thomas.

Introduction

Not so long ago, religion, schools, communities, and families created universal values and norms that carried over into organizational life. Now, these institutions are relatively weak and our values have eroded and changed. This values erosion has occurred in our work lives as well. While corporate America is chock full of rules, policies, and procedures, it is running on empty in terms of norms and values that can provide employees with a reason to believe in their work.

The great turmoil created by downsizing, mergers, and acquisitions has left many organizations in a state of flux. There is growing dissatisfaction with everything from Total Quality Management to worker-empowerment programs that have failed to live up to expectations. To make matters worse, even management doesn't totally believe in its own "fix-it" programs. Indeed, management's uncertainty about how to re-energize its companies has contributed to a lack of competitiveness in America. A values vacuum exists, and most employees are normless. This situation is poisoning corporate America. Leaders need to cultivate norms and values to regain employee commitment, high performance, and productivity.

The problems that plague society are mirrored in the workplace. The disintegration of the family unit and a corresponding erosion of values is paralleled by dysfunctional organizations. This book provides a compelling argument: Employees need values they can believe in. Without a reason to believe that is based on a set of common organizational norms and values, profits and productivity will decline—and our country's competitive position will erode.

A war needs to be waged. A war for values and norms. Normfulness rather than normlessness should be the trophy to the victors. Organizations in America need norms and values that employees can embrace and embody. It is not an impossible task. In fact, we've found that it's eminently manageable.

Our book will speak to the lack of norms and values in today's society and workplace. It will offer a variety of remedies for organizations in America to revive U.S. competitiveness. Everyone from CEOs to entry-level employees will learn how to create a reason to believe.

The Book's Message

A similar period of normlessness emerged at the turn of the century. Anomie was a term coined by the French sociologist Emile Durkheim in 1893. Durkheim observed that in the wake of the Industrial Revolution, increasing specialization of labor left individuals isolated from one another. Without human interaction, people found it impossible to develop and nurture group norms and values. According to Durkheim, anomie was caused by the lack of clear-cut norms and values that guide individual aspirations and group behaviors. He determined that isolated workers lost their sense of being part of a larger group or whole.

The term "anomie" explains the reasons for the growing dissatisfaction resident within U.S. corporations and organizations. There is little motivation for employees to perform well. The importance of each individual is overlooked; the criticality of norms and values is not recognized, and leaders have been unable to develop a values-ful mindset within their organizations. Most employees, from CEOs to mid-level managers, are fed up with their organizations' failures, top-down directives, and downsizing endeavors. They're ready for an alternative to the "That's just the way it is" management status quo.

Most important, senior management doesn't have the answers to fix this employee dissatisfaction. They've tried bottom-up planning, new incentives, teaming, and task forces. By themselves, these techniques don't solve the total problem.

The missing link is knowing how to develop shared norms and values that all employees embrace. This book will teach today's managers the necessary values-based leadership techniques to solve the problem of anomie. Senior management will need to learn how to work within a shared leadership construct. This means that multiple individuals throughout the organization take on various leadership roles in different dimensions and to varying degrees. There are no hierarchical reporting relationships or box-shaped organization chart designs—none is needed. With a cadre of leaders at all levels of a company—all of whom "report" to one another and to themselves—senior managers may query: "What holds the organization together?" The answer lies in developing a shared, agreed-upon, and clearly communicated set of norms and values that guide their daily behavior and methods of interactions with each other in the company. This book will provide a framework of how to implement this kind of "values-ful" leadership within organizations.

Why We Wrote This Book

As employees ourselves, we have worked for more than a dozen different organizations, have created and run two businesses, consulted for more than 100 companies, and raised three boys. Moreover, through our research with more than 200 employees and managers, our leadership seminars and our collective experiences, we have been exposed to and alarmed by the dire need to reinstill norms and values into organizations.

The book is based on several years of research with entry-level, mid-level, and senior managers and leaders from a mix of organizations. We interviewed individuals working at small organizations with only two employees to large bureaucratic organizations with over two hundred thousand employees. Throughout these settings, we discussed the topics of norms, values, and leadership.

The types of organizations we interviewed include investment and commercial banks, the U.S. Army, law firms, private industrial suppliers, hotels, government agencies (city, state, and federal), nonprofit and religious organizations, retailers, accounting firms, universities, medical service providers, restaurants, magazine and newspaper distributors, real estate brokerage firms, consumer packaged goods companies, small and large manufacturers, recording studios, advertising firms, and money management companies.

Furthermore, Susan's doctoral studies on group processes provide a solid theoretical framework for Tom's "real life" examples. Her research about how individuals learn to be members of both a small peer group and of society provides striking parallels to how employees learn to be productive members of a small work group and the larger corporate entity. Norms and values are crucial to the process.

In his growth management, innovation, and new-product development consulting assignments, Tom has worked with hundreds of companies. One critical aspect of his work has been to help clients establish appropriate norms and values that facilitate growth and innovation strategies. The techniques used to establish these norms and values and the case histories that showcase the techniques will be an integral part of the book.

Our purpose in writing this book is threefold:

1. To make people more aware of and help them understand the underlying problem that exists in organizations today;
2. To influence organizational leaders to reignite individual norms and values and develop a leadership style that nurtures a "values-ful" work environment;
3. To help employees gain meaning in their jobs and self-satisfaction from their work environments, which will result in increased competitiveness and effectiveness for their organizations.

This is not an altruistic mission. It's grounded in a holistic belief that the future viability of our country depends upon it. The resultant impact of bringing norms and values back to organizations can change the face and inner fiber of our organizations in the next century. Without it, many organizations will never reach their collective potential. Without it, many other organizations will simply fail. The need to bring norms and values back to American organizations heralds a call to action. We ask organizational leaders to at least be open to the proposed premises and ideas put forth in this book and to discuss them with their employees. Norms and values can serve as the needle and thread to eventually strengthen the fabric and give new shape to the American employee and workplace. For only through the infusion of norms and values into American organizations can we hope to once again restore the solid girders that the great American economy was built on.

It's our personal mission to help make at least a few organizations a better place to work and a more empowering environment for individual employees. If we achieve this, the writing of this book will be well worth it.

Values-Based Leadership may cause controversy with its provocative premise and thought-provoking new concepts. However, norms and values *are* the cure for anomie and the prescription for true employee empowerment. It is the antidote to the dysfunctional organization of today's society.

Susan Smith Kuczmarski
Thomas D. Kuczmarski

Acknowledgment

We would like to express our gratitude to Suzanne Lowe, who provided leadership and guidance at every phase of the project, and to Meridith Epstein, who lent her valuable editorial suggestions. In addition, we would like to thank the following professionals who helped shape this book: Rachel Vecchiotti, Peter Fritz, Jeff Swaddling, Darrell Douglass, Tim Koelzer, Scott Davis, Brenda Rinholm, Carl Bochmann, Craig Terrill, Barton Tretheway, Art Middlebrooks, Loreen Sieroslawski, Michael Petromilli, Peggy Walker, Eva Zelazowski, and Alexa Sehr.

Table of Contents

PART I — THE PROBLEM   1

Chapter 1

Chapter 2

Chapter 3

Chapter 4

PART II — THE FOUNDATION   71

Chapter 5

Part I
The Problem

Searching for a Reason
to Believe

Our Own Norms and Values

Eighteen years ago we married in a Roman Catholic Church. Having written our own vows separately, we presented them to each other in front of 350 people attending our wedding. We made a public statement that our marriage relationship was going to be different from so many others. Our intention was to establish a relationship that was grounded in a set of common values: trust, open spaces, mutual caring, and strong communication with each other. Many people in the reception later awkwardly asked: "When exactly in the ceremony did the priest marry you?" He didn't.

The point in marrying ourselves wasn't to rebel against the Catholic Church, but rather to make the marriage initiative a highly personalized one and to express our reasons to believe in each other as individuals and as partners. We wanted to establish norms and values to guide our relationship, nurture our individual growth, and create our desired family environment.

In effect, the set of values that we expressed on our wedding day provided a common ground of beliefs and a set of norms that identified ways in which we wanted to be treated and to interact with each other. These beliefs, values, and norms have helped us grow personally, professionally and as members of society. Some of our core personal values include:

- Consideration of others.
- Belief in pluralism.
- Open, expressive, and honest communications.
- Trust in each other.
- Desire to help other people.
- Optimistic view of the potential and "good" in others.
- Willingness to be vulnerable.
- Spending quality and quantity time with our children.
- Treating our children as three uniquely different individuals.
- Celebration of the differences in all people.
- Recognition of the need for positive feedback.
- Belief in spiritual power and need to cultivate it.
- Openness to convey love to men and women.

And guess what? It's worked. Sure we've had our hardships and a few downs with many ups. But the vows we made have endured. (See Exhibit 1–1). Our marriage continues to be nurturing, caring, and successful at providing each other with significantly positive feedback almost daily.

Searching for a Reason to Believe

We use the example of our wedding as a way to illustrate the importance of shared values as the foundation of a relationship, an institution, and, yes, even a job. Organizations need norms and values. Individuals need norms and values. And our "societal" organizations, such as families, churches, schools, and neighborhoods, need norms and values. The reason is clear-cut. Our organizations in this country are losing ground; they have become less competitive, less effective, and less rewarding to employee members. Individuals have an increased sense of alienation, isolation, and mistrust, with a corresponding decreased sense of self-confi-

EXHIBIT 1-1

Our Vows

Her Vows

If the expansion of happiness is the purpose of life,
Let us seek this happiness together, through our partnership;
Sharing the pain of personal discoveries, the joys of laughter,
Adjusting to given bends in the road and still retaining a simplicity of living,
Growing still stronger and deeper through a profound sharing and intense giving.

You have the qualities that I value: sensitivity, compassion and strength (of character and body).
You see the beauty in children, their inner sincerity and openness.
You understand the beauty of age, its learned wisdom and purpose.
You are everything I want, all that I need.
Let us be strengthened by a closeness to nature, to give a true appreciation of significance and beauty.
Let us be strengthened by a balance of physical, intellectual and spiritual concerns,
All the time remembering that which is essential to life comes from the heart.
If our hearts are rich, then we will be rewarded with a fuller, ever-growing relationship.

His Vows

No poetry or prose ever written can express my love towards you and intimate desire to be always with you.
For you, Susan, have already become one with me. My deepest concerns, hopes and dreams have already been unlocked by your beauty, sincerity and lovingness.
Our lives, separate from all external forces which might try to encroach upon our unique realm of happiness, will remain growing together and towards each other, while continuing to learn so very much from each other.
Our marriage—unique to all the world—will be filled with music, laughter, joy, disappointments, smiles and tears.
And all will blend into one.
As our marriage grows, I hope that I may become a more complete person through your eyes and my own. For, unless we both develop as individuals as well as partners—friends—we will not hold onto the feelings we know and understand in the present.
Our touching is real. So real, that our hearts, known only to each other, can be heard through our eyes and felt through our minds.
Ours will be different, for we both are, and all needs discovered for each other will be opened to fulfillment by the other's understanding of life and love.
Your givingness, I pray, will be returned in abundance through my knowledge of your beauty, and our fulfillment of each other.

dence, self-worth, satisfaction, and security. Anomie has set in. Our society is clearly failing, with crime accelerating, educational systems deteriorating, and families disintegrating on a daily basis. The situation is severe. Anomie is the cause.

Consequently, as depicted in Exhibit 1–2, we believe that anomie must be eradicated in order to improve our society, organizations, and individual self-worth. Anomie impacts each of these and ultimately makes our organizations dysfunctional. By resolving the anomic dilemma, we will be able to strengthen and fortify individuals, the organizations where they work, and our society. This self-perpetuating anomic disease permeates our total environment and, unless stopped, will continue to cause further erosion and degradation of the very institutions that have helped to build society as we know it.

Why can't work environments embrace a common set of values and norms in their dealings, attitudes, and commitments to employees? Why shouldn't the workplace become a largely personalized experience? We all spend 40 to 50 hours each week surrounded by people with whom we've been conditioned to assume sterile, corporate, and nonemotional relationships. When we both worked in the corporate world, we'd often be admonished, "Just roll with the punches; don't express emotion; and don't rock the boat." It's no wonder that most workers become apathetic, lethargic automatons in their jobs. We're all basically told, "Keep your mouth shut, do your job, and collect your paycheck." That would be about the same as telling your spouse, "Pay the bills, raise the kids, and make sure you love me." How callous! And yet, that same callousness is exactly how millions of employees are treated in organizations.

The current state of our work organizations perpetuates a feeling of helplessness on the part of most and an attitude of entrapment for many. Today many employees feel isolated, deceived, and alienated at work. Nothing personal, nothing emotional, and certainly nothing meaningful. They literally don't believe in their work. How can this situation possibly continue? Well, it can't. We've reached the max in what employees "can swallow," "make the best of," and "put up with." They are undermotivated and stifled. The lack of norms and values and ineffective leadership are negatively impacting their organizational performance and U.S. competitiveness.

EXHIBIT 1-2

The Anomic Dilemma

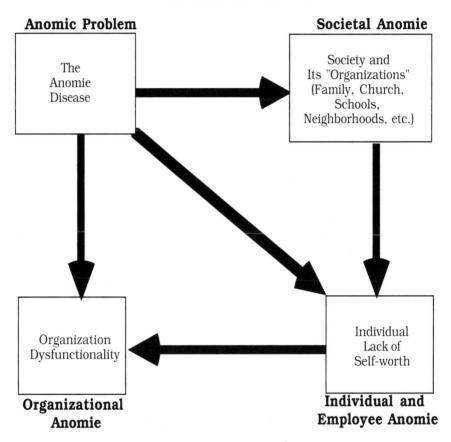

Anomic Problem

The Anomie Disease

Societal Anomie

Society and Its "Organizations" (Family, Church, Schools, Neighborhoods, etc.)

Organization Dysfunctionality

Organizational Anomie

Individual Lack of Self-worth

Individual and Employee Anomie

American Business Is in Trouble

As American business icons such as IBM, Sears, Borden, and General Motors continue to undergo massive internal restructuring and downsizing, the age-old norms of employment security have gone by the wayside. Employees feel betrayed, dismayed, confused, and short-changed. Previously successful corporations aren't cutting it. They're losing profits, losing market share, and losing the spirit, morale, and loyalty of their employee work force. The situation is worse than most are willing to admit. Many are even unaware of the gravity of this phenomenon. After a while, employees just get conditioned to accept things the way they are. They don't question, challenge, or try to change the situation. Most individuals feel virtually impotent compared to the omnipotence of their organizations and dominating management.

Many big companies continue to wallow in their organization's self-deception, believing that problems can be fixed by lowering costs, increasing productivity, and reengineering. How naive! These are short-term Band-Aids that quickly come off. Leaders try to brush away the problem when, in fact, major cavities exist.

Women are leaving corporations in droves to start their own companies, and downsizing has left organizations in varying states of confusion. Corporate restructuring has left some job functions overly specialized and some far too generalized. This condition leaves work meaningless. A creeping alienation transcends all levels of management within companies. Desolation is pervasive and rapidly spreading.

Many people have left the corporate workplace to start their own entrepreneurial business. They have a need for a values system that includes cooperative norms and community values. They have tried to "fit in" to a values-less work environment, but the challenge has been too great, the barriers too insurmountable. Consequently, the only route seemingly left is to form their own work environment and create the desired norms and values that satisfy their needs.

If an organization lacks shared norms and values, it's never going to develop maximum performance and productivity from its people—it takes more than fear of being fired or financial incentives to motivate employees today. This is the root cause of American organizations' suffering from falling revenues and domination by foreign competitors. Without shared norms and values, the workplace cannot bring its employees together to achieve a common goal.

Most employees *do* put up with such pervasive alienation or anomie and try their best to cope. But focusing on ways to cope needs to dramatically change. Rather than finding new methods to cope, we must change the work environment to one that fosters hope. Business leaders in this country need to instill a mindset and way of professional life that gives employees and managers a solid foundation of hope—hope for a caring, meaningful, and self-satisfying job that builds each individual's self-esteem, self-worth, and self-confidence. We need to make organizations credible and trustworthy to employees again. We need to infuse passion and emotion in our workplace. Our new watchword needs to become hope—not cope.

We need to undergo a fundamental shift that reestablishes values and beliefs in our personal and professional lives. We need a set of values that enables us to once again believe in our jobs, companies, and organizations; to believe in our families, churches, and our communities; to believe in our government. And most important, we need rock-solid values to once again believe in ourselves. More than ever before, we live in an age that necessitates our need to find reasons to believe. Who in this country today doesn't have hopes and desires for more happiness, greater self-contentment and a feeling that life needs to be better—more enriching?

For the most part, we all seek ways to better integrate and balance the multi-dimensionality and complexity of our lives. No one's existence is simple or easy. The struggle embraces the mindset of "keep on going, as someday things will get better." This struggle needs to reach its end. The battle is as difficult for the leader in charge of thousands of employees as it is for the newly minted entrepreneur who's seemingly only responsible for himself or herself. The condition of personkind today needs to change. And what's needed is revolutionary, not evolutionary. A few new programs, approaches, or new management styles won't solve the epidemic anomie that pervades our jobs, lives, and organizations of the 1990s.

Do you ever wonder if the people you work with every day really care about you? What do they think of you? Are you respected by coworkers? Do managers in your organization truly appreciate your efforts and contributions? How many people in your organization do you really like to be with every day at work?

It's hoped that the answers to these questions are mostly affirmative or positive. However, we continue to hear responses from managers and employees alike that suggest otherwise. Most employees severely question the intentions, actions, and motives of fellow workers. Distrust is rampant in many organizations. Disloyalty has become a new norm.

The way to fix this is by bringing norms and values back to organizations. This can be accomplished by involving all employees in the development of a set of values they can believe in and norms to guide their behavior. Organization leaders should nurture a common set of norms and values.

We need to change the way work is. In short, we need to give all employees a values base. But the process of developing norms and values to follow professionally takes time. The senior management of an organization cannot be the sole author of values and norms. This would be similar to laying down the Ten Commandments. Employees would view such a move as merely another set of meaningless workplace policies. Norms and values must be developed by virtually all employees—regardless of the size of the organization. The values need to be "bought into," and the norms must be endorsed by most employees in order to enhance the work environment.

Unless this is viewed as a collective undertaking of the entire organization, the norms and values won't gain any traction or provide a credible engine for change.

The essence of happiness—both personal and professional—ultimately comes from a feeling of self-contentment within ourselves. This state is driven by self-accepted and self-endorsed norms and values. Values provide reasons to believe on a daily basis; norms serve as guidelines for our behavior, interaction, and communication with each other.

What values could offer people a reason to believe? Values such as consideration of other people, thoughtfulness, kindness and respect for all individuals. What kind of norms could actually bring meaning to our workplace? Norms such as focusing on development of individuals within corporations rather than exploiting them.

We believe that the cultivation of shared norms and values is no longer an option for managers to casually consider. The fundamental existence of American organizations in the future will depend on it. Simply put: Identify values and beliefs, and shape norms to guide behavior and communication, or involuntarily choose extinction.

Filling the Leadership Void

Along with the need for new norms and values in the workplace is also the dire need for a radically new type of leadership. In most organizations in our country today, there is a severe dearth of leadership that can effectively provide employees with a reason to believe. Leadership is the missing link to tie norms and values together within an organization. It's the linchpin for developing a cohesive, motivated, and productive group of employees. It's the lever for maximizing the collective potential of individual employees.

But even good leaders are often stifled by anomie. Think of five leaders you know who have charisma, vision, effective interpersonal skills, motivational capabilities, and a clearly articulated norms structure and values system. Few come to mind. Right? Many leaders have yet to recognize that their business problems can, in part, be addressed by eradicating anomie and creating a values-ful culture. Others who do acknowledge the problem are unable to reconcile conflicting values and diverging norms. Many leaders try, but the anomic problem is so severe that little headway is made.

Leadership doesn't have to be the way you remember it. The days of autocratic managers who rule with an iron fist are surely gone. So, too, should be the days of emotionless, passionless, and impersonal leaders. A totally new construct needs to fill the leadership void. A values-ful culture needs to be encouraged by organization's leadership.

To help counteract anomie, we need leaders of our organizations to adopt five norms themselves to activate and convey a values-based mindset. These guidelines will serve as the platform for beginning to build a values-based organization.

1. Pluralize the workplace.

Organizations need to support, endorse, and appreciate the differences in people. These include differences in age, gender, ethnicity, religion, social background, personalities, intelligence levels, political beliefs, sexual orientation, race, dexterity, interpersonal skills, and the like. Expressions of diversity need to be appreciated, not judged and categorized. John Gardner, a Harvard professor, believes that everyone draws upon seven potential forms of intelligence. These include linguistic, logical, musical, spatial, kinesthetic, interpersonal, and intrapersonal forms of intelligence.

Consequently, employees come to an organization with a diverse set of different forms of intelligence. No one form is better than another. They're all different, bringing diverse perspectives, benefits, attributes, and power sources to the organizational picture. Leadership needs to encourage the diverse strengths of a pluralistic organization. It's no longer just an issue of representation or accommodation of diversity in the workplace. Leadership must cultivate and leverage diversity to maximize the effectiveness of the organization.

If diversity is endorsed, then the value and importance of all individuals in the organization increases. Only in a workplace that endorses pluralism will its leaders be able to fight anomie.

2. Serve as employee advocates.

Now this is a provocative goal. Leaders need to establish a mindset of serving employees rather than employees serving their organization's leaders. They must develop employee advocacy. This is an important step in setting the stage for eliminating anomie from the organization. Leaders need to change their own mindsets to understand that their new role is to help and support employees in every way possible.

An advocate is defined as "a person who argues for a cause; a supporter or defender; a person who pleads on another's behalf; an intercessor." The leader of the future needs to provide active support to the critical cause of employee satisfaction and enrichment. If employees perceive that management is fair, reciprocal, and striving to serve their best interests, employees will rally around the organization's goals. This means that leaders must help employees ignite their potential, unfold and grow their intelligences, determine their most effective roles, make their jobs meaningful and self-satisfying, and endorse agreed-upon norms and values.

Think about it. We could eliminate all unions if leadership took on a real sense of employee advocacy. Employee contracts could be eliminated if employees trusted leadership to be their personal advocate. While the role of leader as servant has been cited as a new concept for management, we hope the role of leader as employee advocate will become a new management mindset rather than just conceptual philosophy.

3. Be a socratic teacher.

In order to provide learning-ful work environments, leaders need to become teachers. But it is essential that they become socratic teachers, asking questions to elicit understanding. The key to a learning-ful organization is to have employees apply their skills, knowledge, previous experiences, and intelligences to solve problems, suggest solutions, or take specific actions. The role of leader as socratic teacher is to help employees learn through self-discovery. This form of learning has "staying power." It provides the ability to "use" learning over and over again, applying it to different problems, decisions, and situations.

Thus, the socratic teacher creates environments where people learn through their own accomplishments and mistakes. This, of course, requires a risk-taking culture where failures and trial-and-error initiatives are encouraged and, in fact, rewarded.

The socratic teacher-leader needs to provide continuous positive feedback to reinforce learning and its application. Carrots rather than sticks should be the norm for motivating employees in the future. By providing positive feedback, incentives, and reinforcement, employees feel more open to express their values and proactively contribute to the organization. Socratic leaders encourage employees to excel as individuals. Without a belief in individuality, norms and values are rootless.

4. Bridge people to a mission

The verb "bridge" has been carefully chosen. To set up a bridge there must be two free-standing areas or entities that will support it. The same is true for the effective leader who must try to connect or link each individual to the organization. All employees need to design and build a bridge from their values to the organization. These values will ultimately enable an entire work force to understand *why* they go to work in the morning *and* feel good about it.

We frequently hear from younger people about to join an organization: "I want to make an impact; I want to feel as if my work contributions will really count; I want my own personal impact to be felt by the organization." These comments support the benefit of bridging employees to the organization's mission, goals, and achievements. Employees *want* to help their organization establish its mission and achieve its goals. They *want* to feel as if they are making a personal and individualized contribution to its success.

Leaders need to make this happen. By casting employees in the right roles, giving them the training and the disciplined freedom to activate these roles, and rewarding them based upon performance, a bridge to the mission will be built.

5. Evoke professional passion

Leaders need to have professional passion. They need to convey excitement, warmth and emotion in what they do, how they speak, how they act and in all they communicate. Charismatic passion serves as a catalyst for breathing enthusiasm into a values-based organization. Leaders need to help employees get excited about their work, take pride in their jobs, and feel emotionally committed to their colleagues. Expressing emotion rather than suppressing it needs to become a new leadership norm.

Leaders need to reenergize the work force in order to make companies more productive, effective, competitive, and ultimately profitable. Future leadership calls for instilling group-developed norms and values to guide individual behavior, establishing a "values fabric" for employees to adhere to, and providing shared group expectations within the entire organization.

At the beginning of this chapter, we described our own wedding vows as an illustration of a decidedly successful nonanomic institution: a marriage. To achieve similar success in our institutions of work we must allow individuals to activate their personal values, use individual values as the fabric of our organizations' norms and values, and empower leaders who can use values to rejuvenate organizations and employees. Our work organizations can—and must—embody a set of values that will erase anomie and give workers a reason to believe. Until this happens, corporate America will remain in trouble.

Chapter 2

Facing Up to Anomie

anomie ('an - ∂ - me) (1) The lack of purpose, identity, or values in a person or in a society—disorganization, detachment, or rootlessness. (2) Normlessness—condition of society characterized by a breakdown of norms that rule the conduct of people and assure the social order. (3) Personal unrest, alienation, and uncertainty that comes from a lack of purpose or ideals.

Jim Michaelson, the president of a small, growing manufacturing company, recently conveyed to us his confusion regarding low employee morale. He laments:

I just don't get it. We have a business mission, operating plan, and long-range plan. We pay our people well; we give them some extra bonuses when they exceed expectations, and we publish a monthly employee newsletter to keep them informed. For cripes sake, we even have a companywide Christmas party and summer picnic for their entire families. I don't want to sound bitter, but how much more do they want? They don't know how lucky they are to have a good-paying job. Yet all I ever hear is complaints.

Sound familiar? All too often we talk with organization leaders who truly miss the point. Employees are no longer satisfied with just a paycheck. The Depression is over—it's fifty years behind us. Employees want more.

> I'm tired of going to work every day and never feeling as if anyone ever listens to or cares about *me*! The focus is always on achieving the financial numbers and rarely on developing the people who generate the numbers.
>
> —*a 10-year-veteran at this same manufacturing company*

Jim's employees *do* want more, and they earnestly deserve more. They need a work environment that makes them feel good about themselves, their contributions to the organization, and their job activities. They deserve meaningful and fulfilling relationships with coworkers and managers, frequent recognition and feedback and, overall, a sense of belonging and being an integral part of an organization. They need to feel important and special. They need a reason to believe.

The problem that exists today is fourfold: employees are unhappy at work; organizations are failing; society has an eroding values base; and individuals are in a state of anomie. The time has come to rectify this debilitating situation and fix it before it's too late.

Workers of all types need a set of values or beliefs they can hold to. Values that provide employees with professional passion, inspiration, emotion, and motivation. While a mission and operating plan are important tools for describing the purpose and direction of an organization, beliefs and values are vital for providing employees with behavioral and decision-making direction. Beliefs and values are the fuel that can truly drive the competitive engine.

Organizations today haven't created a values system that most employees endorse and adopt as their internal "pledge" to one another. Values haven't been defined to describe the organization's external beliefs toward its customers, distributors, shareholders, and other constituencies. Moreover, organizations have yet to understand the power of developing norms to shoulder the weight of values so that employees have guidelines for decision making, communication, and interpersonal behavior.

Most organizations just give lip service to all of this. We have heard many managers say, "Oh, we understand our employees need to belong to a caring organization. We have a set of values that we came up with over a year or so ago. We even distribute our values annually at the employee banquet." Big deal! Developing a *list* of values is virtually meaningless. These "values" were in fact dictated from the "top" echelons of management "down" to the employee masses. No wonder the list just sits and collects dust and is even potentially harmful to the morale of an organization. The challenge is to find ways to involve employees in the development of a common set of values, reinforce these values, and live them on a daily basis.

So why don't more organizations do this? The answer is because a destructive disease has tainted most organizations—a pervasive disease that we call anomie.

What Is Anomie?

Anomie means alienation. It results from individuals and groups not having values and norms. Anomie leaves individuals feeling isolated, disillusioned, and disjointed. It leaves organizations dysfunctional, divided, and disrupted. It stems from groups and individuals that lack cohesive social and interpersonal guidelines for interaction. Without a solid foundation of values or beliefs, meaningful norms cannot be developed. Without an accompanying set of norms to guide interpersonal communication and behaviors, anomie reigns and runs rampant.

When anomie creeps into an organization, it weakens the ties and social bonds that usually hold workers together and keep them going. When people do not feel compelled to conform to established norms, social cohesion and organizational integrity break down. Anomie appears when individuals are not in some way connected as a group. There is no sense of personal identity, mission, or purpose. Norms and values can provide "bonding power" for individuals within a group. Anomie dilutes and waters down the social glue.

Individuals, organizations, and our society urgently need to become aware of the threatening existence of anomie. Its impact has already been dramatically felt, causing detrimental harm to individuals, their self-worth and communities. It is a complicated dilemma that deserves national attention and individual priority. To a great extent, however, it remains a hidden and infrequently discussed social disease. Anomie stands virtually free and clear of public recognition. Most organizations—as Jim Michaelson discussed earlier in this chapter—don't even recognize that anomie pervades their corridor walls, is prevalent in team meetings, and holds captive the hearts and souls of employees. And if they do catch a glimmer of the symptoms of anomie, it is brushed under the rug and ignored.

We are currently living in a values void. While the topic of and need for values has been frequently raised, we have not yet as a society been able to address this need. Values are continually discussed, but no steps have been taken to initiate and activate a values adoption process.

Does Anomie Really Exist?

The American workplace is filled with people who go about their assigned tasks with little enthusiasm, energy, or creativity. Most are demoralized by their uncertainty about or lack of belief in their jobs and organizations. Meaning and personal satisfaction from their work is gone. Employees feel alienated, isolated, and disconnected from their apathetic colleagues and organizations.

Look around you—how many of your colleagues at work are frustrated about coming to the office or the shop every day? How many of them keep to themselves or bad-mouth management? These are definitive signs that anomie has permeated the workplace.

While new management techniques continue to surface—total quality management, reengineering, quality circles—they all fizzle out and, over time, become ineffective. You just can't plug in a new management technique and expect it to zap all employees to have a changed mindset. This is because the very foundation of the organization, its values structure and norms, is missing, broken, or weakened.

Is the current situation really that severe? Ask yourself how satisfied *you* are with the organization where you draw a paycheck. Do you have a professional passion for your work? Do you participate in decision making? Do you feel as if you are making a significant contribution to the growth of the organization? Have your self-confidence and self-worth increased as a result of your job environment? Do you feel as if you're respected by your fellow employees and managers? Does your job provide you with personal self-satisfaction and intrinsic value? Do others in your organization truly care about your needs, values, and aspirations? Do you feel as if you're in control?

The answers to these often gut-wrenching questions will most likely leave you disturbed and anxious. Unfortunately, most people respond with a resounding *no* to each of them.

A lack of innovation, eroding competitive positioning, a disillusioned, torpid work force, and severe risk aversion by individual employees are typical symptoms seen in organizations that are void of a values-ful culture. Most seriously, employees within these types of companies and organizations watch their "American Dream" disintegrate in front of their eyes.

As a highly paid executive with a leading corporation, Tim has a challenging, fast-track job that most managers would kill for. Not only is the job in line with Tim's career goals, but it dovetails with his experience and expertise. Tim has the right pedigree for the position—an MBA from a top business school; eight years' experience with a leading financial firm, during which time he worked his way up to partner; recruited by his current employer ten years ago, another rapid rise through the corporate ranks to senior vice president of marketing. He is well liked by his superiors and subordinates, is regularly included in elite top-management strategy meetings, and is on the board of his industry's leading association.

Why, then, is Tim simply going through the motions at work? Why is he willing to settle for mere complacency both from himself and from his subordinates? Why is he cynical about management directives and unable to marshal his creativity to come up with innovative solutions to difficult problems? Why did Tim tell his headhunter to "shop him around and look for the highest bidder"? Where is his loyalty to his organization, his pride in doing a superior job?

The answer to all these questions has to do with norms and values. Or, more specifically, the absence of norms and values from his organizational life. All the traditional rewards and challenges are no longer sufficient for Tim. And his participation in his company's gimmicky employee productivity programs has still left him feeling flat. Tim's organization has unknowingly failed to provide him with an environment that meets his needs. He has nothing left to believe in. Abundant perks and a paycheck can't fill the void. His company no longer "stands" for anything. There are no norms to guide his behavior that he can proudly follow, such as consideration for fellow workers or an acceptance of honest failures. There are no values that the company has made its own, such as integrity even at the cost of a lost sale. There's no passion for a job well done.

Without these norms and values, Tim has become nothing more than a mercenary. While he is motivated by money, he is not motivated to work with the requisite energy, enthusiasm, and creativity that defines the highly productive worker. And why should he be? If there is nothing to be committed to or proud of, why break his back?

Tim would break his back for the right organization. Put him in a setting where positive norms are established and shared values are espoused, and he would flourish.

The lack of values and norms has victimized every type of organization. It is not only the large Fortune 500 corporations who have been affected, but small entrepreneurial companies, law firms, banks, retail stores, government agencies, associations, schools, even restaurants. Few organizations are immune. But the disheartening news is that in most organizations, senior managers and employees are virtually unaware of their "values-less" state. They try to cure the disease with programs and strategies that, based on a misdiagnosis, don't work. Employees such as Tim are not looking for yet one more patronizing program to serve as a proxy for the meaning they want from their jobs.

The proof that this values-less ailment—anomie—is prevalent within our organizations is underscored by talking with workers themselves. We asked two hundred employees how they felt about their jobs and their workplace. We tried to uncover their true feelings, often overlooked, overshadowed, and underplayed within their organizations. A candid discussion with a cross-section of employees on this topic taught us some disheartening lessons.

Employees *want* meaningful, self-fulfilling jobs. They want their organizations to be responsive to their needs and to enable their co-workers to be empowered. People make huge life investments in their jobs. They want greater respect as individuals and far greater recognition for their contributions, achievements, loyalty, and dedication. That doesn't seem to be asking too much. Nor does it seem too much to expect from the very organizations that house these individuals for forty to fifty hours each week.

Over a decade ago, an energetic twenty-eight-year-old employee of a financial services firm entered that job filled with pride, high esteem, and unflagging loyalty to the organization. His enthusiasm for the company was so high that he was convinced that some day his own name would be added to the corporate name of the organization. He worked prodigiously, served his clients well, and always supported his colleagues in a team-building way. When he left five years later, his pockets had more money in them, but his heart and soul were empty. He left that firm with his self-confidence broken, aspirations to someday lead that firm squashed, and his spirit and enthusiasm washed away. This real-world example is endemic of our unhealthy organizations and their debilitating impact on individuals.

This needs to change. Even more important than the profound economic reasons for curing this disease are the basically human and socially responsible reasons for doing so. Individuals feel isolated. Social relationships are fragmented. Our society has lost its cohesiveness. Our schools have become caretakers. Our families have separated into disparate pieces.

And without revolutionary change in our workplaces—a fundamental shift in organizational principles and practices—our organizations will gradually, over time, deteriorate and crumble as well. We've already seen the erosion of the once-renowned American "competitive edge."

Anyone who doubted the potential for catastrophe probably assumed that nothing could hurt IBM, Sears, and urban public-school systems. External Band-Aid solutions won't be enough to reverse this pervasive internal cancer. The real problem is not external. It's inside. The "heart and soul" in most organizations is missing—the norms and values that can propel and guide individual and organizational growth are nowhere to be seen. Hope for and belief in a caring, meaningful, and self-satisfying work environment needs to be shared by all employees. Professional passion needs to be infused into the workplace.

We don't mean to make the solution seem easy. It took quite a while for organizational norms and values to erode, and it will take some time to restore them. But it can be done, and this book will provide a model for doing so—a model called values-based leadership.

Values-based leadership can help to restore these norms and values. It can do so without piling on burdensome rules, regulations, and policies, but by creating and endorsing a new belief system.

Before exploring this system, let's first look at anomie within an historical context. Today's erosion of norms and values in the workplace parallels a societal situation described more than 100 years ago.

The History of Anomie

The origin of anomie is attributed to Emile Durkheim, a nineteenth-century French sociologist. The term anomie has been most widely recognized in his work, *The Division of Labor,* published in 1893. Durkheim observed that in the wake of the Industrial Revolution, increasing specialization of labor left individuals feeling isolated from one another. Without human interaction, people found it impossible to develop and propagate cultural norms and values. According to Durkheim, the lack of clear-cut, agreed-upon norms and values left groups without guidelines to shape behavior and conduct.

The ancient Greeks used the word "anomos" as an adjective meaning lawless. Their meaning, somewhat similar to Durkheim's, conveyed the connotations of normlessness, immorality, suffering, and rootlessness. To the Greeks, anomos implied a condition of psychological madness and mental turmoil. It was a painful condition felt by individuals as well as by certain groups in society. Thus, Durkheim's century-old definition of anomie related to thoughts, attitudes, and actions that caused social "contamination" and moral pollution.

Durkheim determined that isolated workers lost their sense of being part of a larger group or whole. The positive feelings of supportiveness and the mental and emotional stimulation that comes from group membership disappeared as labor became more specialized. In Durkheim's classic work, *Suicide*, published in 1897, he showed that the areas with the highest rates of suicide in Europe were the least integrated socially. These people lived in a state of anomie. Without a support structure based on a common set of values, socially deviant acts or even suicide occurred. He observed that alcoholism, drug addiction, and various mental disorders were frequent manifestations of anomie.

Durkheim also discussed the idea of "dual personality," suggesting each person has two consciences. The first involves our individual personality. When we act out of self-interest, our actions and conduct reflect individual needs and concerns. The second involves our membership in a group or society. When we act as a group member, our actions and conduct reflect group needs and concerns. Norms are defined by our membership in the group.

Durkheim viewed anomie as a consequence of "egoistic individualism." This was a focus on satisfying the ego needs of the individual at the exclusion and sacrifice of focus on the group. In short, anomie means self-vested rather than group-responsive. It describes an orientation that centers around individual selfishness, downplaying the importance of group cohesiveness.

Durkheim optimistically saw cures for anomie, however. Anomie could be reduced by developing a values formula that prescribed moral and behavioral guidelines for individuals and groups. He saw an anomic antidote coming from a joining together of both individual and group needs. This would require balancing the egoistic needs of individuals with the collective needs of the group. Anomie could be corrected if both needs were addressed together.

We also believe that for anomie to be eradicated, a genuine equality needs to exist among individuals. This "genuine equality" will become an important tenet surrounding our ultimate solution. It suggests that every individual be elevated to an equal plane with dignity and acceptance. It reflects an intrinsic belief that indeed all persons are created equal within a pluralistic society. The solution, though, will require more than just imposing norms upon a group of individuals. Rather, it will require a total restructuring of the footing upon which all group members stand. Organizations will need to begin by realizing all group members stand equally. Not one individual is "taller" or "higher" than another.

Durkheim's theory of anomie is as applicable and relevant today as it was one hundred years ago. Though times certainly have changed, the condition of normlessness remains the same. It's not that organizations have suddenly forsaken norms and values; it's rather that society has done so continually and insidiously.

Vanishing Codes of Conduct

Not too long ago, individuals had a lot of help in establishing norms: the extended family and family rituals, neighborhood and community leaders, church groups and religious doctrines, and schools and teachers. These institutions and people used to provide each of us with governing behaviors—parameters about what we should and should not do, what was right and what was wrong behavior. We knew what to believe in, and we had good reason to believe.

Those parameters have largely disappeared. Not only have institutions such as churches, schools, and families lost much of their influence over individual behavior, but the increase in divorces, crime, and fragmented families have turned many former "believers" into agnostics.

Organizations, as microcosms of society, mirror these trends—high turnover, mobility, and job-switching have had an especially negative impact on companies of every type. To understand this impact, you don't have to look any further than the downsizing mania that pervades most organizations today. It seems as if every day brings news of another company "rightsizing" thousands of workers. Walk through the corridors of these companies after the downsizing and you'll see morale as low as it can go. But the morale hasn't plummeted just because fellow employees have been fired; it's sunk because all the accepted and established norms and values have been exposed as myths. We know of one national retailer that downsized and centralized its management, turning division presidents (who had previously managed their groups with distinct but effective styles) into corporate staff with greatly diminished authority. Not only were these former organizational leaders dispirited by the norm-shaking changes, but their employees were aghast at the brutality with which a formerly humanistic, entrepreneurial culture was turned into a profit-hungry, callous one. The company quickly experienced a mass exodus of key executives, went into bankruptcy, and has tried to reorganize unsuccessfully to date.

It doesn't have to be this way. The opportunity exists for organizations to reestablish values and norms through their mission, management style, compensation, leadership, and empowerment strategies. But they can't do so without a unified approach that sends and reinforces a message about what they stand for and what types of behavior are acceptable.

The Relationship Between Norms and Values

Values are the shared goals, beliefs, ideals, and purposes of the group. Values often evoke inner convictions among group members. But, in order for a group to maintain a set of values, the group must establish norms that shape and influence the behaviors, attitudes, and activities of its members.

Norms are expected behaviors by members of a group; they are group-decided codes of conduct. A norm is a standard to guide group behavior. It is a predisposition or an attitude on the part of a group to think, feel, and act in a particular way. Norms occur in groups, in contrast to attitudes, which are held by individuals. An example of an attitude is an employee feeling friendly toward another co-worker. The employee is supportive, helpful, and nurturing. If this individual's attitude is shared throughout the entire group, then it serves as a group norm. An example of a norm is a company establishing a culture where employees are expected to be considerate, respectful, and supportive of each other.

Norms involve shared expectations. Norms are the embodiment of group "agreements." When a norm is present, most group members know that their attitude is also held by others and that the others expect them to display that attitude and to think and act accordingly.

Norms don't just happen; they emerge from a three-step process.

- First, there needs to be expression—an honest and openly vulnerable exchange of feelings and emotions between individuals in the group.

- Second, individual group members need to interpret and personally internalize the messages expressed.

- Third, there is a compromising and consensus-building phase where each group member ultimately reaches agreement on the norms and values of the group.

Sociologists have connected the absence of clear norms with individuals' feelings of alienation. If there are very few effective norms or standards guiding personal behavior, then the organization and its behavioral codes of conduct have broken down. This state of normlessness has a devastating impact on the emotional condition of the individual, for whom there are few guidelines and few expectations shared with others. If norms are ambiguous and inconsistent in an organization, expecting employees to work together in productive teams is unrealistic—even detrimental.

Employees on an Island

Isolation runs parallel with anomie. Without norms, people believe that they live and work on an island—totally disconnected psychologically and emotionally from the group, even though physically they are part of one. In order to overcome anomie, one must be able to become a member and feel a part of a group or team. The challenge is determining how best to relate to and interact with other members of the group. In turn, this requires that each member of an organization learns how to interact effectively with each other member. While identifying how best to "fit in" to a group is hard enough, you must also compromise to achieve integration rather than isolation.

Over time, group members have the potential to develop a sense of community. This "community" can be defined as a group of individuals who share common goals, experiences, mission, vision, likes, dislikes, and, most important, values. Without a shared set of norms and values, feelings of isolation are perpetuated and anomie continues.

Schizophrenia exists today in the workplace. Employees have become disconnected from their organizations. There are only superficial connections to the workplace provided by paychecks and the need for employment security. Eventually, this disorder impacts the individual's level of performance and overall productivity. The schizophrenia causes a fragmented series of behaviors from one day of corporate life to the next. By Thursday, employees are able to cope again with their job situation only because the ensuing weekend is just around the corner. However, Monday through Wednesday typically represent "rough" days at the office that are filled with emotional chaos, the "usual" politics, and snafus with communications, directions, and expectations. Without a set of agreed-upon values and norms, behavior and communication become random, inconsistent, and arbitrary. Employees never know from one day to the next how they will be treated by managers and vice-versa. Signals are mixed, communications are misinterpreted, and behavior becomes erratic. People tend to become more and more isolated from each other.

In short, revolutionary and aggressive change needs to be ignited within most organizations. A fundamental and basic shift in the underlying principles, beliefs, and norms of an organization will become a critical component for future organizational survival.

Where, Oh Where, Did Our Values Go?

"In our toughest neighborhoods, on our meanest streets, in our poorest rural areas, we have seen a stunning and simultaneous breakdown of community, family, and work, the heart and soul of civilized society," syndicated columnist Ellen Goodman wrote in January 1994. This observation depicts well the rampant and epidemic disease of anomie that pervades our values fabric today. Values used to be sneezed at or jokingly sneered at as "motherhood" and "apple pie." No more. Rather, values are beginning to be recognized as the essential core of group cohesiveness and group identity. Now we're beginning to see that common values can serve as the super-strength glue holding groups of people together.

Ellen Goodman continues:

> Not long ago, the language of values was spoken almost exclusively by conservatives. Not anymore. Values provide the link with which to connect health care, welfare reform, crime, jobs. These issues are girders to shore up an infrastructure rocked by the earthquakes of social change.

> The cracked societal foundation which currently supports our values structures needs a lot of bricks and mortar. But the process of fixing our values platform needs to begin on an individual and personal basis. People need to be more expressively open about their personal values. Without this candid and, at the same time, vulnerable willingness to discuss our beliefs, group values will remain fragmented.

Does Your Organization Have Anomie?

Remember back to the last time you jumped out of bed in the morning and really looked forward to and were excited about going to work. Depending upon your age, this experiential feeling probably occurred several years ago—when you started your first or a subsequent new job. When you start a new job, you feel a certain exhilaration, anticipation, and excitement. Why? The answer is simple. You're instinctively hoping that this work environment will provide you with self-satisfaction, self-confidence, and a feeling of accomplishment. Unfortunately, within a matter of a few months, this vision of hope is shattered and anomic reality once again sets in. To determine whether anomie exists in your own organization, take the following anomie quiz.

EXHIBIT 2-1

Does Your Organization Have Anomie?

Score 0, 5, or 10 points for each question
(0 - incorrect, 5 - partially correct, 10 - totally correct)

1. Loyalty is not rewarded by my organization. _____

2. Compensation does not reflect individual performance or accomplishments but rather company performance. _____

3. Effective communications and meetings among employees and management are infrequent. _____

4. Profit achievement represents the priority "value" within my company. _____

5. Caring for and consideration of others is not a visibly employed value. Few people ask personalized questions of each other. _____

6. Values and norms are rarely, if ever, discussed within my organization. _____

7. My fellow employees often appear frustrated, angered, or apathetic about their work or managers. _____

8. People tend to keep to themselves and bolt out the door at the end of the day. _____

9. Personalized recognition and positive reinforcement are not management's usual style. _____

10. My fellow employee turnover is relatively high because people don't particularly like working at the organization. _____

Score

Save it	70+	Serious anomic illness pervades your organization
Cure it	50–70	Anomie has crept in and is at risk of spreading
Arrest it	20–50	Anomie is beginning to emerge
Prevent it	Under 20	You're healthy!

How did your organization score? Do you see any signs of anomie? When values are missing from an organization (or if the primary value is self-vested interest by the people at the top), anomie sets in and begins to pervade the entire organization. It's like a chronic and highly contagious disease—never knowing whom it will "hit" next. Going forward, organizations need to recognize and believe that the only truly effective way to fortify, strengthen, and grow their organizations is by motivating and cultivating their most valuable asset—people.

Values and norms need to be instilled within organizations. Employees must be involved in this process so that they embrace and emotionally rally around them. It is not such a formidable challenge or impossible task. In fact, there are scores of organizations, both large and small, that have found ways to change this cancerous state. The key is for management to believe in and make a commitment to complete holistic change. This, of course, requires organization leaders to be open, vulnerable, and responsive. By instilling values and norms in every aspect of our workplace—from creating values-ful products to establishing a values-ful culture—we can hope to cultivate work environments that enable employees to grow, develop, achieve, and once again believe.

It's naive simply to state that values and norms will fix our social ailments. On the other hand, without getting down to the fundamental roots of our problem, that is, *a lack of values*, social programs, reforms, laws, and policies really have no grounding for improvement. Establishing, agreeing to, and living by empowered norms and values is the rudimentary first step in moving personkind up a notch that allows for civilization to move forward again.

Start with Individuals

As we are now entering the twenty-first century, we feel that 100 years is long enough to keep Emile Durkheim's concept of anomie hidden in the closet. We need to develop a heightened awareness and realization that anomie will gradually cause extinction of American corporations as we have known them—the corporate "suicide" rate continues to accelerate. Consequently, now is the appropriate time in our maturing stage of corporate growth to introduce values-based leadership to the business community. In December 1992, a *Chicago Tribune* article highlighted this problem. "Lost in the hand-wringing about American economic decline is the realization that new ground rules are being created almost daily between workers and bosses. As a result, there is a need for a new social compact between employees and workers: a compact that restates how much companies and workers can expect from one another, and how much help they can realistically rely on."

More important, the one steadfast organizational value that employees used to be able to count on in the past is vanishing. The long-held belief that stability and job security is inherent within large U.S. companies is now nothing more than a myth—even it has disappeared. Employees can no longer value job security, as firings and layoffs now occur in the tens of thousands.

Granted, global competition, information systems, new technological advances, and tight credit have had a major impact on corporate profits. But management seems to be moving further and further away from investing in their primary asset: their people. While training budgets are certainly increasing and should be viewed as a form of people investment, to a great extent, they serve only as a Band-Aid to the hemorrhaging caused by the lack of norms and values. A 1992 report of business experts compiled by UCLA's Institute of Industrial Relations cites, "Harsh business conditions have made it easier to get workers to accept cost-cutting. However, each new cut undermines credibility in those companies that try to manage on the basis of mutual respect." Workers soon feel betrayed as company management focuses more attention and capital on ways to cut costs instead of finding ways to increase worker productivity and overall job satisfaction.

Values-based leadership calls for an approach that instills group-developed norms and values to guide individual behavior. It establishes a values fabric for individuals to adhere to and provides shared group expectations for the entire organization. To make values-based leadership work, senior management must accept a shared leadership construct. This means that each individual in the organization, in effect, takes on a leadership role in some dimension. There is no hierarchy—it is unnecessary.

In most large companies, hierarchical reporting relationships have always been a necessary evil because solidifying norms really don't exist. If enriching and nourishing norms and values are lacking, the void is filled with a hierarchical and highly structured reporting and communicating relationship. Structural hierarchy perpetuates anomie, making it impossible for meaningful norms and values to be in place.

The Individual's Impact

Every individual within the workplace can shape, form and influence the organization. The best way to examine this influence is not by trying to figure out the contributions or "value" of each individual to the whole, but, rather, by trying to assess the negative impact on the organization if an individual is not part of a particular group.

Let's try this example. It seems trite to talk about the value of a measly old receptionist in a firm of nationally recognized expert professionals. Oh yeah? Take away the receptionist and watch those professionals answer the phone, field questions, convey a consistent image, and respond effectively to client questions. Try to calibrate and measure the impact of *not* having that individual within the organization. It is a good way to identify the impact and measure the value of that person within the group.

Amazingly, while most employees and managers we interviewed felt that a desire for well-defined norms and values was an important factor in deciding to join an organization, few people ever asked about or explored the company's norms or values in the interviewing process. We found that people are reluctant to ask employers about such "touchy-feely" issues as norms and values.

You can't imagine the number of times we have asked people the question, "What are your personal and professional norms and values?" in an interviewing situation, only to receive a blank stare and a response of "I've never been asked that type of question before."

Without organizational norms and values, individuals will be forced to create their own. In short, norms and values end up looking like a clear summer sky, late at night. While the individual stars are distinct and bright, none are connected to each other. If they were in some way, their brightness would enlighten the sky more powerfully than any light show imaginable. While each individual does have a desired set of personal values, developed primarily from family, religious, and community entities, there is no glue or linkage of those individual norms to each other, nor to the group. When organizations do provide strong collective norms and values that bring individuals out of isolation, collective power results.

This kind of power can truly be felt. You can sense it very clearly in organizations that embody it. Employees have a unique sense of loyalty and dedication to the organization; they enjoy their work and it becomes a meaningful part of their daily lives; it offers self-actualization potential; it satisfies their need for belonging to a group in a meaningful way; it turns apathetic employees into highly motivated ones.

If the power of shared norms and values can do all that, then why don't more organizations embrace it? The answer, unfortunately, is because most individuals, and men in particular, are conditioned to keep feelings, emotions, values, and personal beliefs locked up inside. Promulgated by nonfeeling parents and perpetuated by emotionally brain-dead managers, we end up believing that the "right" behavior is the stolid, sober, "roll with the punches" approach.

Just imagine the power of a senior executive telling a middle-level manager how much he appreciates, respects, and likes him as a professional. Once a company's leadership is able to open up, become more vulnerable, express emotions and feelings and describe its own norms and values, the anomic problems within organizations will begin to subside. Hope can once again be restored.

> There seems to be a natural tendency for every organism to jar apart and become a loose-jointed aggregation of unrelated units unless there is some binding, supervising and coordinating force that continually keeps them in place and makes each unit realize that it is not complete in itself, but merely a part whose greatest service is rendered when it fits perfectly into the whole.

> Webster Robinson
> Harvard Business Review
> April *1925*

Chapter 3

Eroding Societal Norms and Values

The Deterioration of Societal Values

Organizational anomie does not exist in a vacuum. It exists—and grows—from a corresponding values-less society. Literally speaking, we bring anomie to work with us each day. Let's examine the circular nature of anomie in society and its effects on our workplaces. It's clear that the dearth of values in today's society actually fuels the anomie within our organizations. This, in turn, contributes to our dissatisfaction in our jobs and our companies. Finally, the lack of values in today's society is reflected in the workplace itself. A values-less society breeds anomie in a values-less organization.

Just what *is* the state of American society today? Unhealthy, to say the least. Materialism continues to be a goal for some, as humanistic life is declining for most. Cellular phones, answering machines, credit cards, personal computers, and riding lawn mowers enable us to have more time to do other things and make task completion quicker and easier. Moreover, 35-inch televisions, luxury cars, Ferragamo shoes, and Oxford suits may make us feel better about ourselves and enable us to seemingly impress others. But despite these advances, the economic divergence of American society is becoming wider and wider. There is an enlarging segment of Americans who are "have nots." So, yes, ease and materialistic life is improving for Americans who are earning six figures annually, but for the vast majority, the economic struggle is worsening.

This economic and humanistic struggle is reflected in the crime, violence, divorce, chemical dependency, and drug abuse that have all continued to rise during the past twenty years. The evidence is staggering.

People may disagree about the cause of our eroding values in America. Some attribute this phenomenon to economics. Others claim it's due to a decline in morals, beliefs, and norms. A 1993 *Wall Street Journal*/NBC News poll concludes:

> Americans express deep concerns about a range of social problems. But when asked whether they think those problems are mainly the result of a decline in moral values or of financial pressures and strains on families, Americans are split down the middle. Financial pressures are cited by 45%, while 43% cite a decline in moral values.

Vivid Signs of Erosion

The more subtle and yet, in some ways, far more detrimental signs of our values-less society can be seen in the following examples cited by William Bennett, former Secretary of Education and author of *Leading Cultural Indicators*:

- Out of wedlock births have jumped from 5% of all children in 1960 to 30% in 1991.
- The percentage of children living in a single-parent home (90% of them without a live-in father) has tripled in three decades.
- Every year one million children must face the break-up of their parent's marriage.
- Television watching has increased by two hours a day since 1960. Preschoolers see an average of four hours every day.
- The average child watches more than 100,000 acts of TV violence before he/she finishes grade school.

Worse yet, we are abusing, neglecting, and killing our children in this country—daily. Consider the following statistics published in 1994 by the Children's Defense Fund. Every *single* day in America, on average:

- 9 children are murdered.
- 13 children are shot dead.
- 27 children die from poverty.
- 480 teenagers contract syphilis or gonorrhea.
- 1,115 teenagers have abortions.
- 1,234 children run away from home.
- 2,255 children drop out of school.
- 3,325 babies are born to unwed mothers.
- 5,314 children are arrested.

Their report also states that "the steady increase in reported child abuse and neglect is one of the past decade's most troubling trends. More than 2.9 million children were reported abused or neglected in 1992, about triple the number reported in 1980." In short, our values have eroded to such a disgraceful state that we do not even treat our children with respect and human dignity. How could we possibly expect to find meaning in our work environments or communities if, as a society, we behave in such barbaric ways?

As columnist Joan Beck writes: "It is our beliefs, our behavior, and our philosophy that have in many instances changed for the worse. Our injury is self-inflicted." This key message eloquently summarizes the interpersonal and humanistic erosion that has occurred in our society during the past two to three decades. It is painfully clear the great extent to which we have experienced our society's deterioration. The social and cultural erosion of the last three decades is taking a ghastly toll.

Crime doesn't stem from inadequate law enforcement or too few prison cells. Nor does it come from not having enough police or tough enough laws. Crime results from a lack of individual and societal values that are deeply ingrained and firmly planted. People are being shot, stabbed, raped, and wounded. This sounds more like a vicious civil war than just a typical day in the life of American society. As Charles Colson, a convicted felon in the Watergate trial and 1993 recipient of the Templeton Prize for Progress in Religion writes: "Crime is the mirror of a community's mores. Today that mirror reflects a broken consensus. The beliefs that once defined the content of our character have been shattered like glass and Americans are left to pick their way among the jagged edges. Crime is a moral problem which requires a moral solution."

While the news media certainly highlight the societal deterioration that is now snowballing, we still haven't recognized the fundamental solution to fix this situation.

We must begin to better understand the impact of these facts on our values and societal norms. We need to make some big changes, not just some incremental improvements here and there. As columnist Joan Beck insightfully writes: "What's necessary may be a pendulum swing back to earlier family values, to self-reliance, sexual constraint, a renewed sense of social responsibility for one's actions, for lives firmly based on moral principles rather than excuses and self-indulgence. Economic indicators are taken seriously—we need the same kind of vigilance about the social, cultural and moral wellbeing." We can't keep turning to government, social programs, welfare, and attorneys for help. We need to initiate the change on an individual basis. It has to start with each of us. You, me, him, and her.

We must instill norms and values back into societal, community, religious, and family organizations. Once norms and values have been reinstituted in our organizations, individuals will have more support mechanisms in place to let their own personal values burgeon, grow, and develop. If we simultaneously restore individual norms and values while rebuilding them in organizations, anomie can indeed be eradicated.

Easier said than done, however. Activating the solution is the difficult part.

The Values Erosion Era

Our values are in hibernation. They have disappeared, gone underground. Without a set of individual and group-wide values, our work and personal lives will remain shadowed by the shroud of anomie. The trip to the underground hibernation tunnels started about 25 years ago, with the Vietnam War.

Unfortunately, the Vietnam War era was the last time in nearly three decades that our American society *did* voice a set of values and strong beliefs. Simply put, the gradual ground swell of anger and hatred toward killing in Vietnam ignited a luminous "values spark." This spark fueled the social fires of marches, demonstrations, protests, and vociferous expression of feelings, beliefs, and personal points of view. It was great. People were alive, vibrant, in touch with their feelings and willing to express them.

But then a new direction emerged in the late 1970s. Rather than the sixties movement setting in motion a profoundly powerful platform for a values structure, we evolved into a narcissistic and materialistic society. The eighties focused on how to make lots of money quickly, regardless of the ethics involved or approach taken. Witness the evidence: junk bonds, scandalous promotions to positions in top management, stock trades based on insider information, and unfriendly acquisitions that "downsized" massive numbers of loyal employees.

This new self-focused value "structure" has caused the current values erosion. Organizations no longer recognize, reward, or encourage values such as loyalty, dedicated hard work, personal dignity, and honesty. While a few new books and articles have been written about corporate ethics, for the most part they've been left on corporate credenzas, unopened and collecting dust.

The clarity of our current values erosion is best depicted by the 110-outlet chain called Hooters. While this national restaurant chain may serve tasty burgers and chicken wings, that's not the primary reason customers frequent the joint. As the restaurant's name implies, hefty-sized "hooters" are the reason to come to the restaurant—it's the end benefit that's being positioned and sold to customers. "Come see the Hooters!" It's a shocking commentary on the erosion of our current values. We now have a restaurant chain whose main reason for being is to allow men to ogle, giggle, and stare blatantly at women's breasts. The progress made by the feminist movement is certainly set back several years with the introduction of Hooters to our values-eroding society. Without sounding puritanical, could you envision taking your children, or your parents, for that matter, to this "breastaurant"? If not, why not? It's a perfect example of the erosion of our social values.

Now, today's organization or management team is unlikely to admit it is unethical or values-less. And yet, actions speak louder than words. The actions of many managers shout clearly and loudly that their only value is self-vested interest and monetary gain. Otherwise, how could these organizations possibly support such behaviors as autocratic management, sexual harassment, or "profit-saving" employee downsizing?

As the Hooters example effectively shows, many organizations have yet to view their employees as people, let alone put stock in their individual values. The following is another sad illustration of values erosion in action.

A major telecommunications company decided to fire several white-collar folks and, seconds after informing them of their new unemployed status, accompanied each fired employee to the exit door with a security guard. Of course, how could a ten- or twenty-year loyal employee possibly be trusted? The company stripped them of their individual dignity by treating these former colleagues like criminals. As the organization expeditiously escorted their workers out the door (to ensure they didn't steal any important papers or top-secret technologies), they sowed anomie at every step, for the "downsized" workers as well as for those left behind.

Double-Whammy Anomic Impact

The verdict is in. Anomie is causing the erosion of our societal values as well as the decline of our organizations. We call it the Double-Whammy Anomic Impact. As shown in Exhibit 3–1, it illustrates the ailments that result from anomie.

Do you see why we so strongly believe that anomie needs to be diluted and ultimately obliterated? Each of these societal and organizational sicknesses can be improved with sustaining values and norms that are embraced by both individuals and organizations. But it won't be easy.

EXHIBIT 3-1

Double-Whammy Anomic Impact

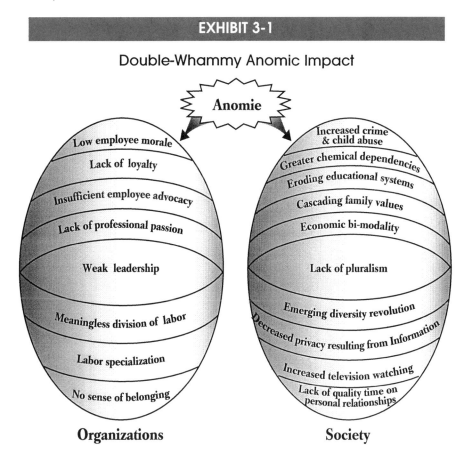

Anomie

Organizations — Low employee morale, Lack of loyalty, Insufficient employee advocacy, Lack of professional passion, Weak leadership, Meaningless division of labor, Labor specialization, No sense of belonging

Society — Increased crime & child abuse, Greater chemical dependencies, Eroding educational systems, Cascading family values, Economic bi-modality, Lack of pluralism, Emerging diversity revolution, Decreased privacy resulting from Information, Increased television watching, Lack of quality time on personal relationships

According to a study conducted by the Roper Organization, cited in the *Chicago Tribune* on December 16, 1992, "Americans by and large view themselves as uncaring, unromantic, materialistic, hard-working and aggressive. Women are more caring than men, and the poor are more caring than the wealthy." This commentary certainly supports our current state of anomie. From a national perspective, Americans have no nourishing values to support the weight of "double-whammy" anomie.

The Roper survey also provides some insight into values Americans hold in the 1990s. Honesty was the most desirable value, cited by 86 percent, followed by getting along with people, responsibility for one's actions, and respect for authority (each receiving 60 percent). Americans think their friends should be trusting, honest, caring, and good listeners. But in order to achieve these personal goals, they first need to be more open to each other as individuals.

Most of our work organizations suppress the expression of feelings, beliefs and values. The usual messages are: "Don't rock the corporate boat," "Roll with the punches," and "Take it like a man (or woman)." We are consistently discouraged to express ourselves. Organizational norms reinforce a "don't express emotion" mindset. This further fosters an inward focus, making individuals more isolated, alienated, and insecure.

We need to be far more open with people. We have evolved into a bunch of emotional deaf-mutes who fear expressing feelings to others. When was the last time you told a friend, colleague, or co-worker, "I really like you"? Well, try it sometime. While you'll probably get a blank stare at first, the person's response back may pleasantly surprise you. Open up!

One way to provide a child with a working values model is to convey the importance of openness—a belief that being spontaneous and candidly straightforward about fears, pleasures, feelings, and emotions is a healthy and appropriate view of the human condition. Jane Smiley, author of *A Thousand Acres,* writes: "A child who is protected from all controversial ideas, including depictions of sex, is as vulnerable as a child who is protected from every germ. The infection, when it comes and it will come, may overwhelm the system, be that the immune system or the belief system."

Interestingly, 55 percent of Americans agree with the idea, as we do, of distributing condoms in schools to prevent diseases and unwanted pregnancies. This is an example of adopting a norm that can reinforce a values belief. This norm eliminates the difficult values decision between abortion or unwed motherhood. It's a norm that recognizes the sexual need in all human beings, yet shows clear-cut respect and consideration for others by not spreading harmful or contagious diseases. Perhaps the advent of the female condom will further accelerate acceptance of the norm.

The state of an organization's health will depend on the reduction and eradication of anomie. We need to replace it with personal and organizational values that provide individuals with a sense that others do care about them and want them to be a part of their group.

Where Do Our Values Come From?

Think about your own values. What is the origin of your own personal beliefs? How did they come about? How have they changed? We believe that values stem over time from four factors: (1) family and childhood experiences, (2) conflict events which evoke self-discovery, (3) major life changes and experiential learning, and (4) personal relationships with "important" individuals. Everyone has different values that are shaped by these four factors. The combination and ongoing occurrence of these various events, combined with our own learning and self-discovery, is what changes and reshapes our values over time. We'll explain each one, so that we can better understand how to influence and positively impact value formation in individuals.

- *Family and childhood experiences*—This source is fairly self-evident. During childhood, our values are shaped by our parents, family members, siblings, peers, teachers, and religious affiliations. Each of these influential people and associations shared their own beliefs with us and transferred their values to us as children. Our childhood experiences from school, family rituals, holidays and celebrations, travel and vacations, as well as daily family practices, styles of interaction, and approaches to discipline—*all* had a major impact on our values formation.

- *Conflict events that evoke self-discovery*—There are two types of conflict events that shape our values. One is societally driven and the other is personally driven. Wars, environmental disasters, community crime, government programs, and legal reforms—these are examples of societal or externally driven sources of potential conflict. Divorce, job loss, school failure, lost lover, hurtful friends, or an unwanted pregnancy—these are examples of personally driven conflict. The issue here is *how* an individual deals with these conflicts and learns from each through self-discovery—not whether each is good or bad. In fact, often a negative conflict experience can sprout some very positive learning and values formation. The conflict itself can set up a situation that requires the individual to confront it. The *way* we handle the conflict can influence certain value shifts or changes. Often, these events will cause a person to question, challenge, and augment his or her previously adopted values.

- *Major life changes and experiential learning*—Marriage, divorce, rearing children, taking a new job or position, moving to a new geographic location, confronting the death of a significant other, or adjusting to the departure of children from home—all are examples of major life changes. The impact of these events is cumulative, often causing a values evolution over time. Individuals are forced to revise their values after experiencing these events. The impact of these major life changes on values formation is monumental.

- *Personal relationships with "important" individuals*—There are a handful of nonfamily members or individuals that we meet in our daily lives who really "connect" with us. We become greatly influenced by them. Teachers, college friends, bosses, friends, or older people are potential "special" people who impact our values. Typically, these people become "role models" whom we look up to, respect, admire, and want to emulate. Impressionable and vulnerable individuals are usually more open to value influences from these people. The existing values and norms of these special people will greatly influence the formation of new values and revisions in existing ones.

So values come from self-learning and self-discovery. Discovering new feelings, emotions, and conflict within ourselves can have a major impact on our values. Beliefs that we have always taken for granted can be seen in a totally new light, when we undergo a type of advanced learning and internal self-discovery. As we learn more about ourselves, others, and how to deal with different persons and conflict situations, we increase our own self-confidence and perception of self-worth. In turn, we better understand our needs, unique characteristics, and shortcomings. For example, a powerful love relationship can often open up huge new avenues to self-discovery. This "uncovering" process can once again influence and alter our values.

Thus, when a combination of these values-shaping factors are at work, often concurrently, they can have a profound impact on our personal values formation and development. Throughout our research, we asked people what influenced and shaped their values. Their answers tended to fall within the four aforementioned categories of potential factors.

Breaking Free from Anomie

The disease of anomie causes individuals to think and act in ways that have a deleterious impact on society and work organizations. As these organizations continue to foster anomie, the symptoms of anomie fester in individuals and further fuel the anomic disease.

Peter Homans, Professor of Religion and Psychological Studies at the University of Chicago Divinity School, says:

> When social structures fall apart and traditional belief systems disintegrate, people engage in "meaning-making" to restore cohesion in their lives. There is a hunger these days, a gnawing dissatisfaction with the answers provided by materialism and scientific progress, a craving for an inner life. Politicians sense it in their constituents and grasp at words like "values."

Implementing organizational programs and policies that don't combat anomie will never work. The long-term solution must be aimed at eliminating anomie and replacing it with individual values and norms. The starting point to resolve anomie begins with the identification and cultivation of group and individual norms and values. Group-derived norms and values will collectively change the mindset and attitudes of individuals within work organizations. By counteracting the key components of anomie, a new social order can evolve. The formula to achieve this includes our need to:

- Instill and cultivate individual and group values.
- Develop norms to guide communications and behaviors.
- Empower individuals to develop meaningful personal relationships.
- Infuse meaning into peoples' jobs.
- Provide individuals with a genuine sense of equality and attachment to work organizations.

Creating Magnetic Values

If we ever hope to fully break away from anomie, we also need to cultivate and create magnetic values. The 1993 *Wall Street Journal*/NBC News Poll cites: "Seventy-five percent of Americans strongly agree that traditional values have grown weaker and need to be strengthened." In roughly equal percentages, agreement is voiced by blacks and whites, men and women, and selected religious groups. That's 75 percent, folks! This startlingly high number surely signifies the widespread recognition that a fundamental breakdown exists in our country today. Perhaps Americans *are* seeking a values formula that reflects more "old-fashioned" family and community values. But we dislike the adjective "old-fashioned" and prefer "contemporary" and "magnetic." There is no need to *return* to the values of the 1950s. That was forty-plus years ago. Life *has* dramatically changed. However, the values void can't continue. We need to develop a 1990s-and-beyond set of new, contemporary, and "magnetic" values.

We propose that Americans develop a new magnetic values system. These are solidifying values that bring groups of people together. These values serve as the infrastructural glue that bonds people to one another. They are compelling or "attaching" values that draw people together. Two magnets will, on their own inertia, move toward each other and connect. The concept of magnetic values achieves the same phenomenon between individuals in a group. Whether it's parents and children in a family, husband and wife in a marriage, teachers and students in schools, managers and employees in a company, or a lieutenant and rookie in the police force, magnetic values can join these groups together and provide a values texture that they can sense, feel, and relate to.

One magnetic value example is a belief in quantity of time with children—not just quality. This value requires spending more time each week with your children than the amount of time you spend watching television! Making the time each week to "activate" this value becomes the norm. The value becomes magnetic in that it helps to strengthen the family unit, bring cohesion to the group, and provide a stronger sense of belonging. The creation of magnetic values is ultimately the solution to anomie.

Another magnetic value is a belief in pluralism. This means an overriding acceptance of all human beings, without any prejudice or discrimination based on gender, age, ethnicity, religion, sexual orientation, or other differences—including geographic location. Really believing in diversity provides an access to people that is full and long lasting. Its benefit is pervasive.

Values Begin with You!

American heroes in the early 1900s tended to include those who gained financial and materialistic success, such as Rockefeller, Astor, and Morgan. Today, heroes are those who are willing to do something about a societal problem.

According to Professor Jack Levin at Northwestern University, "We are beginning to idolize activism—Americans who are willing to give up their seat among the couch potatoes and take charge in the face of government and big business. This may be the beginning of the 'we generation' and the end of the 'me generation.' In the 1980s, people were too busy making a buck to care." His point is a valid and timely one. We are gradually evolving to a society that's going to be "forced" to care for others.

We need to save our organizations and ourselves before we fall into a long-term coma and never wake up. We need to find ways to bring our value system out of hibernation and once again have it surface aboveground. Even though we want to avoid hyperbole, this issue is fundamentally destructive in that it places our organizations on the precipice of annihilation.

Do you get it? We need to bring values back to our daily lives and integrate them into our everyday actions with individuals at home, at work, and in the community. The good news is that our organizations today can place greater emphasis on understanding both the needs of individuals and the collective needs of groups. You'll learn how to accomplish this as we go forward in the book.

Chapter 4

Infusing Norms and Values into Organizations

We've made broad claims about anomie and its devastating effects. We've touched upon the societal aspects that have contributed to an erosion of values within our workplaces. But what exactly does anomie look like in our organizations? We'd like to describe the evidence from our research that supports the disconcerting finding—today's typical employees simply don't have a reason to believe in their organizations.

Egg-Shelling

The 1990s have brought a new breed of workers to American organizations. Employees are getting fed up with their workplaces. They are beginning to refuse to obey orders, blindly and mindlessly. They want norms and values to fortify the cultures in which they work.

This is the good news! What is the bad news? Most employees, unfortunately, have built up a self-protective "shell" around themselves in their work environments. We call this eggshelling. Employees manifest eggshelling in a variety of ways. Increasing sick days, coming in late, or leaving early are all ways to "protect" their job involvement. More subtle signs of eggshelling are: turning co-workers down for lunch—"I've just got too much work to do"; keeping quiet in meetings—"My opinions and comments won't be listened to anyway"; and bad-mouthing management to set up a defensive premise to "protect" themselves from future criticism. With an anomic employee, eggshelling certainly shows up in a performance review. The employee literally doesn't want to hear how others perceive his or her performance. In this situation, the feelings of alienation and isolation are intensified. The eggshell further "thickens" its outer cover.

Eggshelling is both a symptom of anomie and a perpetuator of it. It perpetuates the disillusionment of employees and extends their unhappiness with their organizations. It also fuels anomie because it increases the difficulty of eliciting individual values— the employee is figuratively "unavailable" while they are in their eggshells.

Organizations Need a Norms-and-Values Infusion

Our "believers" research team was sent out to conduct interviews over a period of one year from the fall of 1992 through the fall of 1993. More than 200 employees were interviewed in all kinds of workplaces, ranging in size from small to large organizations. We spoke with entry-level, mid-level, and senior-level employees across a broad range of industries. In trying to summarize some of the observations drawn from this primary research, it became readily apparent that norms and values impacted the way organizations operate. While the range of issues and concerns was broad and diverse, we tried to identify the most common patterns and concerns across the organizations we interviewed.

The following three vignettes from employees depict the need to infuse a set of norms in organizations that will reinforce desired values.

George is a warehouse manager for a large meat-packing operation. He joined the company two years ago and has recently been promoted from warehouse supervisor to manager. His insights on the company's norms and values are fairly representative of our research. He states:

There are no structured norms and values at this company, and management doesn't particularly do a good job of letting employees know when they are performing well or poorly. Management gives out bonuses, but praise and nonmonetary recognition are rarely used here. Employees stay at the company mostly because they cannot find a better job—not because they feel appreciated or enjoy the work in any special way. Management is rather insensitive to employee needs.

His description clearly illustrates the sentiment of most employees: They're seeking a reason to believe in their organizations but can't find one. The biggest concern to us is that George was seemingly happy in this job. His previous job was actually a lot worse. At his former place of employment, his own values and norms did not match those of his company's management. They were in conflict. Employees such as George are generally tolerant and complacent about their work environments. As long as the workplace is anything better than intolerable, and as long as the organization is neutral, run-of-the-mill, and consistent, it becomes a "good enough" place to work.

Bill, who is also relatively happy in his job, describes "materialistic" and "titular" values, which are resident in many organizations. About his workplace he notes:

> I've worked for the Conservation Commission for three years; there's professional conflict and political conflict. It's important that the city not appear to be fighting between departments. It often takes a lot of negotiating work. It seems important to present a unified front . . . It's not codified, but men in the upper levels wear suits while those at my level wear only ties. There is also a correlation between size of office, number of resources, and your title—the higher up you are, the greater status you have. Politics seems to be the major value that's considered and talked about here daily.

Ray, a senior executive at a medical services company, shares the following observations:

There is a general disparity between the values of employees while they [upper managers] themselves practice a different set. Most employees sense this inconsistency between theory and practice. The company norms are simple: Don't confront poor performance directly; listen politely, but use caution before making promises; and hope that people do as they're told, but expect them to not necessarily do so. I think that the president should stop treating us like children. He needs to trust his employees and increase our level of responsibility and freedom to make our own decisions and mistakes. Also, if we revised the measurement and reward system to compensate employees more fairly for their contributions, it would increase enthusiasm and their sense of purpose.

These vignettes present a vivid portrait. Leaders within organizations need to penetrate employees' eggshells and gradually get them to chose to break out of their shells themselves. This is a very important concept. If a manager forces or tries to push an employee out of his or her eggshell, it will most likely shatter. The employee's alienation only increases.

So how can an organizational leader instill a culture where employees will want to work "shell-less"? By doing four things:

1. Establish credible values and norms that employees can see being practiced by others around them.

2. Build employee self-confidence by providing frequent doses of deserved recognition and positive feedback.

3. Convey genuine personal interest in employees—ask them questions that are not *too* personal, yet communicate personal interest in them.

4. Demonstrate that you care about employees—even more than about the organization's well-being; send them a note; give them a call; ask how you can help them.

All these efforts can make a leader fall flat on his or her face if they are not done with genuine caring and a credible attitude. Before discussing the ingredients for increasing job satisfaction, let's present the factors that *decrease* employee satisfaction.

Factors that Decrease Employee Satisfaction

Our interview data uncovered ten areas that employees cited most frequently as factors that reduce their job satisfaction within their organization, as depicted in Exhibit 4-1.

1. Values Gap

There is often a disparity between the values of management and the values of employees within the same organization.

Management preaches one set of values to employees but practices a different set themselves. Employees can sense this

EXHIBIT 4-1

Factors that Decrease Employee Satisfaction

Informal, Unwritten and Unclear Norms and Values

Values-less leadership

Lack of commitment to values

Minimal professional impact and growth

Personal values disconnected from the organization's

Minimal teaching and mentoring

Low self-esteem

Lack of trust

Insufficient feedback, rewards and recognition

Theory differs from practice

Values gap

inconsistency. One interviewee noted the following: "Our organization has many unwritten norms and values, not just one. The management has a set of norms and values, the employees have a set, and owners have a set." When this disparity or "values gap" prevails within organizations, no single set of values for employees and management is followed or adhered to. Confusion results.

2. Theory vs. Practice

Many of the norms and values that are nurtured and developed within organizations are not positive. Rather, they are negative forces that act to create tension between management and the employees.

One interviewee identified this underlining tension: "Norms and values are really screwed up in our company. They are perceived positively by management and very negatively by the employees. There is a difference between what management *thinks* we our cultivating and what the employees are *really* feeling." In the numerous organizations we researched, there appeared to be a difference between the values that managers pressured employees to adopt and the values that managers themselves practiced and cultivated.

3. Insufficient Feedback, Rewards, and Recognition

To understand the impact they are making, employees depend on feedback and view it as an incentive. Management does not do a good job of letting employees know specifically how they are performing; nor do they acknowledge the contributions of their employees. There are few nonfinancial rewards at most companies. Descriptive praise and nonmonetary recognition are rarely used by management.

Insufficient feedback creates employees who are unhappy, prompting them to look for other jobs. Further, there is very little incentive for employees to work when they are not being supervised. Worse, management is rather insensitive to the interests and needs of employees. Employees stay at the organization mostly because they cannot find a better job, not because they feel appreciated or enjoy their work in any special way. The lack of respect with which management treats employees at organizations has led to extraordinarily high turnover rates. The lack of communication and feedback between management and employees has left most employees guessing about what their organization's norms and values really are.

In order to derive satisfaction, employees need and appreciate feedback. Of the individuals we interviewed, most said they depend on feedback to motivate them. Overall, employees desire more feedback than they are getting.

4. Lack of Trust

Many employees are frustrated because they feel management doesn't trust them. Employees perceive that they are not given enough responsibility. They are "ordered" to do monotonous tasks and quickly tire of them.

When an interviewee was asked what would give her an increased sense of purpose in her job, she said: "I'd like more responsibilities and more trust by management to let me make my own decisions. Right now we are treated more like slaves than like intelligent, quick-thinking employees. If I could be given added responsibility and autonomy, I would enjoy this job a lot more." This sentiment was frequently expressed by other interviewees.

5. Low Job Satisfaction and Self-Esteem

Employee job satisfaction is low in many organizational settings because individual self-esteem and perceptions of self-worth are low.

Personal values are important to employee job satisfaction. Notes one interviewee, "I believe in hard work, trying to help my clients as much as I can, asking questions, and learning about the business. If I do these self-prescribed things, that makes me feel good."

When asked how they could develop goals that could increase their satisfaction, another interviewee stated: "Right now I really don't have the power to implement any of my goals. Management is not willing to talk to employees about giving them more responsibility. They just want to make sure the job gets done and the clients get taken care of. This doesn't make me feel good about myself."

6. Minimal Teaching and Mentoring

There is less confusion among employees about their organizational norms and values if leaders are willing to help teach new members how to do their jobs well. In fact, very little teaching occurs within most organizations. Mentoring is almost nonexistent, yet it has the power to transmit knowledge about norms and values to employees and to increase feedback and job satisfaction.

One employee within the hotel industry stated that her first boss was nice, but he didn't teach. She had to learn by observing. Her second boss tried to teach, but came off patronizing, never having a positive word to say.

Another employee noted. "I would like a company that would mentor me from the beginning. They would say, 'Welcome aboard!' and would encourage me to grow. They would show appreciation through promotion, feedback, and through raises. Now it's more 'take it or leave it.' Maybe it's an intimidation thing—an attitude—'we're the best and you're lucky to be working here.'" This employee needed more guidance—a mentor to teach her about the norms and values within her workplace and to provide her with an increased sense of purpose.

7. Personal Values Disconnected to Those of the Organization

If norms and values are established within the workplace, they have the potential to empower employees. If work organizations can get their employees to tie their personal goals to those of the workplace, then they will nurture long-term relationships together.

"Every time I try to express my own point of view, I'm admonished by my peers to just go along with the president's recommendations. How can I continue to assume this organization believes in a respect for individuals when I continually hear this?" recalls another interviewee.

8. Minimal Professional Impact and Growth

Employees seek to make an impact and are happier when they feel they do so. Employees want professional growth.

Most employees derive a sense of satisfaction from making an impact on their organization, whether it is in terms of garnering the respect of their colleagues and superiors, producing high-quality work, or producing products that make a difference with consumers.

Employees desire professional growth, whether it takes the form of increased responsibility or project ownership. Employee empowerment motivates individuals and gives them a sense of purpose. A lack of growth opportunities reduces job satisfaction. Many interviewees viewed training as an essential means to provide employees with the necessary skills to grow professionally.

Some organizations viewed mistakes as learning experiences. They focused on minimizing their recurrence instead of punishing the employee. However, other organizations had a set of "unacceptable" mistakes, which elicited more severe repercussions. Frequently, these were mistakes that had an impact on customers. Most interviewees reacted negatively to being "punished" for mistakes, especially if there were no ostensible positive growth experiences to accompany the punishment.

9. Lack of Commitment to Values

Many organizations are making efforts to create norms and values but are falling short in demonstrating commitment to the values.

Many of the organizations discussed in the interviews are making strides to instill values into the work environment. Some of these efforts include values statements, policy/principle handbooks, and training sessions.

However, many employees detect a divergence between their organization's stated norms and values and the mechanisms to reinforce them. Specifically, most interviewees recognize that their organizations manage to uphold some of the values, but are still aspiring toward others. For example, many organizations express the value of supporting diversity, but have not demonstrated a commitment to hiring minorities or giving them positions of significant responsibility.

To take another example, many organizations expressed a commitment to professional growth and development, but they did little to instill trust in their employees, provide training, or reimburse development courses. Without these tools, some of the employees who aspire to leadership positions do not have the ability to manage effectively.

10. Values-less Leadership

The leadership within the organization does not convey the values that the organization espouses.

If positive norms and values are exemplified by leadership within an organization, then employees can believe in them. When leaders demonstrate the desired norms and values on a daily basis, they lend credibility and authenticity to them. Trust is present. On the other hand, if leadership nurtures a competitive, self-serving, and uncooperative environment, there will not be shared norms and values in the workplace. If management were to adhere to the same values they preach to employees, there would be greater commitment to making the norms work.

An employee states: "Every time I think the company is actually making headway toward openness and candor, I see the vice-presidents remain closed-mouthed as soon as a divisional president challenges them."

There you have it. Our "top ten" list of factors decreasing employee satisfaction. Now the challenge for management is to understand these employee viewpoints and develop norms to improve them.

Conflicting Norms and Values

Most managers are short-sighted. They try to douse the fire without examining the source of the flame. Managers spend too little time trying to understand the underlying causes of why employees are unhappy and too much time trying to achieve their company's organizational goals. If managers focused on employee dissatisfaction, the achievement of organizational goals would occur, with far less effort on the part of managers. By spending more time on employee motivation, recognition, and increased job satisfaction, managers would establish a dynamic culture where employees would push harder than ever to achieve the collective goals of the organization.

In effect, managers have an incredibly powerful *and* sustainable competitive advantage right under their noses: their employees. And yet, for some odd reason, managers seek out new sources of competitive advantages—new technologies, advanced information systems, lower supply costs, and other measures. Why is this? Simply put, organization leaders are not aware of their internal, hidden power: people.

Shakmer Zahra, professor of Strategic Management at George Mason University, conducted a study in 1989 on Executive Values and Ethics of Company Politics. He examined four management attitudes: job satisfaction, life satisfaction, acceptance of others, and anomie. His research supports that while there is confusion concerning the nature of anomie, it implies powerlessness and alienation. He notes that "anomie reflects a person's sense of estrangement within a social system. Executives with a strong sense of anomie will tend to view organizational political behavior as ethical." Interestingly, in Zahra's study, anomie ended up as the most significant variable when examining organization politics. Zahra claims: "It is perhaps this sense of helplessness combined with a strong desire for improved status in life that leads an individual to accept politicking as a mechanism to achieve certain goals." An organization's values are not the only concern of workers we interviewed. It's the organization's accepted norms—behavioral guidelines—that also cause confusion, disillusionment, and insecurity. Norms and values need to converge—not conflict.

We interviewed an individual holding a development position in a professional school at a large private university. She said that she had to motivate herself because there were no mechanisms in place to encourage performance. When asked if she felt there was a system of norms and values at her organization, she replied, "Somewhat . . . at least at some level there is a framework of norms and values." But when pressed for an example of norms and values at her organization, she identified the following behavioral norm:

> One general feeling is that we're better than other departments. There is a feeling that if we need to get something done, we should do it ourselves. Other departments don't do the work because there is no system in place to make them accountable. The alumni office agreed to make ready an alumni mailing list, but they didn't meet the deadline. It was

a simple job. They didn't do what they were supposed to do, and what they did do, they did wrong. Since we were the first ones to use the information, we did it ourselves. We should have done it ourselves in the first place.

Now, this is an odd behavioral norm. It has no connection to knowing the needs and resources of the group. It encourages the school development officer to *not* ask for resources from the centralized departments within the university when there is a need. Instead, do it yourself—that is, *don't* use the resources of the group—even at the risk of duplication of effort.

Another norm that was identified by this same employee was that "nobody wants to be the first one to leave the office. It is an unspoken thing that I should be the last to leave, because I am on the professional staff. Of course, the administrative staff stays because they can earn overtime." This is also an example of an undesirable norm that actually contributes to further disillusionment and isolation. We believe employees should be encouraged to leave the office when they are finished with their work, or they will be unable to work productively as time goes on.

Alleviating Alienation

Karl Marx recognized alienation as a critical issue that employees faced. He argued that employee alienation surfaced along three key dimensions:

- *Alienation from the work product*—when labor becomes so segmented that workers no longer know how their contribution fits into the ultimate product or service delivered.
- *Alienation from coworkers*—a lack of caring, interest in, or desire to interact with colleagues and fellow workers and managers.
- *Alienation from self*—with limited control over or meaningfulness in work; virtually no connection or attachments with other workers causes a perception of lower self-worth and all eventual desire to separate from self.

By effectively infusing norms and values into organizations, each of these three forms of alienation can be greatly reduced. Employees will feel more connected to their jobs and products, more attached to their coworkers, and more in touch with themselves.

According to Roy Payne, professor of Organizational Behavior at the Manchester Business School, culture depends upon two things: "First, the pervasiveness of the norms and behaviors in the explicit culture along with the values and beliefs in the implicit culture; and secondly, the range of beliefs and behaviors which the organization sets out to control." He ties this important idea to what an effective and strong culture can create. He continues, "A corporation with a norms and values clarified culture has employees who believe in its products, customers, and its processes. They sell it willingly because it is part of their own identity."

The way in which alienation is alleviated is by increasing employees' self-confidence and self-worth. This, in turn, provides an openness where connections and attachments can be made to fellow colleagues in the work environment.

Another thought leader, Dr. Paul C. Nystrom, professor of Organizations and Strategic Management in the School of Business Administration, University of Wisconsin-Milwaukee, wrote in 1993:

> Organizational culture has surged in popularity recently. Practicing managers who write about organizational cultures frequently describe more visible aspects such as slogans, ceremonies, and symbols. But they often emphasize that a culture's more powerful and central attributes involve underlying norms and values. Norms refer to unwritten rules that tell members how they should and should not behave. Values refer to beliefs about what outcomes should be desired or preferred. Managers' values shape their processing of information and their behavior.

The strength of an organization's culture refers to the degree of consensus among members about which norms prevail and which values dominate in importance. Organizations with strong cultures provide more meaning and guidance to their employees. A strong set of norms and values can substitute for more bureaucratic coordination and control methods such as hierarchical supervision, plans, budgets, and formal procedures. Thus, organizational culture may be able to infuse members with an ardent feeling of organizational commitment while avoiding the negative reactions so often generated by a bureaucratic approach to management.

The Value of Values

Organizational norms and values can enhance bottom-line performance within companies. But we need to adopt a longer-term return perspective in order for values, which take time to develop, to become sustainable and effective.

Consider the short-term financial pressure that organizations labor under. Most companies, senior managers, and the financial community live and breathe according to quarterly performance. Narrow-minded shareholders have the audacity to slap the wrist of company management based on how well they perform in 90-day increments. Until this devastatingly myopic purview changes, we can never hope to regain U.S. competitiveness or innovative leadership. Of the 15,211 new products introduced into grocery stores last year, more than 13,000 were low-risk, low-investment, short-term oriented line extensions and "me-too, new, and improved" has-been offerings.

This short-term value, which is inculcated into the heads of most U.S. corporate leaders, underscores the failure of management to anticipate and embrace change, or to endorse long-term planning vision. If a longer-term perspective is taken on by management and a shared leadership culture nurtured, then the 90-day choke hold can be broken.

Motorola and General Electric are good examples of companies that have broken the 90-day syndrome. Their strong leadership, decentralized organizations, ability to react to change, empowerment of and respect for their people, and long-term investments (that aren't necessarily expected to yield 12-month paybacks) has resulted in soaring returns to shareholders.

At Motorola, an internal value is anticipation—a doctrine codified in the culture. Competitive intelligence, technology road maps, contingency plans, and breakthrough scanning keep the company ahead of the competition. Moreover, the company has a strong belief in open, verbal confrontation between managers. Employees, in fact, are able to file a "minority report" if their ideas aren't being supported. Reportedly, "engineers are encouraged to dispute their supervisors and one another vigorously at open company meetings." Former CEO George Fisher stated, "It gets wild; the discussions at times get verbally violent." This openness is a value that permeates the organization and supports the belief that every individual counts and is valuable to the success of the enterprise.

In GE CEO Jack Welch's new book *Control Your Destiny or Someone Else Will,* he states: "The only way I know to create trust is by laying out your values and then walking the talk. Trust is enormously powerful in a corporation. People won't do their best unless they believe they'll be treated fairly—that there's no cronyism and everybody has a real shot. You've got to do what you say you'll do, consistently, over time. I think any company that's trying to play in the 1990s has got to find a way to engage the mind of every single employee. If you're not thinking all the time about making every person more valuable, you don't have a chance."

These two short messages offer a high-impact message. First, Welch articulates the values of mutual trust, fairness and consistency. These are motivating values that have stimulated the massive GE work force to accelerate productivity, innovation, and global expansion. Second, Welch describes the value of each individual as an integral and meaningful component of the organization. In short, there is a respect for each employee's brainpower.

Companies such as GE and Motorola don't weave their values out of whole cloth. They're well aware of what individual employees believe and incorporate these beliefs into organization-wide values. According to James Taylor, CEO of Yankelovich Partners, one of the key trends for the 1990s is a renewed thrust by employees to control their destinies.

Only 12% of survey respondents trust public statements made by corporations, but an unprecedented seven out of ten agree: "I'm the one in charge of my life." That's a real change in the psychology of being an employee. It's the price corporations are paying for breaking the loyalty bond.

Corporations will pay a heavy price if the loyalty equation isn't brought back into balance. The value cited by employees of "controlling their destinies" is in effect a powerful one that will impact the inner fabric of an organization.

The Cost of Anomie

There is a premium price to pay for broken employee morale, rattled loyalty, and shaken employee motivation. The missed opportunity costs of anomie are profound and far more costly than most organizations care to realize or certainly ever want to measure. As an investor, would you invest in large corporations where loyalty comes in a distant third, knowing that the talent pool and knowledge base of the company will probably be turning over in the next few years? We don't think so.

And thousands of other potential investors don't think so either. That's why, to a great extent, you've seen precipitous drops in stock prices at companies such as IBM, Sears, Waste Management, Baxter, Hartmarx, Merck, and Apple Computer, to name a few. How is it possible that such well-known, well-respected and resource-laden companies can end up having their equity decline so significantly? Simple—the cost of anomie is recognized by shareholders. They've seen key senior managers leave each of those companies. They've watched turnover increase among the ranks. They know the real story—it's called anomie.

High employee turnover means higher recruiting and training costs, organization instability, erratic customer service, lower morale, less productivity, and stifled creativity.

"Oh, but isn't that all just 'soft' dollars?" they ask. "Aren't these really just missed opportunity costs that are endemic to any business or organization?" The answer, of course, is *no*. Consider Sears, which turned over 119,000 retailing jobs in 1989. Hiring and training costs averaged $900 for each new employee, for a total cost to Sears of $110 million.

Beyond direct costs, a 1990 study showed that "hidden costs" may account for an additional 80 percent or more of tangible out-of-pocket turnover costs. Hidden costs include:

- Inefficiency of incoming employees.
- Disruption and confusion to existing employees from incoming ones.
- Departing employee inefficiencies.
- Negative work efficiency of employees affected by departing employees.
- Negative impact on project completion.

Moreover, research has shown the correlation between *employee* satisfaction and *customer* satisfaction. In particular with service organizations, employees usually *are* the service. Not only do they deliver the service that is being purchased, they embody the service offering itself through their expertise or skill base. Unsatisfied and demoralized employees usually are not able to deliver the quality or service excellence that customers demand. Consequently, companies lose customers to competitors, which results in lost revenues.

Herein lies the huge bottom-line cost to organizations from anomic fallout—lost customers, disgruntled customers, and resultant nonrevenue-generating customers. The big problem and reason why most organizations becomes blasé about this cost is because no one even knows it. Customers don't usually call to tell a service provider that they've decided to move their business elsewhere. Few companies keep careful track of former customers to determine their revenue and profit-attrition rate from lost customers. This is the hidden cost of anomic organizations. This is the cost that must be reduced.

The corporate asset for the twenty-first century is people—not computers, robotics, or automated distribution systems. Therefore, norms and values need to be developed that motivate, inspire, and energize employees. Their positive impact will collectively yield far more bottom-line profits than any new strategy, program, or policy possibly could.

In contrast to Caterpillar, which has had union, competitive, and profit problems, John Deere & Co. achieved robust profits in 1993, and in 1994 net income is expected to reach nearly $400 million, up 35 percent from 1993. How has this turnaround happened? Well, it's a great plug for how the power of norms and values can reenergize a work force, rechannel employees, and gain an employee-led competitive advantage. In 1991, Deere had a $20 million loss. CEO Hans Becherer decided to leverage its work force. He believed that his work force had a lot to offer regarding quality improvements, costs savings, and enhanced customer service. He believed that employees would be more responsive and participatory in improving efficiency if they felt part of the process. In his view, employees needed to be the leaders rather than the recipients of change.

"We have damn good employees," Becherer stated in a Business Week interview. "We can compete with anyone in the world." Four key initiatives helped to drive Deere's work force into a more efficient team:

- Increased education and training by linking pay raises to completing technical courses.
- Aligning workers to non-traditional jobs allowing for more crossover into customer service and other areas.
- Customer-contact exposure by bringing hourly workers to farms to have them see how customers actually use their equipment.
- Sessions with suppliers and assembly-line workers to help cut costs and improve delivery times.

In short, the values message sent to Deere's employees are ones that support a respect and recognition of the contributions that hourly employees can make to the success of a company. Actually enabling and empowering increased training, customer contact, and the like to occur does a lot more than just turn employees into customer-smart ones. It converts them to a synergistic energy source where two plus two does equal five.

Perhaps these reasons may be enough to motivate corporate leaders to better understand and appreciate the precious cost of anomie: declining stock prices, lower returns on equity, and less year-end bonus money in their pockets. Shareholders and investors are getting a lot smarter. They can't be easily fooled. And, more and more, they are seeing through the thin veil that some corporate CEOs wear to disguise their organization's anomie.

Factors that Increase Job Satisfaction

We've cited several thought leaders who summarize the cure for organizational anomie. But it is the workers themselves who told us—directly—how to break out of the eggshell. For when the eggshell is cracked open, employees cite several methods for enhancing job satisfaction, as depicted in Exhibit 4-2. We'll close this chapter as we began it—with employees' desire for bringing norms and values back into their organization.

- *Leaders who set the example.* It cannot be assumed that if management sets a good example for its employees, they will adopt the norms and values the company espouses through observation. Management did set a good example in many companies, but, in most cases, the employees were still uncertain about what the norms and values were that they should adopt. Norms and values must be consistently activated if they are to be understood and adopted by employees. Leaders who set the example provide a role model for other employees to follow.

- *Visibly practiced norms and values.* You'll recall our research found that most employees *readily* noticed and identified discrepancies between what management put forth as norms and values and what was actually practiced by employees. The norms and values in most companies are unwritten and, most times, uncommunicated. This leaves employees and managers guessing about what they might be. Few employees or managers seem to be particularly confident about what the norms and values actually are in their com-

EXHIBIT 4-2

Employee-cited Desires
Leading to Increased Job Satisfaction

Leaders who set
the example

Visibly practiced norms and values

Greater responsibility

Lower turnover

More direct, yet constructive confrontation

Personal values linked to job

Increased motivation and trust

Values training and discussion

Recognition and fairness

Pluralism and diversity
demonstrated

panies. When asked, few were able to come up with a "list" of norms and values. In part, this is because norms in practice conflict with stated norms. Employees want to see and experience the norms and values—daily—not just hear management talk about them.

- *Greater responsibility.* As we've seen earlier, many of the low- and mid-level managers we interviewed cited "a desire for greater responsibilities in the company" as the one thing that would contribute most to improving their overall job satisfaction. Other commonly mentioned and desired interests were greater budget control and assignment of more resources to them, signs of increased responsibility.

- *Lower turnover.* Organizations with clear guidelines for interaction or a distinct system of norms and values have lower employee turnover rates. Employees are generally more satisfied than are those working in settings with undefined, uncommunicated norms and values. Employees want to work where turnover is low. This enables them to develop and keep relationships and work patterns with co-workers. They want and need consistency.

- *More direct, yet constructive confrontation.* A negative norm cited was the tendency for employees and managers to avoid direct confrontations or conflicts within the workplace. Managers tended to avoid confronting employees directly if they made a mistake. Similarly, employees who had a conflict or problem with another employee's actions or work were not likely to deal with that situation directly. Therefore, there was a substantial amount of uncertainty regarding employee performance. But employees truly want to know "where they stand." It's that simple. Employees "expect" confrontation and especially want to see it happen with co-workers who are underperforming or negatively impacting the effectiveness of a work team.

- *Personal values linked to job.* Very few people said their workplace had contributed to shaping their personal norms and values. Instead, most cited family and friends as having the greatest impact on their norms-and-values formation. Nevertheless, most employees want to see a greater connec-

tion between their individual personal values and those in the
workplace.

- *Increased motivation and trust.* Employees at organizations
  with a fairly clear set of norms and values most often worked
  hard even when they were not being supervised by management. The magnetic values in their workplace served as a
  source of motivation. In contrast, at companies with few or
  no norms and values, employees tended to "goof off" whenever they had the chance to do so. Employees who feel and
  believe that their bosses trust them are far more motivated
  and perform more effectively.

- *Values training and discussions.* "Talking and walking" values are perceived as beneficial by employees. This means
  that actions support the words. Coming up with an annual list
  of values just doesn't cut it. But discussing them and acting
  upon them does. Open discussions play an integral role in
  conveying company norms and values—especially when discussion is both formal and informal.

- *Recognition and fairness.* In terms of an "increasing sense of
  purpose," most interviewees were in agreement that recognition and fairness of treatment are paramount to nurturing
  contentment and commitment. Furthermore, there is a need
  to be told the truth—to not be left confused—as to what is
  expected and what can be accomplished.

- *Pluralism and diversity demonstrated.* While there were
  diverse opinions on this topic, employees *did* want a workplace that was void of discrimination. Recruitment and promotion practices need to support and reinforce a belief in pluralism and demonstrate support for diversity. Actions and
  words need to consistently portray and reinforce a pluralistic
  mindset and attitude.

Taken together, these ten employee desires, cited by interviewees themselves, help to describe the urgent need to infuse
norms and values into organizations, allow employees to break out
of their eggshells, and increase employees' job satisfaction.

Part II
The Foundation

Chapter 5

Laying the Foundation

In the previous chapter, we examined the specific norms and values gaps that employees encounter in the workplace. We explored the way anomie begins to take hold in organizations. We summarized the specific ways employees would like to reduce their alienation from their company and increase their job satisfaction. But developing organizational values to alleviate anomie cannot be imposed from "on high" by senior management. It all starts with the individual.

Developing Individual Values

Values are not born overnight. It takes time to identify and cultivate beliefs. Moreover, personal values change over time. They evolve, shift, and constantly migrate to a refined set that keeps some previously established values and adds new ones. Before an organization can develop and articulate the norms and values of its group members, individuals need to think about and spend adequate time determining their personal values. But to accomplish this, we strongly believe that individuals need unencumbered time—a series of small respites, relaxed time, unstressed time, focused time.

We all waste a lot of time every week on activities that rob rather than enrich our lives. We lack self-rejuvenating time. We need this time to charge up our internal batteries and provide an open spot in our minds that is not overrun by innumerable daily burdens, hassles, and problems. Beyond increasing the balance between work and play, we feel *all* Americans need more time to focus on values, norms, and personal self-development.

We've already discovered that Band-Aid solutions won't work for curing anomie. The problems of anomie have become deeply rooted and entrenched. Too many people have developed a severe case of apathy. This mindset says "it's not my problem—I can't do anything about it." Therefore, the solutions must be penetrating and, quite frankly, radical. Any one specific program, change, law, or cultural shift won't be enough. Instead, each individual must heed a call to action that will help society bring back values and fill anomie's vacuous void.

But can each of us—as individuals—make the difference? Well, maybe, just maybe, we can. Only when we as individuals focus on our own values can we develop values within organizations. We need to restructure our lives so that as individuals we have the time to focus on values. We should try to overcome our own apathy before our children develop a drug addiction, we lose our job, our best friend is severely discriminated against, our co-worker's depression gets worse, or our house gets robbed by values-less thugs. Sure, once one of those conflict events take place, then we're ready for action. Well, how about before they happen? How about now?

We suggest seven initiatives we believe can help get a values-ful mindset started in our society. They are provocative and forward-thinking. Their goal is to make more time that can be focused on the development and cultivation of personal values. These initiatives are also intended to stimulate *your* thinking and serve more as a starting point than as a finish line.

Seven Initiatives to Build a Values Mindset

1. Decrease TV watching and charge a 100% "sin" tax on all domestic and foreign televisions as a deterrent to television

OWNERSHIP.   The television is an ever-increasing usurper of valuable "down-time." Rather than reading, thinking, writing, drawing, or just conversing with other individuals, Americans spend, on average, over 29 hours per week planted in front of the "one-way dialogue-only" television set. Imagine it. People spend more than four hours each day passively watching the television. It's simply an amazingly negative energy drain and time waster.

While we hear from people that "I relax and can wind down when watching TV," there is nothing further from the truth. It's a scam; a charade. How can you relax watching people getting killed, buildings set on fire, or insultingly stupid sitcoms that put people down?

Children, in particular, can demonstrate vividly how time is used when there is no television available. They play games, engage in sports, read, cook, ride bicycles, draw, use the computer, and talk. When children and adults *don't* have a television, they *do* find other things to engage in. They become active listeners, participants of a group, or they engage in a self-directed activity. They don't sit on a sofa and stare blankly at a wall. They actually talk with other family members. This missing ingredient—down time—is a vital component for values development. Without time alone, as well as without genuine dialogue with other people who are interested in you and who care about you, it's difficult to develop a values framework or reference points to adhere them to. Consequently, elimination of or drastic reduction in time spent watching the brown tube will open up time for values. This will be far better for building and cultivating values than is TV gaping.

Television is a major contributor to our societal state of anomie. It causes even further fragmentation and individual isolation. "Did you see Letterman last night?" "Wasn't Seinfeld a riot the other night?" Instead of social conversations about individuals' thoughts, needs, opinions, and feelings, we substitute more meaningful dialogue with reviews and "ratings" on the previous evening's television shows or soap operas.

Our society's major institutions—families, schools, churches, the workplace, marriage, and neighborhood communities—have become weakened. They have far less influence today in shaping our norms and values. TV has taken up the slack. Television serves as one more nail to drive into the anomie coffin.

So what can we do? We propose that the government provide an economic dis-incentive to television purchasing. By charging a 100 percent penalty or "sin" tax to every television, we may end up discouraging the perpetuation of this mindless activity. This tax, which might be earmarked for improving our educational systems, will signal to Americans that TVs *are* harmful to our emotional and "values-ful" selves. The sin tax will serve, at the very least, as a psychological deterrent, if not a financial one.

Decreasing or, yes, banning television is one right step toward giving individuals time to develop their own values and beliefs and allowing them to cultivate and evolve their own personal norms. Now, of course, another viable alternative is to eliminate all television violence. That alternative definitely has merit, but our vote is to just drop all television from our anomic lives, eliminating the problem from the outset.

2. CLOSE ALL RETAIL STORES ON SATURDAY *OR* SUNDAY.   Can you remember back when you couldn't go shopping or errand hopping on Sunday? We need to restore that sacred block of time again. It seems as if, in our quest to make it more convenient for shoppers to increase their available purchasing power, we've forgotten what we sacrificed in the process.

Sundays used to be far more focused on participating in social institutions that provided people with environments that offered values—institutions such as churches, families, neighborhoods, friends, and social communities. Institutions such as shopping malls, strip malls, and supermarkets offer no such values. Whatever we've forgotten to purchase on Saturday can certainly wait until Monday. Perhaps, as a nod toward our need for food and medicine, some convenience stores should stay open on Sunday, along with a few drug stores to have access to medicine. But the rest of the stores should be closed down.

We can envision, for example, a Nordstrom's newspaper ad in the future:

> Nordstrom's respects your need to spend time with your family, friends, and with yourself. Consequently, we are closing our stores on Sundays to provide you with quiet time. Spend it wisely! However, to accommodate your working and busy schedules, our stores will be open until 9:00 P.M. Monday–Saturday.

In this way, total available shopping time really hasn't decreased, nor is the convenience factor for customers dissipated. Rather, this re-scheduling of shopping time provides one day each week for people to focus on personal values and more time to participate in social institutions that can be enriching rather than materialistic.

Perhaps a progressive state could encourage closing all retail stores on Sunday. It could tout: "New Jersey—The Back to Values State." We have nothing against the wonderful diversity of retail store offerings. We're just trying to find tangible reminders that all individuals need to focus more time and attention on values development. Perhaps having Sundays free from shopping excursions will give us the chance to do so.

3. INCREASE VACATIONS TO FOUR WEEKS AND ENABLE ALL EMPLOYEES TO TAKE A TWO-MONTH SABBATICAL AFTER SEVEN YEARS OF EMPLOYMENT. Loyalty is a value that many organizations have abandoned, forgotten about, or grossly neglected. It's a value that had been in place for years and provided employees with security, self-confidence, and a sense of belonging. But it's become an overlooked value by many organizations as well as by many employees.

Our third suggested initiative to help build a values mindset is aimed at providing more values-cultivation time to individuals, as well as rewarding and reinforcing the value of loyalty throughout an organization. First, companies should reexamine their vacation policies and develop a four-weeks' vacation policy for all employees after two years of full-time employment. Four weeks is far more time than the norm of two weeks, which is the average for American workers today. Only after decades of loyalty and dedication can most workers look forward to a four- or five-week vacation schedule. Today's senior managers always get at least four weeks at the outset. We believe this initiative should be adopted for all employees throughout the organization.

If you are an employer reading this suggestion, remember this: regardless of the amount of payroll increases you think you'll incur, you will more than offset that cost with more loyal, motivated, productive, and values-ful employees.

But don't stop there. A two-month paid sabbatical after every seven consecutive years of full-time employment will provide employees with a period of adequate time to do something that can have long-term benefit and payback for themselves and for the company. It's a long enough time away from work that a major professional project or initiative could be undertaken.

4. ESTABLISH A NATIONALLY CELEBRATED FAMILY VALUES WEEKEND. The purpose of this national holiday would be aimed at increasing awareness of the need to spend concentrated time discussing and "living" family values. The point of this initiative is not to spend only one weekend a year on family values, but rather to raise it to a higher level of consciousness. This initiative could ultimately be escalated to become a weekly endeavor. The members of the family can be defined however you choose. The emphasis shouldn't be on who but rather on *what* is discussed and agreed upon. Now, how do you start a conversation about values? Try asking your children what they like and don't like in other people. Ask them what their needs are. Ask them about their heroes, whom they look up to and why. Ask them about something they're proud of. Tell them about one of your failures. Ask them about two of their fears. Get to know them—and yourself—a bit better in the process.

5. IDENTIFY AND CONSISTENTLY ACTIVATE FAMILY RITUALS WITH ALL FAMILY MEMBERS. What are families? Single parent. Divorced parent. Gay parents. Multi-ethnic parents. They are *all* part of families in the 1990s. Family can no longer be defined as the traditional "working dad and stay-at-home mom." That definition is naive and dinosaurlike. What is relevant, though, is recognizing that a family, regardless of its composition, is a sacred, powerful, and significant energy source that can have monumental impact on each member's values.

One way to nurture values is to consistently partake in family rituals. Rituals offer children, in particular, a sense of stability, security, and sense of belonging. Rituals give them emotional anchors, which help them to cope with the other uneven aspects of life. Examples of family rituals are Sunday night dinners, Saturday afternoon movies, weekly religious attendance, holiday celebrations, birthday parties, and morning breakfasts together. The key is to choose some and stick to them—consistently.

6. INITIATE AN IN-DEPTH RELATIONSHIP WITH SOMEONE FROM A DIVERSE GROUP. No, this is not a "token" initiative. It's a significant step. Under normal life circumstances, many of us, unfortunately, do not readily have an in-depth relationship with a person from a group that is not "just like ourselves." Diversity comes in many types—socioeconomic class, national origin, ethnicity, political beliefs, gender, religion, race, age, sexual orientation, or personal philosophy. In fact, individuals we know who have taken this initiative have ended up being far more disposed toward pluralism than they were prior to this experience.

First, try eating a meal with this person—perhaps a breakfast or lunch. Try to have the meal in a relaxed setting, without wearing any pseudo-security masks. Ask the person about his or her childhood, siblings, and parents. Ask the person what motivates him or her, demotivates him or her. Ask the person about his or her needs, fears, and likes. Get to know the person better and then ask yourself if your previously prejudicial views were accurate or inaccurate. And then get together with the same person two or three times more and ask more questions. This type of initiative is aimed at increasing the level of understanding about the "unknown" minority. They tend to be "unknowns" because others outside of their group just don't take the time to get to know them better. It's simply as sad as that. But, with enhanced knowledge and insight, false-grounded feelings will likely float away. If individuals take this initiative, organizations will eventually welcome and encourage a wide range of expressions of diversity.

7. HOLD A PARTY AND INVITE TEN NEIGHBORS WHO LIVE IN YOUR NEIGHBORHOOD. Do you even know ten neighbors who, day in and day out, live next to you? Well, if you don't, it's time you did. It's important to restore and reestablish a sense of community. But this can be achieved only through individual grassroots initiatives. A group of people, living next to one another (or often in the same condominium building), may keep to themselves and remain on separate "islands." For a group of people to ever hope to progress into a team, a community, or a neighborhood, they need to know one another. For most of us today, we don't know even five neighbors who live but a few yards away from us. Shouldn't we try to get to know them?

Granted, some of these initiatives will require some government and organization assistance, but several can be activated on an individual basis. What are some of your ideas? Please write us and tell us some of your ideas for reducing anomie and for improving our society and its organizations to be more values-ful. We'd be pleased to pass on your responses to others in future writings.

The Need for the 3 S's

As employees and managers, we are deprived of establishing meaning, values, and norms in our work lives. These, however, are the needed ingredients to enable us to develop the 3 S's: self-confidence, satisfaction, and security. Each one of these ingredients can help fix our shaken, fragmented, uncertain selves. Our inner lack of confidence is one of the many negative impacts of anomie. Without norms and values to lay a foundation for our inner feelings and insecurities, our self-confidence cracks and gradually erodes.

We have entered a values erosion era, perpetuated by a reversal of personal values. There is a lack of respect for individual needs and beliefs. We tend to care far less today about other people than we care for our own self-aggrandizement and materialistic gain. Think about it. When you're in a conversation with your boss, colleague, or neighbor, how many *personal* questions do they ask you that genuinely conveys an interest in you as an individual? Usually, not many. Most often, none at all. Why should they? Because you are a unique and totally fascinating person with fascinating opinions, thoughts, ideas, and feelings. When you meet people that *do* convey interest in you, your immediate reaction is usually a positive, endearing, and engaging one. The reason is simple: They're giving you a reason to believe in yourself and a demonstration of your worth as an individual. This, in turn, increases your self-confidence, personal satisfaction, and sense of security. Developing these three S's can fortify individuals, giving them meaning, a sense of belonging, and personal contentment.

To give employees in an organization a reason to believe they must have a sense of purpose and belonging. Once these two key ingredients have been established, an employee's self-confidence and inner security will be dramatically increased, enabling self-satisfaction to flourish. Leaders must pay close attention to the 3 S's. They can use norms and values as pneumatic pumps to keep self-confidence, satisfaction, and security buoyant and alive.

But rather than merely focusing on the end result (that is, whether employees are satisfied or not), organizations need to discover the underlying cause of each and better understand the specific series of events leading up to the contentment or discomfort. When doing so, they will likely find a major mismatch of perceived and desired norms and values among employees combined with an overall employee need to define, reinforce, and substantiate these norms and values.

By developing a values mission statement or people pledge, leadership both signals to the organization the need for norms and values, as well as provides a tangible way to reinforce and encourage them. Leadership needs to clarify them and promote those values that enable employees to once again believe.

Not surprisingly, both management and the board of directors of most organizations provide a thick layer of insulation around themselves. They avoid asking their three most important constituencies about what they think are the appropriate norms and values for their company: employees, consumers, and shareholders. Why not hold small-group forums or focus groups or administer a survey to each to solicit their input or advice on desirable norms and values for their organization? Ask each constituent and listen.

Andrew Campbell offers the following advice in *The Power of Mission: Aligning Strategy and Culture:* "Manage the link between belief and behavior. By giving people a reason for new behavior that fits their beliefs, you make change easy." He eloquently explains the linkage that exists between values and behaviors, and describes the power of norms and values to affect positive change within organizations.

The Values Foundation Prescription

Organization management needs to stimulate an environment and establish a mindset that says, "We want each and every employee to vocalize their needs, wants, fears, concerns, frustrations, hot-buttons, and dislikes." In this way, through risk-free communication, we can begin to lay the foundation for shaping and conveying to others our individual beliefs and values. Once the cement has dried and some values are solidified, the task of developing norms and expected behavioral patterns can be started.

So let's now turn to a potential prescription for beginning to cure anomie, lay the foundation, and open up the collective set of imprisoned values that can reenergize any organization. The overall starting point includes the following ten recommendations for improved values and norms health:

The Values Foundation Prescription

1. Promote an overall mindset that recognizes the intrinsic value, strengths, and merit of each individual.

2. Develop and promulgate a written statement of the organization's values that is visible and believed in by employees.

3. Activate rewards and recognition that reinforce, support, and encourage the values cited.

4. Cultivate credible leaders who set the example by regularly displaying the values of the company through tangible actions.

5. Establish norms that encourage open discussions and expressions of feelings, fears, wants, and needs.

6. Develop leadership-supported norms that encourage and reinforce loyalty and dedication by employees.

7. Define and integrate a norms that convey the values of the company and its employees through the company's products and services to the customers served.

8. Craft and activate recruiting policies and norms that support pluralism and hiring of employees whose values closely match those of the organization.

9. Establish shared leadership and a shared-values culture that is generated from the bottom-up, endorsed by all, and embodied in group accepted norms. Create an action plan for turn-

ing every leader into a "values spokesperson" for the organization.

10. Nurture norms that reinforce teamness, diversity, risk taking, innovation, integrity, individualized control, and customer/client satisfaction.

As stated by Barry Posner and Warren Schmidt in a 1992 article, *Values and the American Manager: An Update Updated,* "We refer to managerial values as the *silent* power in personal and organizational life. Values are at the core of our personality, influencing the choices we make, the people we trust, the appeals we respond to, and the way we invest our time and energy. In turbulent times, values can give a sense of direction amid conflicting views and demands." In short, this emerging new interest in and recognition of the benefits of shared values will provide employees with a reason to believe.

There is no doubt that the silent power that Posner and Schmidt refer to is similar to our own intense belief. It's a belief we have espoused for a long time. This book's co-author, Dr. Susan Smith Kuczmarski, stated in a 1983 speech:

"Values make the person and values-ful persons make the organization—it's as simple as that. But the values need to be shared and agreed upon by *all* the members of an organization—not pontificated by a few anointed managers at the top."

As Robert Haas, the chairman and CEO of Levi Strauss & Co., has stated: "The alignment between organizational values and personal values is the key driver of corporate success." Yes, yes, yes! We totally agree. The starting point for all of this begins with individual personal values. Unless we "expose" ourselves—our inner selves—we won't lay a foundation that is real, meaningful, and long-lasting.

Develop a Value System that Serves

The days of self-centeredness must end. Managers need to develop a servant's mindset, a mindset that suggests the reason why we go to work every day is to serve others—not to have others serve us. The "to serve" orientation means looking after the needs of many different groups, including employees, consumers, suppliers, and shareholders. In short, the purpose of our daily activities should reinforce an attitude and mindset that tries to identify the needs, meet or exceed the expectations of, and improve the overall satisfaction level of the following constituencies:

Shareholders (owners, investors, etc.)
Employees (managers, leaders, workers, etc.)
Retailers (dealers, distributors, salespersons, etc.)
VIP suppliers (vendors, partners)
End-users (consumers, members, students, etc.)

These groups can be segmented according to their "proximity" to the organization itself:

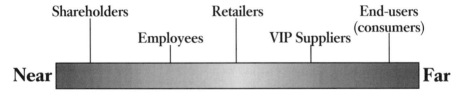

Proximity to Organization

The challenge becomes more difficult as we move further away from the organization itself, that is, as we try to satisfy consumers. It's fascinating that most organizations do a much better job, though, of satisfying the two ends of the spectrum: their shareholders and end-users, than the constituencies in the middle which should be easier to satisfy.

Going forward, employees will need a reason to be loyal, want far more independence and satisfaction from their work, more personal empowerment, and a better organizational lifestyle. Employees need to identify and reinforce the values and norms that will accomplish this change. This axiom applies to organizations and companies as well as to individuals. Organizations as well must develop a values system that defines specific norms and values for each internal and external group. The development of employee-based norms and values is only the starting point.

Chapter 6

Energizing Organizations

In this chapter, we'll examine a series of issues that serve as cornerstones for effectively energizing organizations. We'll touch upon the way organizations can structure themselves to provide a bridge to an effective participatory and shared leadership construct. Next, we'll introduce a new concept called "peoplequity" which values the contributions of an organization's biggest asset—its people. We'll also discuss a critical concept—teaming in a shared values environment—as a foundation for helping organizations evolve into values-ful cultures. You'll have a chance to assess how values-ful your own organization is today. Finally, we'll show you the ten building blocks of a values-based organization.

Values-Based Organizations Are Energized Organizations

How values-ful is your own organization? Norms and values collectively make up a large portion of an organization's culture. In fact, the prevalence of norms and values directly translates to the strength or weakness of an organization and its employees. This, in turn, will determine how committed and productive employees are relative to the goals and strategies of the organization. If an organization has a cohesive and distinct norms-and-values system, it will have the basic building blocks for creating a strong culture and powerful organization. With this in place, employees will feel a sense of attachment and belonging. They will then believe their work really adds value to the whole, and they will be reenergized to *want* to come to work each day.

If a supportive culture is absent, many employees will not be focused on the organization's mission and goals. Rather, they will work to promote their *own* goals and objectives, which may be incongruous with the goals of the organization. Therefore, establishing commonly agreed-upon norms and values is a critical step for aligning the goals of the organization with the personal goals of employees.

Having effective norms and values can be greatly beneficial in linking employees together without the need for bureaucratic rules, corporate regulations, and hierarchical organization structures. With motivating compensation programs that are performance-based and norms and values that serve as "fasteners," linking employees to each other and the organization, there isn't the need for so many rules. Employees will do what they are supposed to do because they want to—not because they are coerced or because they have to.

> A 34-year-old marketing executive at a $200 million manufacturing firm told us, "I feel as if I'm part of the management team at our company. They respect me both as an individual and as a professional. What I say really does count. I *am* able to make decisions which aren't second-guessed. My annual compensation reflects how well I've been able to move the organization closer to achieving its goals, and I get recognized with praise and peer recognition in doing so. While I technically report to the COO, I don't ever feel as if he is my boss or manager. I guess I really feel as if he and I are partners—in this thing together. Yes we do share a common set of values."

The foregoing example is a wonderful one of a values-based organization. It demonstrates the energy and power that can permeate an employee base that believes in the organization and its culture. The key to a truly energized organization is, of course, norms and values.

In fact, norms and values can replace the traditional and linear reporting hierarchy. Imagine eliminating a tiered, layered organization. Employees and leaders end up working together more as equals—as partners. For sure, each will bring different skills, forms of intelligence, and contributions to the organization "party," but each will no longer feel like a subordinate *underneath* someone else in the organization. Future organizations will readily recognize the positive energy and effectiveness of creating values-based organizations. Let's look at the evolution that's been occurring to date in leadership styles and organization structures.

As depicted in Exhibit 6–1, a traditional hierarchical structure was the guiding principle for most organizations from the 1950s through the 1980s. Now, of course, there are still many organizations today that have this archaic hierarchy in place, but many more progressive companies have evolved to a more participatory style of leadership. The big problem with the hierarchical structure (see Table A) is that it needs an autocratic, top-down, and often dominating leadership style. This style further propels anomie, makes employees lose self-confidence and feel "small," and disconnects their inner motivations from the organization.

While Harold Geneen was able to lead ITT for many years with an autocratic and iron fist, once he left, the company began to slide downward. Why? With an autocratic leader, employees are made helpless. They take orders, do what they're told, express no emotion, don't rock the boat, and certainly don't think for themselves. Self-confidence is usurped, self-worth is devalued, and self-satisfaction is effaced. As long as the autocratic leader is in place, motivation by fear and intimidation will continue to drive employees to strive toward achieving their leader's goals. But when he or she leaves, employees virtually don't know how to act, think, or behave. Few relationships have been built and no value structure and norms exist to tie the organization together. With the autocratic leader now gone, there is no social glue.

Many organizations are recognizing that succession planning requires developing the leadership skills and effectiveness of many employees—not just a select few. You shouldn't just have a handful of senior people waiting in the wings to take over some day. Leaders should exist at all levels throughout organizations. Here's another example. From 1992 to early 1994, eight out of

EXHIBIT 6-1

Evolving Leadership Styles and Organization Structures

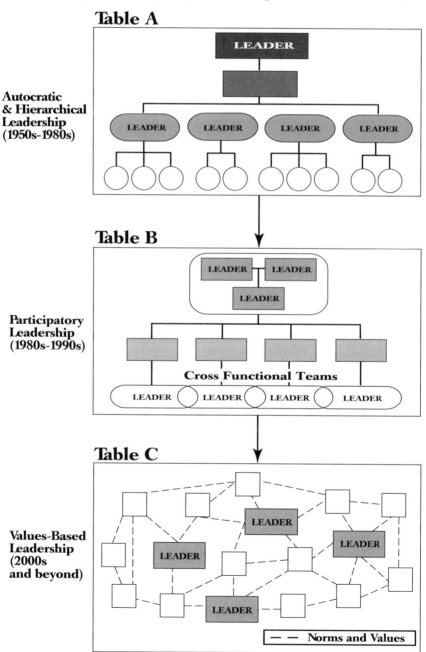

Table A

Autocratic & Hierarchical Leadership (1950s-1980s)

Table B

Participatory Leadership (1980s-1990s)

Cross Functional Teams

Table C

Values-Based Leadership (2000s and beyond)

– – – Norms and Values

nine senior executives left a Fortune 500 medical products company. That left one person at the top—the chairman. Oh, by the way, the stock has declined over 40 percent during the same time period. Sure doesn't look like a shared leadership style at the top, now, does it? It takes a long time to cultivate employees into leaders. Cultures must be created where people want to stay in the same organization for long periods of time. Without tenure, even the right norms and values won't yield positive results because "churning" managers over does not allow for consistency and continuity.

Smart organizations have been evolving toward participatory, team, and shared leadership structures as depicted in Table B. Sometimes a group of senior managers at the top will form an Office of the Chairman or a Senior Management Executive Team. This is a good start at establishing a shared leadership construct, because it encourages shared decision making and responsibility. But for an organization to be truly participatory and to honestly cultivate a shared leadership mindset throughout an organization, multiple leaders need to be established on teams, projects, products, and functions. We strongly encourage cross-functional teams with team leaders coming from a variety of backgrounds.

This type of leadership fosters teams as an effective way of capturing and leveraging the skills and capabilities of individuals across departments, functions, and even divisions. The use of cross-functional or multidisciplinary teams helps to perpetuate the shared leadership approach throughout the organization.

We've used Table C to graphically portray a values-based leadership approach. While this leadership style may first appear to be random, it's actually not. What appear to be scattered and sporadic reporting relationships are actually solid, integrated, and cohesive ones. In fact, employees and leaders are far more closely aligned and more effectively related to each other than in the previous two constructs. A strong sense of "partnership" exists. Values-based leadership brings out the best in employees because they are able to perform at their maximum potential. They don't have to play politics, play games, or play the good organizational "soldier." They can play themselves. They can express their professional passion.

A great sense of individual respect, equality, and endorsement of diversity becomes the values cornerstone. Employees and leaders aren't looking behind their backs to see if someone is about to "stab" them. Rather, they are looking forward, knowing that the people who surround them are also "rowing with them," not against them. Anomie is dissipated.

The "glue" that binds each employee together, and collectively to the organization, allowing linkages to be actualized, is mutually agreed-upon norms and values. Designated leaders of the various groups aren't just positioned at the "top" of the organization, but rather are integrated throughout it. This instills greater commitment from all employees. To a great extent, it does indeed suggest that every single employee is a critical part of the whole organization. The values fabric will have holes in it and will become separated unless all employees participate in holding it together. A chain is only as strong as its weakest link, and a team is only as strong as its weakest member.

The Ultimate Value—Peoplequity

Many years ago a vice-president was appalled to see the way Jim Dickerson, a black consultant, was being treated by senior partners at the firm. She fully recognized and was aware of Jim's analytical smarts, dedication to the firm, and intense desire to serve and satisfy clients. However, Jim had a slight speech impediment. You can't believe how quickly and self-righteously those partners set out to find ways to "legally" ask Jim to leave the firm and find other employment. What is the message we can interpret from this example?

Clearly, their values focused far more on cosmetics than on Jim's initiative, smarts, and dedication. How could a company be so callous, myopic, and careless? Simple—because anomie was resident, and because the company was blind to its real asset: people. We propose that organizations consider a new concept for measuring the economic worth of its people. We call this concept "peoplequity."

Peoplequity is a new concept that future values-based organizations should consider. Peoplequity is the economic value of people. Nowhere on company balance sheets is there a regular line item that reflects the economic worth of people. Think about it.

Balance sheets depict the assets, liabilities, and net worth of a company. On the asset side of the balance sheets, accountants include receivables, plants, equipment, inventory, cash, computers, and the like. For the most part, the "assets" are tangible bricks and mortar, machines, money, and other hard goods that can be converted into an economic worth. Depreciation is used to account for their decline in value over time due to use and deterioration. So all these tangible assets represent the "plus" side of the balance sheet. But wait a minute—intangibles are also included. Accountants do place an economic value on such things as patents, proprietary technology, distribution networks, and sometimes even on customer lists, brand equity, and goodwill. Astonishingly, these intangibles often represent the major line items on the balance sheet. For example, in 1992, the Black & Decker Corporation showed a total of $5.4 billion in total assets. Guess what represented $2.5 billion of that total? You guessed it— goodwill. If we are able to calculate an economic worth for goodwill, then why aren't we defining a separate economic worth for the number *one* and *most* valuable asset—people?

Peoplequity needs to become an accepted accounting practice for measuring and valuing the worth of an organization's employee asset base. We place goodwill value on brand names, company recognition and image, and other intangibles. But many companies consistently undervalue or, worse yet, don't value at all the key asset that really counts for bringing long-term competitive advantage to an organization—its people. Although the accounting practice of valuing the intangible contributions of people is calculated as goodwill during the acquisition or sale of a company, most companies do not follow this practice on a regular financial accounting basis.

Interestingly, the stock market does tend to recognize the peoplequity value at least of CEOs. Look at how stock prices fluctuate when a new CEO comes to or leaves a company. The stock will often jump or decline by as much as 5 percent or 10 percent. Examples abound: Take a look at IBM, Apple, Merck, Baxter, and Borden within the past two years. Each company has had major senior management turnover that pounded their stock prices down. The financial community is, in effect, placing an economic worth, a tangible financial value, on that individual CEO. Without necessarily knowing it, the financial community has effectively illustrated the importance of peoplequity.

But the way to think about peoplequity is in terms of all the employees of a company—not just the CEO. Granted, developing a measurement system for determining the economic value and contributing worth of each individual is not easy. However, finance and accounting experts have created a way to do it with depreciating machinery. It seems as if we should be able to find a way to do so with appreciating human "assets."

Peoplequity needs to become a regularly used, standard economic measurement of the worth of an organization's people. It needs to be added to the balance sheet. Our accounting practices need to develop an innovative approach for assessing the economic value of people within companies. We need to find a way to better measure the unique talents, skills, leverageable competencies, and competitive advantages of our people—not just our plants, equipment, and technologies. Let's explore some specific suggestions.

Peoplequity could be determined by an individual's tenure, historical accomplishments, skills assessment, and previous bottom-line performance. As the productivity and performance of a work force increases, the worth of those individuals should concomitantly increase in value to the organization.

Perhaps we could develop a formula that, for example, includes several of these factors—a *skills- and experience-based* calculation. Or alternatively, how about calculating the economic value based on an employee's *replacement* cost? This calculation would include recruiting, training, and professional development costs, as well as a new-employee compensation package. Let us provide two illustrative examples. Please keep in mind that the intention of these examples is meant only to provide greater understanding of the peoplequity concept. We are not recommending the methodology of either one—the accounting community will need to do that.

The underlying assumption in peoplequity is that individuals can indeed increase the economic worth of an organization. Under the first scenario, a skills- and experience-based formula (see Exhibit 6-2), an organization employs four criteria to serve as the basis of its peoplequity measurement. These criteria are as follows: First, an individual's years of experience in a related field is a key

EXHIBIT 6-2

Peoplequity: Skills- and Experience-based Formula

Criteria	Economic Worth Conversion Factor	32-year-old Marketer		51-year-old Chief Operating Officer	
		Criteria	Economic Worth	Criteria	Economic Worth
Years of experience in related field	$10,000 per year	5 yrs	$50,000	25 yrs	$250,000
Cumulative net profits generated from all organizations previously led	$100 per million of net profits generated	$3.5 million	$35,000	$34 million	$340,000
Value of skills-- both functional and leadership	A-$200,000 B-$100,000 C-$50,000 D-$25,000	C	$50,000	A	$200,000
Concrete, finite accomplishments that relate to projects impacting bottom-line profit performance	$1000 per accomplishment	12	$12,000	94	$94,000
Total Peoplequity Value			$147,000		$884,000

factor and includes a guesstimate of future potential. Experience does have economic worth. Second, the cumulative net profits generated from all of the organizations that an individual has previously led. This criterion demonstrates the hard-core, bottom-line performance of the individual. Past performance does have economic worth. Third, the value of the individual's functional and leadership skills is qualitatively and subjectively assessed. Fourth, the specific finite accomplishments of an individual is measured by the number of projects that have yielded a bottom-line profit benefit to the organization. In the Skills- and Experience-based Formula example, the combination of the two employees cited would represent $1,031,000 worth of people economic value or peoplequity.

Now let's look at a replacement cost formula alternative as depicted in Exhibit 6–3. Here, the key cost categories we've assumed include: (1) base salary, (2) bonuses, (3) perks, (4) stock equity, (5) recruiting costs, and (6) the first two years of training and development costs for the individual employee.

Under this replacement cost formula, the combined peoplequity is identical to the skills and experience-based formula—resulting in a combined value of $1,031,000 even though the values of both managers are slightly different. Again, this is not to suggest that one formula is better than the other, nor that either is legitimate from an accounting standpoint. Their purpose, rather, is to illustrate the concept of peoplequity and give future leaders some food for thought regarding the concept and the need to recognize the worth of individuals within organizations.

Peoplequity sends a clear-cut message to employees: "Our people are worth something." Understanding and recognizing the worth and potential of each individual within an organization is the starting point for developing norms and values to rid the workplace of anomie.

Teaming in a Values-Based Environment

In our work as consultants, we have long maintained that the best new product development leader is a *renaissance* person. With a broader, multi-faceted perspective, his or her vision is not derived from the limited view of a single function. As new-product development becomes more complicated, and in many companies it is appropriately becoming a separate function, we see a heavier reliance on teaming to ensure a sufficient mix of necessary skills. Those companies and organizations that rely on interfunctional teams will, out of necessity, have to learn how to develop values-based leadership. In doing so, they will also help facilitate shared leadership and conflict resolution.

We believe the differences and varying perspectives that exist between functions are essential to innovation. Could the tensions

EXHIBIT 6-3

Replacement Cost Formula

Cost Categories	Assumptions		Replacement Cost	
	32-year-old Marketer	51-year-old Chief Operating Officer	32-year-old Marketer	51-year-old Chief Operating Officer
Base salary			$75,000	$350,000
Bonus	15% of base	40% of base	11,250	140,000
Perks	Equivalent to 12% of base	Equivalent to 20% of base	9,000	70,000
Stock equity	None	10,000 stock options[*]	-0-	200,000
Recruiting costs	33% of base	33% of base	24,750	115,500
Training and development costs	Years 1 and 2 at $5,250 per year	Years 1 and 2 at $12,500 per year	10,500	25,000
Total Peoplequity Base			$130,500	$900,500

[*]Valued at $20 per share

that exist between individuals as a result of having different values and personal beliefs be additive and important to innovation? We believe so. But members of the team need to establish a group set of norms and values that every team member can buy into while acknowledging the differences of each person.

Teaming in a shared-values environment calls for each individual team member to answer a set of personal questions:

• What are my major fears of being part of the team?

- What do I personally want to achieve by being a member of the team?
- What do I want the team to accomplish?
- How will I measure my success or failure on the team?
- How will I measure the success or failure of the team?
- How do I want to interact with each team member?
- What values do I want to have other team members establish?
- What norms do I want to operate within?

It is important to note that each question is self-focused and initially based on individual, personal issues. This first step must occur before the team as a whole can begin sharing, compromising, and developing group norms and values. Sharing this type of personal information with each team member begins to plant norms and values in the only ground where they can grow—from within individuals.

Consequently, teaming in a values-based environment fosters an organization that instills norms and values jointly developed by employees. Alienation and isolation will be offset. In turn, organizational norms and values will provide the basis for all employees to have a "rallying point." Behavioral expectations will be set. Employees will have a better understanding of how best to interact with one another.

Energized Organizations: The Foundation for the Anomie Solution

James Todd, M.D., the executive vice president of the American Medical Association, is a progressive and values-ful leader. He believes strongly that "leaders need to set a tone within organizations that give employees a reason to believe in their *own* value and contributions in order to achieve the established goals of the organization." He supports the idea that values-based leadership is "right on target for addressing the culture and atmosphere dilemma that many organizations currently face."

The foundation for a values-based nonanomic organization includes:

- Developing adhered-to norms and values that recognize the unique benefits and strengths of each individual.
- Encouraging a sharing of leadership throughout all areas of an organization.
- Cultivating a culture that breeds employee loyalty and commitment, and "keeps" and offers continuity to employees.
- Using norms and values as the "structure" to hold the organization together.

Jerry Fisher, vice-president of Applied Sciences for Baxter Healthcare Corporation, a worldwide leader in the health-care industry, believes that anomie "describes the symptoms of a business management culture that is devoid of the nutrients that provide homeostasis for a healthy management infrastructure." Jerry's insight provides a superb perspective on the malady that winds its way throughout most American businesses today. Thinking of norms and values as nutrients for a healthy organism is an appropriate analogy. Just as is a person who is starving and whose body undergoes deterioration, so too does the organization gradually deteriorate without life-sustaining values. Jerry summarizes three key deficiencies in organizations: "lack of understanding and skills with which to accept, initiate, and manage change; lack of adaptive and practiced leadership processes; and absence of well thought out and sensitively communicated group values and norms."

Our hope is that American business quickly finds a way of reversing the damage that has been done. Companies have extracted too many pounds of flesh and taken too much blood from most of their employees. They have not fed them or provided them with a life-giving norms-and-values transfusion. The key to strengthening and restoring the endogenous damage is to formulate agreed-upon values and norms that will guide the behavior and communications of all group members in any organization.

Measuring Your Organization's Values-Fulness

Now you can evaluate your own organization's "values-ful" qualities and characteristics. We have developed the following quiz (see
Exhibit 6–4) to illustrate the key attributes found in a values-based
organization. Take the quiz and see how well your organization
scores.

EXHIBIT 6-4

How "Values-Ful" Is Your Organization?

Measure your organization's "values-ful" qualities. Evaluate it
using the following twenty descriptive characteristics. Score five
points if the characteristic exists within your organization, two
and one-half points if it is only partially present, or zero points if
it doesn't exist at all. Then add your scores, and refer to the scoreboard below. **(Score 5 points if 100%; 2.5 points if 50%; 0 if 0%)**

1. Management and employees jointly develop annual and long-
   term financial goals and strategic objectives for our business.

2. Our mission statement is commonly known, understood, and
   adopted by all employees.

3. Our organization has a commonly agreed-upon and understood People Pledge or values statement that defines what's
   important to each member of the organization.

4. Our People Pledge or values doctrine is visibly displayed in
   our office.

5. Individual employees have objectives that describe their personal and professional goals for the next year.

6. Policies, procedures, regulations and rules exist, but are not
   an overstated, overused part of our organization mindset.

7. Our culture is highly supportive of and greatly respects individual differences, needs, and issues.

8. Our organization adopts a totally pluralistic hiring philosophy.

9. Our organization endorses and schedules at least five social
   events annually for employees and their spouses/friends to
   better understand the nonworking side of employees.

10. Our management and employees effectively know each other personally.

11. Our organization encourages change and realizes that short-term failure may have positive long-term consequences.

12. Our organization accepts a shared leadership construct; that is, each individual takes on a leadership role in some dimension, with very little hierarchy present.

13. Individual employees are rewarded for creativity, innovation, and teaming.

14. Our leadership style incorporates conflict resolution and interfunctional teaming.

15. There is a strong message throughout the organization that consideration of others is appropriate, even encouraged.

16. Emotions, feelings, and personal beliefs are not locked inside but are openly communicated.

17. Compensation incentive systems are tied to risk-taking and to performance criteria—with high returns for high performance and risk taking.

18. Employees feel a strong sense of mutual trust, fairness, and consistency.

19. The value of the individual is an integral and meaningful component of our organization.

20. Intuitive thinking is encouraged in the decision-making processes.

Scoreboard

60+	You have a strong values-ful environment. However, values-based leadership will further leverage the already strong culture that exists.
40–60	Problems exist. Senior management needs to be actively involved and must buy into the need for effective values-based leadership.
Below 40	Stop! Take a deep breath and go back over each question. Begin developing an action plan that will address each issue.

A Flexible Scorecard

Use your test results as a helpful but by no means permanent scorecard of how your organization is doing in its battle against anomie. Remember that your score can easily change. On the negative side, a top-management decision that violates employee beliefs can quickly destroy months of value-building. On the positive side, a commitment to values-based leadership can eradicate years of employee cynicism and apathy.

We must learn to be as vigilant against the erosion of norms and values as we are against the erosion of market share. Even after you've mastered the techniques and tactics of values-based leadership and successfully implemented them in your organization, don't stop there. You can always do something else to strengthen the beliefs of your organization and reinforce the behaviors of your employees and colleagues.

In the coming chapters, we'll provide you with numerous suggestions for doing so. For now, all that we ask is that you objectively analyze your values-ful condition and be open to the new and sometimes unorthodox strategies we propose.

What is the source for energizing organizations? Individuals and their collective values. Shared values represent the future super glue to link employees together. "To get the job done, we have to have the same values," states Lawrence Bossidy, CEO of Allied Signal. This need for shared values is depicted well in a December 1993 *Fortune* article, "How Will We Live with the Tumult?" "Once the bureaucracy is gone, the organization flattened and workers empowered, shared values provide the only practical way to ensure that everyone is pointed in the same direction. And the values some corporate folk espouse sound good: candor, integrity, facing reality, taking responsibility, being accountable, investing in education and respecting diversity. The value most needed is a sense of community—loving your neighbor as yourself."

The Ten Building Blocks of a Values-Based Organization —The Energy Pyramid

We need to instill professional passion back into employees and their work organizations. We need to see emotion and feelings

EXHIBIT 6–5

Values-Based Organization Energy Pyramid

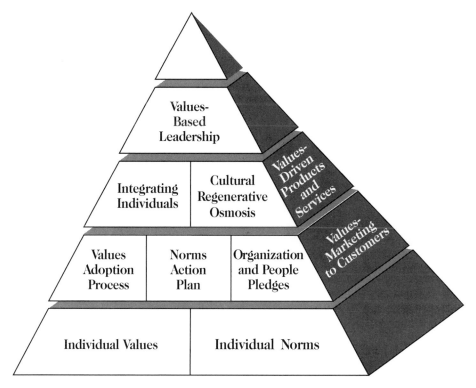

The Ten Building Blocks for Creating Values-ful Organizations

being expressed and communicated. We need to reenergize our work force. The platform for the revolutionary change that needs to occur is a recognition of and appreciation for *individual* norms and values. The key value *is* the individual.

The way to energize organizations is through values-based leadership. The Energy Pyramid, depicted in Exhibit 6–5, illustrates the ten building blocks for creating a values-ful organization. The face of the pyramid is comprised of eight building blocks aimed at energizing the organization internally. The bottom two building blocks—Individual Values and Individual Norms—activate the next tier of blocks—the Values Adoption Process, the Norms Action Plan, and the Organization and People Pledges (Chapters 8 and 9). The third tier of building blocks includes concepts that are important for raising the dignity and respect of all employees (Chapter 10). They are represented in an organization that supports cultural regenerative osmosis and adopts practices that integrate individuals into groups (Chapter 11). The top building block encompasses all the concepts captured through values-based leadership (Chapters 12 through 15).

On the side of the Energy Pyramid are two building blocks that are greatly influenced by an organization's internal culture, yet have a major impact on external customers. Developing values to guide the design and development of products and services, along with undertaking values-marketing (Chapter 17) completes the Energy Pyramid. If employees have and convey values that customers can identify with, they'll be the best company spokespersons possible. An organization that puts these ten building blocks in place will be well on its way to becoming a successful values-based organization—and one that has indefatigable energy.

Part III
The Solution

Chapter 7

Activating a Highly Personal Process

The difficulty in building a shared set of values and commensurate norms in an organization is ensuring that all employees truly feel as if they have been active participants and meaningful contributors in shaping them. Without an approach, that, at a minimum, offers a multistaged opportunity for employees to participate, values will *not* be "bought into" and norms will not be adhered to.

The leadership of an organization cannot dictate a set of norms and values and expect any benefit to accrue. Management cannot cram a set of its desired values down employees' throats and expect any good to come from it. These values just won't stick. Participation by group members in their development, however, yields energizing power. The collective development of norms and values—a highly personal process in and of itself—sets the stage for a values-ful culture that is credible, actionable, and meaningful. Anything less is virtually a waste of time and effort. Moreover, a short-cut approach can actually make employees even more frustrated, isolated, and alienated within the organization. This fosters discontent and unrest.

However, building an organization's set of norms and values in this highly personal way is indeed a challenge. Consensus,

105

therefore, is crucial. And so is following a specific framework of defined steps.

A CEO recently told us: "Our company has already established a set of family values that guides our culture. Any employee who doesn't believe in them or does not want to subscribe to them should leave and find work elsewhere." This rather myopic view is a perfect example of how just *having* a set of values in a company is virtually worthless. Anybody can develop a laundry list of values that mirrors the Boy Scout Oath. While those values might very well be a potentially viable list of appropriate values, the entire organization needs to develop them rather than the "holier-than-thou CEO" at the top.

Unless norms and values ultimately are shared across divisions, departments, layers of management, project teams, and the like, their survival is short-lived at best. Worse yet is the common situation that we see where top management will "talk" norms and values but never embrace actions, activities, incentives, or behaviors that endorse and reinforce them. They give lip service to the whole thing, which even worsens employees' negative perceptions and increases the personalized emptiness they feel.

Developing Shared Values and Norms—The VAP© and NAP©

We have developed two systematic, step-wise processes for developing shared values and desired norms for any organization. The two processes work in concert with each other because the key objective and purpose of norms is to reinforce and support agreed-upon core values. The Values Adoption Process (VAP©) describes a methodology—in effect, it provides a blueprint to help guide an organization through a series of steps, exercises, and discussions for developing a shared set of values. Similarly, the Norms Action Plan (NAP©) is a step-wise process for developing a desired set of behavioral and communication guidelines that reinforce the identified values.

These step-wise processes are comprised of a series of several discussions that will need to be held with a multilayered group of managers and employees. We recommend that an organization form a Values Task Force to lead the entire Values Adoption Process and Norms Action Plan development. A task force comprised of six to eight employees and one to two managers can be formed to serve as the coordinator to spearhead and shepherd the organization through these processes.

One or two individuals of the task force needs to be designated as the leader(s) of this process. It's very important to maintain consistency in the leadership of the VAP and NAP processes. You should not start and stop, start up again, and stop these processes. Once begun, they need to be completed to enable the organization to understand and begin to see the benefits of undertaking these initiatives.

Don't automatically assume that the VP of Human Resources or the Personnel Director is the most appropriate person to lead this process. You may want to "elect" a leader or a task-force member to guide the process. Or you may want to have a team of five comprised of one representative from each layer of management within the organization. Better still would be to seek volunteers, who by the nature of their stepping forward are clearly committed to the initiative.

Many subjective and highly interpretive issues will surface during the values-and-norms development process. Maintaining the same leader or leaders throughout the process will facilitate a smoother development of its ultimate output—the People Values Pledge and the Organization Values Pledge.

A good way for the task force to start the planning is to come together to discuss a set of twelve questions. These questions can be used as guidelines to foster a candid and frank discussion. Some of the issues may later be addressed in some of the communications to employees regarding the activation of these processes within the organization. The questions are usually difficult and complex for any organization to resolve. They are listed here.

1. Why should our organization undertake a Values Adoption Process and a Norms Action Plan? Do gaps exist in our culture that we want to fill?

2. What are some of the organization's most significant problems?

3. What is the current level of effectiveness of leadership within the organization?

4. How is employee morale and how would you describe employees' overall mental state-of-health?

5. What behavioral areas, in particular, should the Values Adoption Process and the Norms Action Plan focus on?

6. What have recent employee complaints centered on?

7. How would you describe the emotional tenor and tone of the organization during the past six months?

8. What are two to three major cultural shifts, if any, that have occurred in the organization during the past year? How have these affected employees?

9. What expectations does the group have for the impact of activating a Values Adoption Process and a Norms Action Plan?

10. What will be the communications approach taken to inform employees that the organization is undertaking a Values Adoption Process and a Norms Action Plan initiative?

11. What are the appropriate timetable, involvement of employees, and measurement criteria that will be used to assess the implementation effectiveness of the Values Adoption Process and the Norms Action Plan?

12. How will we know if this endeavor has had a positive impact on the organization?

Some of the questions that may be raised during this preliminary phase of values-and-norms development is "What's in it for us?" and "Why *should we* do this?" We believe there is a compelling reason to undertake this initiative.

Overall Benefits of Developing Values-Ful Cultures

By developing values-ful cultures through a thorough, organization-wide process that builds the personal expression of individual norms and values, companies can effectively combat anomie. The VAP and NAP are two such approaches that can provide high-impact and long-lasting benefits to an organization. Yes, VAP and NAP will significantly reduce and eventually eliminate anomie. An organization that has no anomie will look, act, and perform radically differently from one that is full of it. Because of this, instilling norms and values becomes the most critical initiative an organization can undertake to gain long-term competitive advantage. Let's examine some specifics. Over time, VAP and NAP would accrue the following benefits to organizations:

- Dilute anomie within the organization.
- Increase consciousness (organization-wide) of the positive impact of instilling norms and values.
- Increase employee performance, security, self-confidence, and self-esteem.
- Enhance employee and manager job satisfaction.
- Improve employee morale and increase productivity.
- Improve teamwork among managers and employees, and among divisions and departments throughout the organization.
- Accelerate more effective decision making and employee empowerment.
- Improve work quality and foster high-impact interactions with customers.
- Increase communication effectiveness within and across work groups and teams.
- Heighten sensitivity to and interest in adopting organization-specific norms and values.
- Increase competitive advantage and improve bottom-line performance because of highly motivated employees.

There is no type of investment that can be made that can generate such a powerful set of end results and a higher return to an organization.

The Consensus-Building Challenge

As we've learned, individuals bring their own personal values with them into the workplace. Having built these highly personal beliefs over a lifetime, the reconciliation of disparate norms and values among a group of employees can be a formidable challenge. Undoubtedly, within every organization and often among small groups, individuals will express values and norms that will conflict with others. But this is exactly why the processes need to give people time to think about differing values, compromise their own a bit, shift some of their thinking, and strive to find at least some common values to be adopted by the majority.

Consensus building needs to have enough gestation time to allow people with different points of view to corroborate and reach a common ground. This is why we have developed the Values Adoption Process and Norms Action Plan as iterative, time-intensive, and people-involved processes. The total "investment" required to complete each process is approximately fifteen to twenty-five hours of meetings to allow adequate discussion among employees, scheduled over a three- to four-month period of time. And this is a minimum. Depending upon the size of the organization, level of desired involvement and participation complexity of the issues, and potential number of conflicting values, both processes may very well take six to nine months to complete. Therefore, if an organization wants to undertake these two processes, and we believe strongly that every organization should, top management needs to be fully committed to having employees spend the time needed to do it right. Don't expect to hold two meetings on norms and values and hope that your culture will be transformed and anomie will have disappeared. It takes a much greater time investment than that.

Consensus building is needed to reach a mutually satisfying set of values among employees. Margaret Thatcher contends in her recent book, *The Downing Street Years,* that "consensus is the process of abandoning all beliefs, principles, values and policies in search of something in which no one believes, but to which no one objects." We do not agree with her. This rather satirical definition suggests that the consensus process turns group opinions into a pile of mush. This is not true. Successful consensus results when each employee feels that his or her individual beliefs and ideas have been incorporated into the group definition.

Consensus building should enable individual values to be strengthened and fortified once they have been embraced and adopted by the group. The concept of community depends upon consensus. Without it, there is no linchpin to support an already fragile group of people.

The way to build consensus is by first reaching agreement on the values that a group can endorse. This process requires defining and discussing the strengths, weaknesses, advantages, and disadvantages of conflicting values. The group must make a unanimous decision on the ultimate values to be accepted. The process leader or task-force members cannot "step in" and close the discussion or make a decision. This would defeat the ownership-building process. Consensus building should be viewed as the glue to bond individual norms and values together within an organization. It is worth the substantial time investment.

But how do we build consensus when conflicts exist? We suggest a five-fold approach.

1. Encourage each person with conflicting points of view to discuss his or her "side" of the argument, providing perceived pros and cons to his or her stated value, its potential benefits and possible drawbacks to the group.

2. Foster a discussion with each group member in which he or she restates and paraphrases, in his or her own words, the points of view expressed by the previous individuals.

3. Lead a brainstorming discussion with all members of the group, focusing on positive, proactive ideas and solutions that seek a compromise to each conflicting value.

4. Prioritize the potential compromises and have the groups come up with one recommendation that best satisfies the needs of *most* group members, but not *all* of them. The key here is to build ownership for the solution so the group feels all members will buy into it.

5. Develop a specific working definition or statement of the group-generated value, one that is commonly understood and shared by all members.

This process requires employees not to interrupt or put down others in group discussions. Moreover, generating as many ideas or solutions as possible can help the group build ownership for the values finally selected.

A Highly Personal Process

Values are personal beliefs. Therefore, an organization needs to identify values for itself that reflect and represent the collective personal values of the individuals who work there. In order for values to "stick," employees must feel as if their own beliefs are respected, embraced and endorsed by the organization. Now, of course, you can't accommodate every single employee's value, but one of the key benefits of the Values Adoption Process is surfacing all employees' values and using those as the foundation for organization values.

By now, you're probably wondering, "This sounds great, but when will we learn the specifics of VAP and NAP?" We'll describe the details of implementing each process in the next two chapters. But first, let's explore the most critical aspect for success—identifying values as a *highly personal* process.

In a recent issue of the *Economist* (April 1993), the article "The Death of Corporate Loyalty" contends that the values of job security, lifetime employment, and loyalty to the corporation have disappeared in many organizations. The unprecedented job cutting, downsizing, and reduction of employees in our largest corporations have altered the values of those employees who remain. Perhaps IBM is the best example: between 1987 and 1994 it reduced its number of employees from more than 400,000 down to 200,000. In the "old" corporate culture, employees looked forward to (and valued) a value of full lifetime employment. Twenty years' employment within a single firm used to be expected—a norm. The hierarchy within large corporations was also valued. It offered definite career advancement within the corporate setting. If one did well and demonstrated loyalty by investing years with the company, then clear rewards were expected. These included the reward of promotion to a better position, higher salary, larger offices, and greater access to resources. These *were* prized corporate values. What will the values for our work settings be in the future?

The primary value should become the professional and personal development of the individual worker. This "business" of development is a highly personal process. Personal values identification is the starting point. Opportunities must be given to individual employees to develop and learn new skills. Management must encourage each employee to carve out personally fulfilling goals that go *beyond* traditional objectives such as hitting budgets and achieving financial targets. The goal for each employee is to eliminate the feeling of powerlessness spawned by anomie. By making one's job more relevant and more personal, and by allowing personal norms and values to flourish, the employee gains a measure of control.

Control is a key part of crafting highly personal norms and values. In the past, the control has always been placed in the hands of the organizational leaders, especially within corporate settings. If an employee wanted an answer to almost any question—whether the company could hire a new person or purchase a much-needed office supply—then approval was required from the "top dogs." The people within work settings were left powerless. Imagine! The very people who need to call the shots and are best able to see the needs of the group are left with no authority to do so. This characteristic is extremely detrimental to any organization. Why? Because if a person is in control, then he or she feels happy, positive, and self-confident about himself or herself. He or she will do a better job because of these feelings. Most important, if an employee is given control, then the norms and values of the workplace can be crafted to become highly personal ones. They help to develop each person within the workplace.

One of the best ways to understand the personal values of employees is to ask them. But getting into a discussion of personal values is tough to do. Often, it seems to be an awkward and uncomfortable topic to explore with employees. A good way to initiate this discussion is for task-force leaders to facilitate a discussion about the needs and characteristics of each member in a group. This begins a dialogue about individual professional needs and characteristics that are unique to each person.

Knowing the Needs and Characteristics of the Group

An individual in any group setting must be able to give attention to his or her own needs and interests. At the same time, an individual must interact with the other members of the group who can also help that individual address his or her needs and interests. As group members, we must learn to do some things for ourselves and some things for other group members. Work settings must encourage their members to have this double focus. Because development of values and norms is undertaken in a group setting, it is crucial to understand the interplay between individuals and the group they join. As the Values Adoption Process and Norms Action Plan development are initiated, this context becomes paramount. As you will see from the following exercise (see Exhibit 7-1), having a double focus, both on the group and on the individual, involves a highly personal process.

This exercise can best be completed in a small-group setting. Task-force leaders should ask individuals to complete the section "Who Am I?" by noting characteristics that best describe them personally. After doing some more deep-down thinking, the leader(s) would proceed next with a discussion on "What Are My Needs?" Some examples are illustrated in Exhibit 7-1, but the page should be blank when conducting the exercise.

Next, the group should break up into pairs. Participants should focus on "Who Are You?" and "What Are Your Needs?" by noting those characteristics that they feel best describe their partner. When both have completed their descriptions of each other, it is important to share this information. How accurate was your description of the other compared to his or her own description? In some cases, they may be very close. In others, quite different. Why? We may not spend enough time or express enough interest in our co-workers. Or, some individuals may try to hide their highly personal characteristics. We need to understand and be sensitive to others in the group and become aware of their needs and characteristics. We need to know them. As the group goes forward, members will become more aware of each other's needs and characteristics.

What do we do with this information? Knowing who you are and what your needs are can help to identify activities for personal growth. What do you want to achieve, learn, acquire, and master in the workplace? How can you find ways to achieve your personal goals? What can the work environment do to facilitate this personal growth? The workplace should value something other than bottom-line growth and security. It must become a pathway to personal growth.

EXHIBIT 7–1

Who am I?

| "Sensititve" | "Considerate to others" | "Intelligent" |

What are my needs?

| "To be respected by others" | "To have people treat me fairly" | "To be part of an effective team" |

Who are you?

| | | |

What are your needs?

| | | |

If you are a teacher and need to improve your teaching style, then you could take a course covering different ways to introduce and present material and practice new teaching styles. In a work or business setting, the need might be to gain greater peer recognition. The action might be to become the team leader of an important project and motivate other team members to exceed their expectations. In time, the individual's peers will provide the leader with well-deserved recognition.

The context for this needs-and-characteristics exercise should be grounded in understanding the balance that will eventually have to be achieved between self-interests and individual commitments to the group. It is important that this balance be maintained when developing group values. Equilibrium needs to be maintained between individual needs and group needs.

Every individual characteristic and need can be matched with at least one activity or action. These become our individual growth goals and plans. The group can also address our individual needs by focusing on who we are. At the same time, we can focus on and learn about others in the group.

The VAP and NAP—An Overview

The Values Adoption Process—as a highly personal initiative—provides for participation and involvement by all employees and requires consensus building as a key part of this iterative process. It is intended to enable a sustainable values system to be activated within an organization. Values need to be cultivated over a long time period—at least three to five years. The time investment made up front in doing it right is well worth the positive returns that can be yielded in the future. The values shouldn't change annually like a business plan. So, get employees and managers to actively participate in shaping them.

There are several important outputs that result from undertaking the Values Adoption Process. The end results of the VAP include: (1) a definition of individual and small-group values and beliefs, (2) a People Values Pledge, a contract defining employee commitment to a certain set of values, and (3) an Organization Values Pledge, which describes the organization's commitment to live up to a set of agreed-upon values. Often, the People Values

Pledge and Organization Values Pledge articulate some overlapping values. Both should work together—not against each other.

Tied closely to the Values Adoption Process is the Norms Action Plan (NAP). Like VAP, it is an iterative group process. The end results from completing this process include: (1) a definition of individual and group norms, desired and undesired; (2) recognition of rewards to reinforce behavioral norms; and (3) a cultural transformation activities plan that defines the people, practices, and training systems necessary to achieve the transformation. Over time these outputs will breathe life into the desired norms. Let's now examine the specifics of these processes in the next two chapters.

Chapter 8

Launching the Values Adoption Process

People need to create institutions they can be proud of. Pride comes with developing a values-ful product, sharing profits with employees, and shaping an internal environment that increases the self-confidence and self-worth of all employees. Organizations need to be viewed as living and breathing organisms. The first part of the word organization—"organ"—describes the concept we want to convey. For an "organ" to function well, it needs to have strong and healthy employees. The process of developing a values-ful organization can indeed reenergize an organization.

It's time for us to put our faith back in the people who work with us daily. We need to view them as a deeply respected community of individuals who all want to share a common vision and common set of values. We need passion and spirit to be rekindled in our workplaces—we need to give employees a reason to believe.

Let's first explore the process of adopting values within an organization based upon individual values.

Stage I—Individual Values Development

The identification of individual values is critical to the success of the Values Adoption Process (VAP©). Therefore, we begin with the

119

recognition and development of personal values. Organizations need to activate several initiatives simultaneously to launch this most critical stage, as depicted in Exhibit 8–1, which graphically illustrates the entire VAP© process.

Step 1—Inform organization and list personal values and beliefs.

VAP leaders should distribute a letter from senior management describing the purpose of this entire initiative. Then they should hold a series of small-group workshops explaining the Values Adoption Process to the entire organization. These initial meetings by a VAP leader or a designated facilitator must be conducted face to face with all employees. The message that the organization is undertaking this process is best conveyed in person because it's a highly personal process. Employees and managers need to gain a perspective on the intended impact and benefits of the process as well as understand the purpose, use, and intentions of this values-setting endeavor.

The VAP workshop leaders will ask each employee to write down his or her personal values that he or she would want to embrace and be shared by their co-workers in the work environment. It may be helpful to refer back to the five sources of values discussed in Chapter 3. Examining these factors can help employees to better understand what has shaped their own values. Self-discovery can provide a new level of values recognition.

Step 2—Prioritize top five values desired in workplace.

Each employee will then be asked to prioritize his or her own top values, indicating which ones he or she would like to have in the work environment. Employees should select values they'd like to see activated on a daily basis and, as with the preceeding step, values that can be shared by their co-workers.

Step 3—Publish a list of all employee values segmented by category areas.

VAP leaders next should gather the top priority values of all employees and publish a list of the collective responses. All

EXHIBIT 8-1

Values Adoption Process(VAP©)

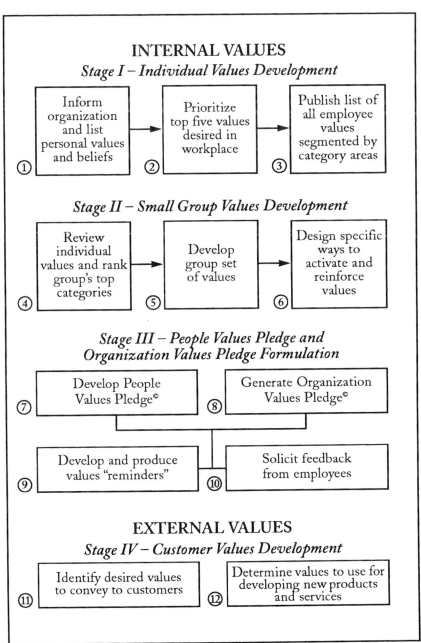

responses should be kept anonymous. Usually, most employee values end up falling into a distinct number of broad categories. Even small companies might find that there might be fifteen to twenty broad groupings of values. For large organizations, responses may be computerized and tabulated to determine the frequency of most commonly cited values.

Individual values can also be segmented according to divisions, functions, work groups, teams, and other organizational divisions. For example, in a highly decentralized company, comparing the similarities and differences among subsidiaries may be beneficial and insightful. Similarly, the separate schools of a very large university might have differing values. So, in short, VAP facilitators should summarize these collective individual values in a way which can be used most effectively as the process unfolds. As we'll see next, these values summaries will be examined by employee groups in Stage II.

Stage II—Small Group Values Development

Once the steps of individual values identification, prioritization, and segmentation have been completed, the Values Adoption Process enters its second state—Small Group Values Development. VAP leaders should form small groups consisting of eight to twelve employees and one or two managers. We find that some of the best groups are those that cut across and include several layers of managers and employees. At a minimum, there should be three two-hour meetings on the topic of group values with each group.

Step 4—Review individual values and rank group's top categories.

In the first meeting, each group should review the previously published individual values and identify the most important categories. As in earlier steps, VAP leaders can facilitate these meetings. Indeed, by this step, the VAP facilitators may begin to see volunteers for further VAP leadership. Volunteering should be encouraged and welcomed.

Step 5—Develop group set of values.

Then, after a couple of weeks pass by (three at most), the group's second meeting should concentrate on developing a list of the specific values that that particular group wants to adopt. These will eventually become the Group Value Statements.

*Step 6—Design specific ways to activate
and reinforce values.*

At the third meeting, VAP leaders should guide the finalization of this list. All group values statements across the organization should be prioritized into top-tier and second-tier values. Thanks to the advent of computers, those group values statements can be patterned and synthesized fairly quickly and easily. The VAP leaders will need to make some subjective decisions and conduct some interpretive analysis in order to represent the values of both individuals and groups. The top ten should represent "must have" values and the second ten should depict "would like to have" values. This list of roughly twenty values should be reviewed by each group in a subsequent meeting. As each group reviews this list, they will revisit their group-developed set and discuss any changes they feel are appropriate to make.

The groups should also develop concrete, tangible ways to activate and reinforce the desired values on a daily basis. As we'll see later, these action suggestions will form the basis for the Norms Action Plan, which will be developed to further strengthen and reinforce these values.

Stage III—People Values Pledge and Organization Values Pledge Formulation

One of the most effective ways of providing to all employees a tangible and "living" reminder of the organization's desired values is by developing two documents—the People Values Pledge and the Organization Values Pledge. The significance of having two separate pledges is key to successful long-term values inculcation. In a concrete way, a mutually agreed-upon series of commitments are being expressed. The People Values Pledge cites the values commitment, which is intended to be made by employees to one another—in effect, a values "contract" by each individual to all other members of the organization. Both the People Values Pledge and the Organization Values Pledge must be developed in a way that employees can buy into and live by. Now, the hard work comes. This is the stage where the Values Adoption Process leaders begin to draft these two documents. Both are based on the collective values of the employees and will ultimately be published as the internal values statement for the organization.

In turn, the Organization Values Pledge is the set of values and behavioral commitments that top management and the organization as a whole make to all employees. In this manner, the values framework implicitly provides a foundation for the Norms Action Plan (see next chapter), which further translates values into personnel practices, communication approaches, career advancement methods, feedback mechanisms, hiring practices, and compensation systems. In concert, these two pledges demonstrate to all employees that values are important and will drive the company's internal culture and personality.

The pledges, for the most part, should be viewed as three-year agreements. They should not radically change from one year to the next. It often takes several years for norms and values to be truly inculcated into and adopted by a culture. If they change every year, enough traction will not be secured, nor will adequate "ripening" of the desired values take place. So, once the pledges are developed, it is wise to wait three years before undertaking a whole new look at them again.

Step 7—Develop a People Values Pledge.

The values identification work previously conducted in the small groups provides the foundation for developing this pledge. The People Values Pledge often describes the company's values along the following dimensions:

- Ways to interact and communicate with all employees.
- Expected behaviors of all individuals within the organization.
- Group values and team beliefs.
- Feedback styles and approaches.
- Specific values-based behavioral guidelines.

To provide a few examples of what a People Values Pledge looks like, we have included pledges from two organizations of different size.

Mid-Size Organization People Values Pledge

- Share good news with everyone, but convey constructive criticism *directly*.
- Take pressure off being "perfect"—recognize that we're not perfect.
- Depersonalize criticism.
- Support me—believe in me.
- Treat everyone fairly.
- Keep trying to fix it; work it out.
- Start and stop meetings on time.
- Be tolerant—no finger wagging.
- Set egos aside to accept others' ideas.
- Emphasize positive growth.
- Take risks and get rewards.
- "Rally" the team—once we decide to do something, it will get done.
- Provide humor—keep it in perspective.
- Emphasize personal growth opportunities.

Step 8—Generate Organization Values Pledge.

Assuming the People Values Pledge has been thoughtfully and iteratively developed, the Values Adoption Process will have ascertained and expressed the most commonly shared internal values by all participating employees. It is now appropriate to convey the values that the entire organization, as its own entity, will embrace. For organizations as we know them today, this Organization Values Pledge includes senior management's pledge to employees. To some degree, these values need to support, reinforce, and endorse the People Values Pledge. However, most often

---

Large Organization People Values Pledge

- Focus on customers.
- Respect people.
- Support teamwork.
- Strive for quality.
- Communicate openly and effectively.
- Value diversity.
- Be decisive and effective problem solvers.
- Act with high integrity.
- Develop vision and strategic focus.
- Be innovative and adaptable.
- Develop self and others.

---

the Organization Values Pledge describes values that codify the basis for promotions, rewards, and style of management interaction with others. Some Organization Values Pledges will also include a values statement regarding customer relationships.

The process for developing an Organization Values Pledge is, like the development of the People Values Pledge, an iterative series of steps. Each step goes beyond the previous one until a finalized set of Organization Values is identified and endorsed by all.

It's important to remember that there are no right or wrong *statements* regarding organization values. However, there are wrong *approaches*. If the Organization Values Pledge is developed in a senior management vacuum, without infusing the small-group values, then it will be empty and meaningless. Making the pledges credible is absolutely essential. Unless employees believe management will act and behave in ways that reinforce the agreed-upon values, all authenticity is lost.

In some companies, we've seen top management write up an Organization Values Pledge, announce it to all employees, and then watch it fall flat on its face. That's because the only way to build authenticity into a values platform is to have all employees and management build the platform together. The Organization Values Pledge must capture the core values desired by the various groups. Without broad participation, active listening, and thorough integration, the pledge may actually do more harm than good. Once employees see management give lip service to values, all future credibility is lost. Distrust and anomie will reign. Four examples of Organization Values Pledges follow. These include Paladin, a small marketing staffing firm in Chicago; the IBM Consulting Group, a division of IBM Corporation; our own firm, Kuczmarski & Associates; and Norcross Footwear, a privately held manufacturer. Their uniqueness and variety illustrate how highly personal this process truly is.

Paladin Organization Values Pledge

- Paladin business is always conducted with a deep and abiding respect for the value of each individual with whom we come in contact, be they co-worker, customer, or associate.

- Paladin business is conducted day to day and over the long term in a manner that demonstrates both the company's and each individual's commitment to an ethical, honest, and aboveboard approach in all dealings, with all audiences.

- Paladin business is conducted in such a manner as to ensure the complete satisfaction of our customers in terms of the absolute appropriateness of the candidates we present, the courtesy and professionalism of our service, and the accuracy and efficiency of our payroll, billing, and reporting systems.

- The best and most productive work environments are those that encourage creativity, self-challenge, appropriate risk-taking, and questioning of the status quo.

- To ensure short-term and long-term success, employees must share a relationship in which information is freely shared, advice is freely given, and ideas are freely exchanged both informally and formally.

- Paladin is a new, but long-term player in the staffing industry. As such, it is critical that the evolution and development of management be part of annual business planning.

IBM Consulting Group Organization Values Pledge

Vision

The vision of IBM Consulting Group is to use our knowledge and technology to accelerate the transformation of our clients into sustainable, successful organizations. Thus, all our actions will be measured by how successful we make our clients. Our aim is to become the world's preeminent firm in this business.

Our Values

The values of our worldwide consulting practices parallel IBM's Basic Beliefs:

- In consulting, **people working in teams are our key asset,** resonating IBM's "respect for the individual."
- **Our consulting clients come first,** and equates to IBM's belief in providing "the best possible customer service."
- And finally, we translate IBM's "pursuit of excellence" into **striving for superior results in everything we do.**

Kuczmarski & Associates' Organization Values Pledge

- Recognize and reward excellence and outstanding performance for each individual.
- Build and maintain a team environment based on a common set of norms and values as well as trust relationships.
- Encourage every team member to take risks, make decisions, and never be afraid to make mistakes.
- Hold team members accountable for results but enable creative and flexible approaches to achieve results.
- Provide adequate training on a continual basis.
- Promote on merit.
- Always be considerate of other people and never try to move ahead at the expense of others.
- Have fun building our company!

Norcross Footwear Company Pledge

- We recognize that our people are our most valuable and important asset.
- We are committed to setting the standard of excellence in every facet of our business and in everything we do.
- We recognize that it is our customers who keep us in business and their 100% satisfaction is our reason for being.
- We will never apologize for price when the quality of our products and services consistently exceeds our customers' expectations.
- We will share a responsibility for the company's profitability, and we recognize its importance for our survival and growth.
- We are professionals, and we will always conduct ourselves accordingly.
- We believe that anything we do is worth doing well, every time.
- We believe it is essential that we make our company fun for all Norcross Footwear associates.

Employees at each of these organizations have jointly developed these shared values. They believe in them and try to live their daily professional lives according to these principles. These pledges represent a set of values or beliefs that help to guide their organizational behavior.

Step 9—Develop and Produce Values "Reminders."

Developing, producing, and distributing pledge "reminders" —visible communication of the text or spirit of the pledges—is an important part of reinforcing the values. Some reminders we find effective include:

- Printing one or more of the pledges on the back of business cards.

- Including both pledge statements in annual business and long-range plans.

- Distributing individual plaques or paperweights engraved with the pledges for each employee.

- Displaying an entryway or lobby wall plaque describing the two pledges.

- Discussing or writing about the Values Pledge in the organization's newsletter.

- Including the pledge statements in employee paychecks and customer invoices.

- Giving annual awards to individuals and teams who consistently embrace and demonstrate a belief in the cited values. Have judges elected by co-workers.

- Recognizing employees who exemplify the Organization Values Pledge in their daily actions.

The list is endless. The important point is to find ways to keep the pledges in front of all workers—regardless of level or function—on a regular basis. If the two pledges are developed and then filed away, they will provide little power to change or enhance the culture.

Step 10—Solicit feedback from employees.

The final step in the internal Values Adoption Process, before integrating these values into a Norms Action Plan, is to provide a critical closure point to the process. Employee feedback should be obtained before the final values pledges are distributed and then again immediately afterward. Once people begin to live with the agreed-upon values, they can better see ways to enhance, modify, or strengthen parts of the pledges.

Usually, there is a need to clarify some of the values and provide further interpretation of others. Soliciting feedback from employees serves two major purposes: First, it helps employees see that this is an iterative process, not merely a time-filling wasted exercise. Employee feedback helps to effectively integrate the changing and evolving values of an organization and its people. Second, it acknowledges that employees who live and breathe these values daily are best suited to evaluate their effectiveness and to identify any potential need for alterations or adaptations. Often the feedback can be obtained by holding one small-group session with the original groups.

Stage IV—Customer Values Development

This stage is aimed at converting the values identified internally into externally perceived values that customers will recognize. This provides the foundation for values-marketing programs and acts as the cornerstone for future new products and services, which we discuss in Chapter 17. In reality, customers can readily see and experience the values of an organization. Values are conveyed by the way customers are treated, the quality of products produced, the caliber of the services delivered, the responsiveness of an organization to customer queries or complaints, and the overall reputation and image of an organization in the minds of its customers.

In the 1970s and early 1980s, consumers readily sensed and insightfully recognized the values conveyed by major American automobile manufacturers. Their values, in effect, said that Detroit knows best, customers don't really know what's good for them, big is better, and price and value don't count that much. Moreover, quality of manufacturing, reliability of cars produced, and escalating sticker prices further communicated Detroit's rather ego-oriented, "who cares about the customer" values. At the same time, as we all know, the Japanese conveyed a different set of values to customers. These included values of quality, consistency, reliability, comfort, price/value, and functional performance. These values were "built into" the products the Japanese produced. When customers bought a Japanese car, they bought the values as well.

And now perhaps the American auto industry has finally caught on. In the winter of 1994, General Motors embarked upon a massive "values" corporate image advertising campaign. Some samples of the ads are included in Chapter 17. These ads imply that the internal values of the company influence and permeate the way in which cars are made. They communicate responsiveness to customers, and the "care" that employees take in the company's cars and manufacturing process. While keeping these advertised "promises" may be a challenge to pull off, it's an interesting example of communicating the values that an organization wants its customers to recognize.

Step 11— Identify desired values to convey to customers.

One of the best starting points to activate this step is to go out and talk with customers about four major topics: (1) what values do they perceive the organization currently conveys through its products, positioning, and service delivery; (2) what values would they want the organization to convey; (3) which one value should be the top priority for the organization, and (4) which new value would customers want the organization to adopt and convey.

The research approach for this step would once again be guided by a defined number of voluntary Values Adoption Leaders. The approach for securing this information from customers can take a variety of different forms, including a mail survey, phone survey, formal focus groups, or small internal discussion groups. Any traditional form of market research is fine. The key, however, is to do research that will give customers a hand in shaping the values topics.

Once this research has been conducted, the external VAP leader should collect and develop a preliminary list of customer values. The first draft should be distributed to the organization's employees. VAP leaders should then conduct small-group discussions to solicit feedback and suggestions from all employees. This step is important because it bridges the internal values of the organization to the external environment. Like the People and Organization Pledges, a Customer Values Pledge can now be developed and distributed throughout the organization.

Step 12— Determine values to use for developing new products and services.

Organizations can leverage the customer research on values to determine which values should guide new-product development. Products and services need to be values-based too. At first, it may seem a bit strange to be talking about product values. Yet the people who design products and services, shape them and

IBM Consulting Group's Customer Values Pledge

- Our people:
    - Work well with clients.
    - Will have a good fit and chemistry.
    - Are experienced and knowledgeable.
- Our process:
    - Includes teams that collaborate with the client's people.
    - Incorporates proven approaches.
    - Is based on best practices.
- Our performance:
    - Will result in realistic and viable recommendations.
    - Will exceed our clients' expectations.
    - Enables our clients to achieve their objectives.
- Our "promise" to our clients is that we will:
    - Work with their people as part of their team.
    - Bring the right expertise for their needs.
    - Deliver implementable recommendations.
    - Perform above their expectations.
    - Help them achieve their objectives.

make them, need to have guidelines for their development. The identification of values for designing products and services is similar to the process for developing an organization's internal values.

Once again, an organization must identify voluntary values leaders to facilitate this external values determination process. Begin by defining the *benefits* of the organization's products and services to customers. Describe the benefits, as perceived by customers, that the products and services provide them. Then compare the list of potential benefits to the benefits of competitive or "near proximity" products. This will determine the unique benefits of your products and services relative to the benefits of competitive offerings substituted. These points of differentiation often signify some of the values that differentiate your organization's products from others on the market.

A few examples might be helpful. Rubbermaid has established the value of durability for its new products. Every Rubbermaid employee, from marketers to industrial design engineers, values durability as a key component of any consumer product the company develops. Here is another example: Federal Express conveys the value of reliability in its service delivery. They provide their customers with consistency in overnight delivery. This axiom is the focus of the company's systems and people. Once this step is completed, the organization will have successfully developed a list of values that will guide the future design of all new products and services. As we learn later in Chapter 17, that's a powerful position to be in and one that offers organizations a distinct competitive edge.

It's time for organizations to make this time investment. Developing values, internally and externally, can bring meaning to employees and their jobs. The Values Adoption Process is not a game or a face-saving management tactic. The attitude of top management in this endeavor is critical to success. Management must express a strong commitment and support for the Values Adoption Process. There needs to be a fundamental respect for and trust in all individuals, beginning with a basic interest in including all employees in the process. Employees invest their lives in the workplace. They need to feel it's all worth it. They need an invitation to participate and deserve praise for their involvement. The Values Adoption Process gives them this invitation to help shape the future values of the organization.

Chapter 9

Developing
a Norms Action Plan (NAP©)

The Norms Action Plan (NAP©) builds on the Values Adoption Process. Crafting the NAP defines norms that will reinforce the desired values and will translate them into behavioral actions and attitudinal mindsets. Simply put, values alone won't work. Behavioral norms must be established to provide tangible and concrete signs that bolster and activate desired values.

Norms are *expectations* about behavior that are shared by the members of a particular group. They are social rules that specify what behavior is appropriate and what behavior is inappropriate. Norms inform the group members of what they should and should not do. They serve as a means for guiding individual actions so that these actions might fit the actions of others. They permit or discourage certain behaviors and require or prohibit other behaviors. Thus, norms are guidelines for interaction. They act as a social tool or blueprint to create joint actions among group members.

But, norms are also ends. They become social standards or goals to which we align our actions or behavior. They dictate conduct in formal and informal situations. They tell us how to behave in and out of staff meetings, how to act, and what to say. They clearly tell us what is permissible behavior. Norms emerge when a group, through its own experiences, identifies a particular behavior to be good or bad for its members. If the behavior is good for the group, it receives a positive value and is encouraged. If it is bad, the group discourages, perhaps even forbids, it.

A norm, then, is a guideline that shapes group behavior. Norms motivate and drive groups to behave and communicate in agreed-upon ways. They define the shared expectations of the group. Norms are group "agreements" that inform individuals how to act and behave in particular situations. A Norms Action Plan is a process that fosters the creation of behavioral guidelines specifically designed to match the values adopted during the Values Adoption Process. The end result of the VAP and NAP is a valuesful organization that has reduced anomie.

In any organization we need to identify the desired set of norms and behaviors that we want all employees to live by and act on daily. Once identified, an organization then needs to develop a concrete and tangible "tool box" of rewards and "avoiders" to shape, reinforce or discourage different behaviors. As the following matrix (Exhibit 9–1) depicts, there are four different actions that can be taken to modify current norms and create new norms.

This matrix can help to categorize norms and behaviors into the desired and undesired norms for an organization. Using this matrix will provide a framework for prioritizing the norms and behaviors that will ultimately become part of the behavioral and communications fabric of the organization.

The actual process of creating a Norms Action Plan is nearly a mirror image of the Values Adoption Process. Similar to the Values Adoption Process, an iterative series of small-group discussions led by an NAP facilitator should be held with employees to create the desired norms as well as ideas for appropriate rewards and "reminders." The previously identified Values Task Force will need to remain actively involved throughout the formulation of the Norms Action Plan. Their presence provides continuity and consistency in designing the NAP. In addition, senior management will need to approve and endorse the NAP because many of the actions will impact compensation and overall personnel policies.

The Norms Action Plan has three key stages of development. Stage I is Individual Norms Identification—the articulation by each employee of norms they want and like, as well as norms they dislike and want to discourage. Stage II is Rewards Formulation—

	EXHIBIT 9-1	

	Rewards	**Avoiders**
Current Norms	① Reinforce and Maintain	② Discourage
New Norms	③ Create and Establish	④ Eliminate or Block

description of the potential tools that an organization can use to reinforce desired norms and discourage undesired ones. The combination of identified norms and defined rewards represents the key ingredients for developing the Norms Action Plan. Stage III is called Infusing Norms into the Organization, which converts this process into company-wide practices impacting a number of key company areas including compensation, personnel practices, information systems, and communications approaches.

As the process gets under way, participants may need to be clear on the context for developing a Norms Action Plan. In effect, norms serve as "translators" of the values, providing a tangible, visual, and real interpretation of values into daily behavior and communications. Without norms, values can end up just being a list of beliefs. As we all know, actions speak louder than words. The values are the words; the norms are the actions. Values are internal—within individuals; norms are external—demonstrated by individuals.

NAP—NORMS ACTION PLAN©

Stage I—Norms Identification

The overall process for developing a Norms Action Plan is depicted in Exhibit 9–2. As with the VAP, several steps occur nearly simultaneously in the initial stages of NAP. The careful—and caring—facilitation of these steps becomes increasingly important as

Norms Action Plan (NAP©)

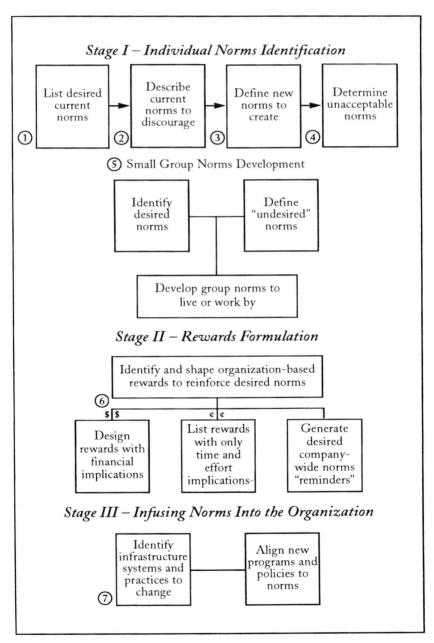

Stage I – Individual Norms Identification

| ① List desired current norms | ② Describe current norms to discourage | ③ Define new norms to create | ④ Determine unacceptable norms |

⑤ Small Group Norms Development

Identify desired norms

Define "undesired" norms

Develop group norms to live or work by

Stage II – Rewards Formulation

Identify and shape organization-based rewards to reinforce desired norms

⑥

Design rewards with financial implications

List rewards with only time and effort implications

Generate desired company-wide norms "reminders"

Stage III – Infusing Norms Into the Organization

⑦ Identify infrastructure systems and practices to change

Align new programs and policies to norms

the process of NAP unfolds. A successfully implemented Norms Action Plan has the power to provide an enormous energy "kick" to an organization. Stage I comprises the identification of individual and group norms.

Step 1: List desired current norms.

Ask each employee to list those norms and behaviors their organization currently endorses and that they, as individuals, want to be further reinforced. The list should comprise the top five to six behavioral norms that are most important and meaningful to each employee. The norms should also support the individual's values, serve as a source of self-satisfaction, and provide a sense of belonging to the group.

Listed here are selected examples of some desired norms cited by employees who have participated in developing a Norms Action Plan for their company:

- Start and stop meetings on time. Being punctual conveys respect of others' time and commitments.
- Provide positive feedback and constructive criticism *through-out* a project, instead of just evaluating performance after the project ends. Intermittent feedback reinforces the value of developing people and helps others to learn and improve.
- Give *both* verbal and written comments on performance. Use positive reinforcement to encourage and motivate employees for their contributions.
- Provide frequent training to employees that is customized to their individual skills and developmental needs.
- Keep time commitments made to other employees. For example, reinforce this belief by delivering reports on time.
- Establish team bonus programs that reward the value of team contributions and performance.

An excellent example of a desired norm at a company comes from McDonnell Douglas. This worldwide organization does a marvelous job of demonstrating its belief in fostering individual growth. The company reinforces this value by offering self-improvement courses on the premises after hours.

Step 2: Describe current norms to discourage.

Next, have employees list those organizational norms and behaviors that they dislike and would prefer to eliminate from their workplace. There should be a listing of the top four to five behaviors that currently exist, which should be discouraged or frowned upon. These norms are typically categorized as those that create a demotivating work environment.

An example of a norm that might be viewed by some employees as demotivating could include the strict dress code that employees of Chicago's Fairmont Hotel must follow. If a female employee arrives at work in slacks, she is required to go home to change into a skirt or dress before returning to work.

A few examples of other norms to discourage that surfaced in our own research include:

• Patronizing employees or "putting them down."
• Putting in "face time" at the office to impress others versus productive time that focuses on performance contribution.
• Speaking disparagingly about fellow co-workers.
• Masking feelings and emotions about an issue or action because of fear of reprimand.
• Promoting employees based on how well they "manage up" rather than how well they perform or produce quality work.
• Communicating only through written memos or "phone mail" rather than directly and in person.

Step 3: Define new norms to create.

Employees should identify three to four new norms that they would like to have others adopt as daily practices to guide their behavior, interaction, and communication with others. These should be norms that most people in the organization currently do not convey or activate. An example of a new norm that frequently surfaced from our research was using more descriptive praise and positive feedback to reinforce desired behaviors and achievements.

Step 4: Determine unacceptable norms.

This final set of norms should be the three to four behaviors that are clearly unacceptable to an employee. When we use the term "unacceptable," we mean those practices that, under any circumstances, would be enough to cause an employee to leave the organization voluntarily. There may very well be far more than three to four norms that are viewed as extremely unattractive or that must be eliminated for an employee to feel good about his or her work environment. However, the task here is to identify the three to four behaviors that are indeed totally unacceptable.

For example, Deloitte and Touche, an international accounting firm, maintains that harassment is an unacceptable behavior. Any employee who is found to have harassed another, regardless of performance, is relieved of his or her job and must leave the firm.

An example of the Individual Norms Identification exercise, follows. This matrix framework is identical to the one depicted in Exhibit 9-1, but shows how an employee might complete this task. The illustrative norms identified are shown in Exhibit 9-3.

EXHIBIT 9-3

Examples of Norms

	¹ **Reinforce and Maintain**	² **Discourage**
Current Norms	• Communicating openly and directly • Displaying mutual respect • Allowing for honest mistakes • Genuinely caring about others' needs	• Causing embarrassment • Taking credit for others' ideas • Destructive criticism • Sexually oriented jokes • Insensitivity to others' needs • Patronizing others
	³ **Create and Establish**	⁴ **Eliminate or Block**
New Norms	• Doing anything possible to please customers • Confronting people tactfully • Allowing people to control their priorities • Providing frequent positive feedback • Supporting cross-functional teams • Enabling employees to set their own work hours	• Discrimination • Harassment • Lying • Lacking consideration for others • Discouraging others from expressing their opinions • Forcing others to conform to one leader's personal style

Step 5: Develop small-group norms.

Once individually developed norms have been summarized, small-group discussions should be conducted similar to those in the Values Adoption Process. NAP leaders should convene a series of small groups, which should include a mix of senior managers, mid-level managers, and employees from various levels and positions within the organization.

It's important to note that these discussions can take place in conjunction with the Values Adoption Process. However, it's well worth the time invested to separately conduct the Norms Action Plan small-group discussion. Each small group of eight to twelve people should meet twice for two hours. The first small-group session should be aimed at identifying and describing the group's shared set of desired and undesired norms.

During these first sessions, NAP leaders should initiate small-group discussions on norms by having the group conduct the norms exercise on Building Relationships (see Exhibit 9-4). This exercise enables individuals to better understand what norms mean in the context of shaping a professional relationship with another person. Individuals in the group should pair up with someone they know fairly well and have worked with in the past.

EXHIBIT 9-4

Norms Exercise—Building Relationships

1. I would like the following type of professional relationship with you: _____
   _____

2. My needs in maintaining and growing the relationship include: _____
   _____

3. My greatest fear about our relationship is: _____
   _____

4. Three actions or behaviors that I'd ask you to consider are:
   _____
   _____

5. I would like to get the following benefits from a relationship with you: _____

6. Three things I'd ask you not to do relative to our relationship are: _____
_____
_____

— —

7. How would I describe the type of professional relationship I think you want with me: _____
_____

8. I think your needs in maintaining and growing our relationship include: _____
_____

9. I believe your greatest fear about our relationship is: _____
_____

10. Three actions or behaviors I think you'd want me to consider are: _____
_____

11. I think you would like to get the following benefits from a relationship with me: _____
_____

12. Three things that I believe you'd ask me not to do relative to our relationship are: _____
_____
_____

The questionnaire is divided into two sections. The first six questions allow an employee to convey information about himself or herself. The next six allow the individual to speculate—in writing—about the way he or she believes their colleague might think, act, or feel.

Each person should write down the answers to the twelve questions before sharing his or her responses with one another. Then, each individual should share his or her answers to the first six questions so that each person understands how the other would like to expand the professional relationship. Next, the last six responses should be shared. This part of the exercise often pinpoints that there is a dearth of understanding about the other person. It's hard enough for us to define our *own* desired norms, never mind trying to identify the desires of others. But that's the whole point of the exercise. Individuals need to express their own desired norms as well as understand those of their co-workers. Without this kind of sensitive and insightful understanding, the staying power of established norms will be short-lived.

Obviously, there are no right or wrong answers. However, several misperceptions about other people frequently surface. The final step of the Building Relationships exercise is for both individuals to reach agreement on a set of norms that they wish to adopt in further developing their relationship together.

NAP leaders should then reconvene the small groups for a lively discussion to identify the behavioral norms that are desired by the group, as well as those undesirable norms that they want to discourage or totally curtail. NAP leaders should capture all brainstormed suggestions, which will become the foundation for the second round of discussions in this step of small-groups norms development.

During the second meeting, each small group should summarize and rank those high-priority norms to professionally live and work by. Norms should be finalized, distributed to each group member, and shared with other small groups.

NAP leaders will then collect these small-group norms, synthesize them, and develop a draft set of norms for the organization. This preliminary document should be distributed to all small-group NAP leaders for input and then finalized into a document called, for instance, "Organizational Norms to Work By." As the organization progresses through the development of its own Norms Action Plan, these organizational norms will be reinforced through rewards and later kept top of mind with "reminders." Still later, in Stage III, these group-developed norms will be infused into the organization's infrastructure through program and policy changes. An example of our consulting firm's "Organizational Norms to Work By" follows:

Kuczmarski & Associates Norms to Work By

- Keep commitments to one another.
- Accept and deliver a "no" as a well-thought-out and honest answer.
- Confront and give constructive feedback when appropriate.
- Use positive feedback and recognition with one another regularly.
- Lead by example.
- Treat one another with respect, honesty, professionalism, courtesy, and integrity.
- Use open communication as the norm, not the exception.
- Remember we are individuals first, K&Aers second—it's okay to be different.
- Establish and maintain personal/trust relationships with other K&Aers and endorse pluralism.
- Continue to use humor often.
- Listen to one another interpretively.
- Understand and accept K&A's growth and change over time.
- Believe in the strength of the team, that no individual can ever be stronger than the team, and that the team is only as strong as its weakest member.

Stage II—Rewards Formulation

Companies often fall short at this stage of the Norms Action Plan—when management needs to put some money where its mouth is. Rewards, incentives, reinforcers, and reminders must be created in order to bring credibility and action to this process. We are not suggesting that thousands of dollars be spent on this endeavor. However, rewards need to be significant enough to provide substantive and adequate recognition. In the steps that comprise this stage, the Norms and Values task force should develop a set of financial and nonfinancial rewards that can be activated by the organization. Of paramount importance to the success of this stage is tangible commitment by senior management. They must not only communicate their endorsement of these rewards, but must utilize them visibly and regularly.

> *Step 6: Identify and shape organization-based rewards to reinforce desired norms.*

The company-wide list of desired norms becomes the blueprint to guide the creation and application of rewards that will reinforce them. Financial and nonfinancial rewards need to align with the group's desired norms. Although many of these rewards should cost virtually nothing, they should provide peer recognition and prestige to bolster and strengthen the organization's norms. Some examples of reward categories that can be used are depicted in Exhibit 9–5.

Norms "reminders" also need to be developed by the task force. The group-developed "Organizational Norms to Work By" can be turned into reminders similar to those identified for values (such as posters, plaque cards, banners, or notecards). Suggestions for norms "reminders" should also be collected at company quarterly review and annual planning meetings as well as at occasional staff or employee meetings.

Stage III—Infusing Norms into the Organization

The final stage in the Norms Action Plan process is to now transform these norms into company policies, procedures, systems, and

EXHIBIT 9–5

Examples of Organization-Based Rewards

	Financial-Based Rewards	**Non-Financial-Based Rewards**
Desired Norms • _____ • _____ • _____ • _____ • _____	• Cash awards for outstanding demonstration of norms activation • Team performance-based bonuses • Individual bonuses • Profit-sharing bonuses • Cash awards for task completion • Group trips and travel awards • New product stock "options" • Equity investment programs and bonuses	• Increased training and development • Written notes of recognition • Increased decision-making accountability • Special peer recognition plaques, honors and awards • Increased job responsibilities • Greater budgetary control • Group social events • Meals with senior management

Internal Personal Benefits That Accrue

• Increased pride

• Peer recognition

• Increased self-5confidence and self-worth

• Greater motivation to perform

• Increased effectiveness of personal interaction

• Heightened awareness of desired norms

• Reduced anomie and greater job satisfaction

• Enhanced self-accomplishment

people practices. Unless these norms and values are driven home—throughout the infrastructure of the organization—they won't stick and become woven into the fabric of the organization.

Step 7—Identify infrastructure systems and practices and align to norms.

Here's where the "rubber hits the road." Unless fundamental infrastructure changes are also made to substantiate the desired norms, the entire process will lack credibility and authenticity. We propose three infrastructure categories to align with desired norms: (1) people systems, (2) policies and practices, and (3) "physical" systems. As depicted in Exhibit 9–6, each of these categories will contain a variety of subcategories such as rewards, performance evaluations, recruiting practices, communication mechanisms, and others.

Making changes and developing new-program policies and procedures across these categories will signal to the organization that the norms and values game is for "keeps." A few posters and plaques alone won't cut it. Tangible and meaningful infrastructure changes will create a values-ful mindset and culture within the organization. However, this will require the task force to work closely with senior management to design and activate the new infrastructure changes and practices. A series of discussions will need to take place with a couple of cross-functional teams whose members represent all functions or key departments of the organization. Again, employee feedback should be secured before finalizing any new programs or policies.

The Values Adoption Process and Norms Action Plan are the tools to assist an organization in bringing greater meaning, security, and self-satisfaction to the workplace. We strongly believe that VAP and NAP will indeed accelerate the construction of a solid norms-and-values foundation. Development of norms and values represents the beginning of positive long-term change. However, while these processes provide the basis for initiating a norms-and-values-ful culture, this is not the end point. The finish line is a long way off, but at least the race has begun.

EXHIBIT 9-6

Infusing Norms into Organizations

INFRASTRUCTURE SYSTEMS & PRACTICES	EXAMPLES OF NORMS		
	Hire and promote based upon merit	Encourage employees to be innovative and take risks	Encourage and enable employees to satisfy customers
PEOPLE SYSTEMS			
Education & Training		X	X
Compensation		X	X
Reward & Recognition		X	X
Performance Evaluation	X	X	X
Promotion & Career Management	X	X	X
POLICIES & PRACTICES			
Employee Selection and Recruiting Practices	X		
Management Style & Decision Making		X	X
Employee Participation		X	X
"PHYSICAL" SYSTEMS			
Organization Structure			X
Job Descriptions & Skills			X
Communication	X		
Information Systems			X

X = Suggests high degree of alignment between desired norm and infrastructure system or practice.

Chapter 10

Establishing Norms
to Get Groups Going

A values-based organization must be founded on group norms and values that stem from and reflect individual norms and values. Establishing norms that provide motivation and satisfaction to members is one way to propel the power and potential of a group, increase employee job satisfaction, and counteract anomie. The right set of norms for any group will be those that maximize the potential of the individuals that comprise it.

We consistently find that five norms in particular tend to foster group behavior, enabling individuals to flourish. These norms include encouraging intuitive thinking, cultivating a caring community, providing recognition, developing one's own gifts, and creating learning communities. These are the norms that can accelerate the potential of group members, get groups going, and energize endogenous growth.

Endogenous Norms

Norms can energize a group. With norms, the "guesswork" is taken out of how best to interact with group members. Ignorance is *not* bliss. If a group has not established norms to "live by," group members will waste a lot of trial-and-error time. Moreover, each person will most likely experience frustration because agreed-upon norms have not been established. Without norms, behaviors can become counterproductive, confusing, and conflicting.

When norms are established by groups, four major benefits accrue: (1) group members are more effective; (2) groups get more accomplished; (3) individuals increase their self-confidence because they deal better with people through clear-cut norms; and (4) groups complete their tasks more quickly and significantly increase their probability of goal attainment and success.

So, behavioral norms can increase effectiveness, maximize results, foster self-confidence, and expedite performance. Wow! This seems to be too good to be true. Why, then, don't more groups spend time developing and shaping group norms? Most often, it's simply attributable to group members not recognizing the need, or fearing or avoiding norms development. Of course, if the group consists of ego-centered, self-focused individuals, norm-setting will provide minimal benefit. For norms to be effective, group members must have some degree of interest in one another and in the potential of the group or team.

We haven't explained why we need more productive group behavior, only individual behavior. The process of activating norms that energize a group can turn a formerly dispirited, contentious group into a highly motivated, consensus-building one. It is a powerful experience, one that enjoys a positive payback for every member of the group. Group members are both happier human beings and more involved group members.

But not only is the impact felt by each individual. The group itself experiences an empowering process. There is growth from within. Medical doctors describe this type of growth as *endogenous*. It comes from within the cell wall. It is deep tissue growth that provides longevity. Endogenous growth is caused by factors inside the system or organism. If endogenous growth happens in a group, a metamorphosis takes place. Group members are uplifted and become spirited, energized, and united.

Matching Endogenous Norms with Personal Values

Group norms become internalized. Individuals follow norms, believing it is the right way to behave. When they do not follow their group norms, they feel that their behavior is inappropriate. If norms involve how people should act, feel, or think, then values involve what one believes is right and good. Values are more individualistic, personal, and abstract. They are connected to our beliefs, which are based on emotion. This means that our sources of values (as discussed in Chapter 5) all have a strong emotional base, stemming from our inner self. Our values are as basic as sexual instincts, which over time become more refined and controlled. However, in effect, the raw emotional base of both norms and values continue to exist throughout our lives and influence the development of our personal values and passionate feelings.

So, personal values are those that are grounded in deep-seated emotion. Once we have identified our core, deep-rooted, emotional values as individuals, we can begin to match those values to norms that will reinforce the values.

When we value something, we are saying that we believe in it. This means it is good or important to us, our group, or our organization. For example, if a small manufacturing firm believes that its employees should be treated equally, then it values a pluralistic and shared leadership style. These values will drive related norms. If the manufacturing company values this shared leadership, then it develops specific norms or guidelines that describe to the employee how to behave, formally and informally, in specific situations within the company. For example, all employees are encouraged to participate in all meetings and to verbally express their ideas and points of view without any negative, future repercussions to them or their career.

At some point, values and norms become so intertwined that it is difficult to identify which comes first. Whether one comes before the other is not important. What is critical to note is their major difference. Norms are prescriptions for *behavior*—what behavior is expected within the group and by individual members.

Values express personal *beliefs*—what is good, right, and desirable. These personal beliefs cause us to adopt guidelines for interaction—group norms—that reinforce the values.

Five Group Norms that Allow Individuals to Grow and Develop

1. Encourage intuitive thinking.

Developing and identifying values begins with acting and thinking intuitively. Intuitive thinking enables individuals to tap into their emotions and better leverage their values in decision making. Applying intuitive thinking to decision making is becoming more and more popular and desirable. There is greater recognition that it can be a powerful technique. Intuitive thinking differs markedly from our more accepted ways of thinking and professional training. We are repeatedly taught and encouraged to employ analytical, linear, and fact-based approaches. However, more successful leaders and more effective team members recognize the benefits of using intuition. Intuition bridges both feelings and emotional inputs. Along with some hard data and facts, intuition is then "peppered" with the individual's experience base and values structure. It is an effective, underutilized tool.

Why don't more leaders and group members use intuition? First, as a society, we have perpetuated with archaic stupidity a perception that intuition is a feminine trait. Creative intuitive thinking is perceived as not manly or rugged enough for strong, serious male leaders. This is insanity. If tough male leaders would open up, express some emotion, convey their inner feelings, and begin to care for their "soul," then their intuitive powers would develop quickly and deeply. Intuitive thinking could actually assist them in decision making, communications, leadership, motivating others, and building trust.

How do we develop and choose values? Hunter Lewis in *A Question of Values* has written an insightful book providing an excellent discussion of six ways we make personal choices. He identifies six ways of thinking about how values are developed. They certainly blend nicely with our five sources of values, discussed in Chapter 5. Lewis describes each as a mode by which knowledge is acquired. We find them interesting ways to think about values and their origins. Values come from authority, deductive logic, sense experiences, emotions, intuition, and science.

Lewis defines authority as taking someone else's word or having faith in the actions of a boss, or the church, or the Bible. He defines deductive logic as knowing something is true because it has undergone a number of consistency tests, so it follows that it must be true. He describes science by combining a number of the modes; the scientific technique requires the collection of observable facts, the formation of a testable hypothesis, and the use of logic to develop and test the experiment.

As the means to most personal decision making within their boundaries, most organizational settings gather decision-making information in three ways: authority, logic, and science. We want to extend the influence of intuition, feelings, and sense experiences on decision making. Organizations tend to discourage intuition, emotion, and sensing. Children have greater skills in these three ways of learning. They are really better than adults at using unconscious thinking (intuition) to feel that something is true (emotion), or know it is true because they touched it, heard it, smelled it, tasted it, or saw it (sense experience). New recruits in an organization may be better at learning in these ways, too. Organizations should give new employees greater respect. Often, their perspectives are far more intuitive, objective, and insightful. In fact, their arrival may infuse a new intuitive energy, fresh perspective, and creativity into the group. Managers end up letting their intuition get flabby. Intuitive thinking gets weak and flaccid when it is not exercised at all.

Promoting other ways of "knowing" is critical. Members of the organization feel a greater sense of freedom. By allowing other ways of arriving at information, individuals in the organization become open to new perspectives. Intuitive thinking, feeling, and sensing are quite a contrast from the emphasis on knowing via authority, logic, and science. Yet, most managers discourage these behaviors. Or they view them as frivolous, requesting greater substantial evidence prior to making a decision. Managers want evidence acquired by authority, logic, or scientific thinking. What is lost in this process is the very ingredient we are searching for—inner emotionally-charged intuitive energy, vision, and insight, which brings a new perspective on issues.

Allowing individuals to exercise their intuition empowers them. Individual insights are valuable. Encouraging employees to be intuitive communicates that individuals are appreciated for their value. There are ways to awaken intuition, emotion, and sensing. For now, it is imperative to know that they can serve as a means to infuse energy, happiness, and spirit into the organization. And important, intuition can serve as a glue to unite individuals within a group and help get the group going. This norm—the development of greater facilities of intuition, emotion, and sensing—will promote endogenous or deep tissue growth.

2. Cultivate a caring community.

"Never doubt that a small group of thoughtful, committed citizens can change the world. Indeed, it's the only thing that ever has," stated Margaret Mead, the well-known and respected anthropologist.

We both had the unique and personally rewarding and enriching experience of taking a graduate course with Margaret Mead at Columbia University when we were attending the School of International Affairs. Her course was very different from most. She evoked passion in every class she lectured, correcting and making comments *herself* on every student's term paper. Unlike other professors, she didn't use a graduate student "grader." She communicated that she cared about her students' learning and about her messages and "lessons." She cultivated a caring attitude and caring classroom community—even at age 72. This resulted in a highly enriched and motivated group of students.

As an anthropologist, she was exposed to scores of different cultures and a diverse mix of ethnic groups from around the world. We believe strongly, as she did, in the power of a cohesive group, bound by a common set of norms and values. Mead observed that when these groups of people were functioning optimally, they created a special kind of caring for each member of the group. Caring makes individuals gain respect for one another.

Think about it. When you really know that someone *cares* about you and for you—whether it's professional or personal caring—you respond to and behave differently with that person. Typically, you are more open, trusting, and secure. In a caring environment, individuals are motivated, productive, and happy. This allows for more open and direct dialogue and communications, limits greatly any sporadic outbursts of anomie, and helps to build trust in the relationship. It's this caring attribute that often distinguishes effective groups from massively dysfunctional ones.

If we want to create values-based leadership, there must be a strong sense of a caring community. Hundreds of social scientists have focused on the concept of community over the past twenty-five years. A community provides an internal feeling of purpose and sense of individual security. There are shared goals, values, a mission, and related activities. The community provides a strong sense of support for its members. If the supportive foundation is in place, members can take risks and experiment freely. Group members provide for their members' needs, interests and feelings. This is defined as caring. Caring needs to serve as the guideline for the way we interact with one another within our work settings.

In *On Caring* by Milton Mayeroff, the author defines caring as the way we help others grow. He conveys in his book, "Caring has a way of ordering activities and values around itself; it becomes primary and other activities and values come to be secondary. When a man who has been unable to care or had no one or nothing to care for comes to care for some other, many matters previously felt to be important fade in significance, and those related to *caring* take on new importance." If the demonstration of caring exists in one's work, then other important matters may seem less significant. These might include larger amounts of money, status, or promotional opportunities.

Once caring is experienced, the individual seeks out conditions that make caring possible and highly desirable. The employee undergoes a "liberating" process, excluding what is incompatible with caring and its conditions. This brings the individual in better touch with what is important in his or her life. It fine tunes genuine and significant interests and helps to focus on what is really important. Mayeroff says that this liberating process requires giving up certain things and activities. "Caring, then, provides a center around which my activities and experiences are integrated. This results in a harmonizing of the self with the world that is deep-seated and enduring." Caring orders other values around itself, and allows the individual to be "in place" in the world or in the workplace.

How do we "do" caring? How do we activate it? It first starts by developing a caring attitude and mindset. Asking people personal questions that convey genuine interest, helping someone address a problem or issue with concrete action steps, hugging a co-worker, and feeling someone's support for and belief in your point of view are all tangible forms of caring.

Additionally, a view of the world that sets up a personal responsibility for *you* to care about others unconditionally is key. Caring cannot mandate reciprocity or expect "benefits" back in return. A caring attitude conveys a desire to give to others, be considerate of others, and convey genuine empathy and interest in others. Caring mindsets are essential for "doing" caring.

The ways in which you can "do" caring are endless. However, there are three key characteristics or principles that should underscore all "caring" communications and actions. First is the need for consistency. Employees can't convey caring on Monday and be uncaring on Tuesday. People feel mistrust when inconsistent caring is demonstrated. Second, caring has to be genuine. There's nothing worse than someone who rather dispassionately and insensitively "manufactures " some so-called "'caring." Unless the caring is truly genuine and is perceived as such, the actions and words will be meaningless and in many ways more harmful. Third, caring has to be universal and broadly applied. If cultivation of a caring community or group is to be achieved, it can't be rationed out to a select few. Caring needs to be conveyed to all members of the group by each member within the group.

3. Provide recognition.

The third norm needed to get groups going is to encourage recognition and provide extensive positive feedback. Teachers and parents do this all the time. Isn't it peculiar to have omitted it from our work settings? Over a lifetime we spend as much—or more—time at work as we do in our homes and schools. When we tell our three sons that they have done an especially good job at something, their whole being lights up. When they send back one of their smiles, the giver is rewarded for providing recognition. Work settings must do the same for employees. Providing recognition is as rewarding to the giver as it is to the receiver. Both feel better. After a while, providing recognition becomes as self-satisfying as receiving it.

Just because you are older now doesn't mean you don't need your efforts to be recognized. Have employers forgotten how to do this? If the conditions have badly deteriorated within the work setting, we will need to jump start the recognition wire. No doubt, in some organizations this lack of recognition does exist. Just getting started on recognition will help dramatically.

Here are a few ideas. A verbal thank you, of course, is the easiest and quickest to give. When was the last time you wrote a brief note thanking the persons who helped you with the assignment? Maybe they will even write one to you, expressing gratitude for the opportunity to work with you or the team. Describe what you want them to know they did particularly well.

Recognition is indeed different from providing feedback to an individual. Recognition implicitly conveys a sense of appreciation and continued encouragement to the individual as a person. It's fine for the focus of recognition to be on the task completed, comment spoken, gesture made, or goal achieved. But for recognition to provide maximum benefit, it's important to have the individual feel greater self-worth about himself or herself—not just about his or her action being recognized. Greater self-worth contributes to greater satisfaction with one's contributions.

Recognition can be offered in a variety of ways and under different circumstances. Recognition can also occur at different stages of a task. Providing positive reinforcement to employees along the way is far more motivating than waiting until after the task has been accomplished. Thus, recognizing an employee's insight for identifying a problem area, understanding the difficulties encountered during creative solution generation, and recognizing the benefits accrued from pinpointing solutions to the problem offer three different points where positive reinforcement can be given.

An effective leader is always hunting for and seeking ways to provide recognition to others. But so often, we woefully underrecognize others. We hear managers lament, "But, you don't want to make people feel overconfident or think they're too good because then they'll be asking you for more money." How naive. Recognition, when it's genuine and legitimate, doesn't cause egoinflation. Instead, it bolsters and strengthens the inner core of individuals. It enables them to feel better about themselves and in turn to actually perform more effectively and efficiently. When people are filled with self-doubt and question themselves, they underperform. Their concentration becomes fragmented because time and energy is spent wondering if their actions will be recognized, positively or not.

Team or group leaders need to give far more thought on effective ways to provide their team members with recognition. But group members also have a responsibility to provide their leaders with positive recognition and reinforcement, too. Most people expect the flow of recognition to stem from the top down. How often have you complimented your boss for a job well done? Probably, infrequently. And yet, providing recognition to those at the top can be as enabling and motivating for them. In short, providing frequent recognition is a completely beneficial initiative, which leaves groups stronger, more confident, and better motivated to perform productively. Consequently, performance can be better focused on the tasks at hand rather than on worrisome self-doubt. The key here is to view recognition as a powerful, high-octane fuel that really can get individuals motivated and collectively keep groups going.

4. Develop one's own gifts.

Wise parents let their children be themselves. Yet, quite a large number of parents want their children to be just like them in terms of habits, interests, values, and mindsets. Every person is different and has his or her own strengths and weaknesses. Our fourth norm to get groups going is to encourage each person to develop his or her own gifts or talents. Although this may seem simple to accomplish, great barriers exist. Managers want their employees to be just like them, to support them—as if they come from similar genealogical profiles. Managers want "subordinates" to do it their way, just as most parents wanted their children to do it their way and become just like them. But, this is not the best way to establish norms that get groups going.

Parents can't claim ownership of their children. These little individuals have identities of their own. Similarly, employers can't "own" their employees or subject them to their wishes. The best parents and employers can do is to encourage the development of an individual's innate gifts and strengths and to focus on areas for improvement and change. The best arena to nurture and develop the individual is in a "learning community." Before we take a look at these communities, let's take a close-up look at how work settings can facilitate developing one's own gifts.

One of the key components for letting people develop one's own gifts is by allowing them to make mistakes. People must make mistakes to learn. You can't become an avid and competent swimmer by reading a swimming manual and listening to an instructor tell you how to swim. You need to do it often, practice, make loads of "mistakes" in the learning process, and do it some more before you can swim. The same is true for just about any task in a work environment. Making decisions, writing reports, giving presentations, conducting meetings, leading project teams, and acquiring new skills can all draw upon our unique talents and inner gifts. We need to create an environment that supports people taking "risks," falling down, and not being scolded by a "superior" for having stumbled or fallen along the way.

Another aspect of developing one's own gifts is helping to develop the talents in other individuals. Highlight for them some of their strengths. Talk to them about the potential you see. Don't be afraid to enter their "personal zone." You have to get involved with an individual if you're talking to them about their inner gifts. Too often, we have been conditioned in organizations to avoid getting too personal. For sure, it's inappropriate to discuss people's sexual preferences. But it's appropriate to discuss inner talents and strengths.

Empowering others to develop their own uniquely individual gifts is yet another powerful tool to get groups going and further eliminate anomie.

5. Create learning communities.

Learning communities are thought to exist only within schools. We take a different point of view. We believe individual development and learning should consistently take place. Leaders should do more to further developmental growth in their employees. Factories should become "schools," offices should become "schools," conference rooms should become "schools," and work organizations should become "schools."

In 1938, John Dewey wrote *Experience and Education*. He felt that the aim of schools and education should be "development from within." Student-centered learning and active learning were key concepts to Dewey because they underscored the nature of teaching and the learning process. He viewed learning as individual development, not as acquiring information poured in from a dogmatic teacher. Dewey was the father of the active learning model. A teacher was a leader of a group activity, rather than an authority figure who imparted knowledge.

In *How We Think,* a book published in 1940, Dewey described education as a social process of "shared inquiry." His concept can be translated to work organizations—individual employees solving problems together within a group. Rather than the authoritative manager demanding "the answer" ASAP, the small group takes ownership of the problem and works out a solution, after discussing alternative ideas and approaches. This involves a group process of working together to resolve a problem. It requires asking questions, gathering information, and jointly coming up with solutions. It conveys the power of the team.

Human beings do not learn by having information poured into their heads by authoritative teachers standing in front of classrooms. This process results only in silence. These authoritative or traditional approaches to learning increase the distance between the learner and the teacher. In recognizing learning as an inherently social process, education is a very active and participatory process. Employees do not learn by having the answer given to them by upper-level managers. If given the opportunity to resolve a problem at work, the team or small group can work together to come up with a solution, possibly better than the one dictated by upper management.

An effective leader should not simply impart knowledge. Rather, the "teacher-leader" is a partner in the learning process. Similarly, managers should not impart their solutions to problems. Rather, the manager is a partner in the problem-solving process. Employees come to the workplace with unique backgrounds, interests, aspirations, and experiences. All these must be seen as important when structuring a learning community in which the learner and the "teacher-leader" collaborate. Employees bring their own baggage—-interests, goals, and past experience—and each unique participant augments the group with its problem-solving perspectives.

"Development from within" should be a top aim of the organizational setting in which one works. Work settings need to be viewed from the perspective of creating opportunities for "active learning." Places of work can focus on the active involvement and development of employees, rather than be stale, boring, passive places where work offers few learning opportunities. Work settings can easily give greater attention to the individual needs and learning of each employee. Where one works should also be where one learns. This is the workplace of the future—where anomie no longer exists.

Groups become learning centers, or places where employees join to accomplish needs of the organizations as well as direct energy toward individual employee needs. All types of work groups are opportunities for learning—teams, committees, task forces, administrative meetings, special-interest groups, even staff meetings. Group leaders—teachers—collaborate with the learners or group members in a process of shared inquiry. The development of the individual employee is the ultimate aim of this process. Of course, the group tasks at hand are fundamental and are not overlooked! Just as the curriculum within a classroom setting is critical, the learning that takes place, not the books used, is the goal.

The sad note about most corporate environments is their lack of interest in the individual development of their employees. Employers tell their employees what to do, rather than facilitate development and learning geared to the employee's needs and growth. Instead, most work settings have those elements of traditional classrooms where the teacher is the one who imparts his or her knowledge to the student—pours it out—thinking this is how learning occurs.

Endogenous Growth Through Energizing Norms

Organizations must develop a sense of urgency in cultivating the effectiveness of groups. This chapter has identified five norms to get groups going. The goal is to energize the group—to infuse it with *spirit*. We called this deep-tissue growth endogenous, or growth caused from inside the social fabric of individuals and groups. To summarize, the energizing norms are:

1. Encourage intuitive thinking.
2. Cultivate a caring community.
3. Provide recognition.
4. Develop one's own gifts.
5. Create learning communities.

These five norms set up an attitude of sharing ideas freely, caring for and providing support for one another, taking ownership, risk taking, asking questions, expressing different points of view, making knowledge and learning meaningful, and providing recognition to all group members. The process of shared inquiry within the learning community causes a surge of energy. Instilling these group norms in organizations provides an environment that allows individuals to personally grow and develop.

This energy is also a by-product of belonging to a group. Groups, per se, offer a sense of belonging and personal security, especially those that have activated these five norms. They extend opportunities for collaborative learning, or they explore an idea or problem together and come up with a solution. Effective groups also convey an appreciation for another's point of view. Hearing the perspective of a fellow group member may lead one to rethink one's own point of view. New energy is infused into the group in this process. Effective, nurturing groups can help to eliminate anomie from organizations.

Furthermore, when a person does a particularly fine job in a collaborative or group effort, the group feedback becomes a powerful motivator. This creates an intellectual energy—"I have done a fine job"—and builds personal confidence. Group work also facilitates the understanding of something that is very complex. Working together, building knowledge to the point of developing a thorough understanding of its complexity, is invaluable. The group inquiry process puts the learner in touch with the organization or group, with fellow peers, and with himself or herself. It is a highly inspiring process—one that gives employees a reason to believe.

Chapter 11

Integrating Individuals into Organizations

To escape isolation, a person must be able to become a member of a group, and this is not just a problem of finding a group. The capacity for relating one's self easily to other men and women is not inborn, but a result of experience and training, and that experience and training is itself social.

George C. Homans in *The Human Group* underscores the importance of learning how to become a member of a particular group. In this chapter, we will relate it to learning how to become an employee in a work organization.

To remove anomie from organizations in the future, employees need to feel attached, connected, and part of the group. They need to know and feel that they belong and that they play a critically important role in the growth of their organization. They need to be involved in shaping the culture in which they work.

Many times, culture means one thing to senior management and something very different to employees. Our research confirmed that without norms and values that are agreed upon, adopted, and effectively utilized within organizations, a widening cultural gap exists between leaders and employees. Too often in our interviews, employees viewed "culture" as the environment created by top management. Organizational leaders, on the other hand, viewed culture as the way in which employees interacted with one other. This scenario is yet another illustration of the disconnect that exists between workers and management. We need to create organizations with clear norms and values that provide a pattern for weaving and linking all individuals into an organization together and that ultimately blur the line between the traditional hierarchies and organizational "layers."

Cultural traditions, rituals, and work habits often seem to originate with upper managers, but employees don't always recognize or accept management's conclusions. Employees may not find value in these upper-management-driven traditions and attitudes. And why should they? The culture doesn't reflect the employee's values or beliefs—only senior management's.

At other times, however, a culture sends mixed messages, and employees either cynically reject the culture or choose to selectively take certain things away from it and adapt them differently. The key is to integrate shared norms and values into an existing culture by translating past traditions into ones that provide meaning and benchmarks to guide behavior for current and future employees.

We learned in Chapter 7, Activating a Highly Personal Process, about how to create an environment that caters to and builds upon the values of all employees. Now, we want to encourage employees to understand how their organization's culture became what it is, to draw up and describe their own definition of culture, and to lay out their own future behavioral road map of their organization. Specifically, we want employees to take part in establishing their own cultural values and norms in order to tightly weave themselves into the "fabric" of the organization. The organization therefore becomes *their* organization. We strongly believe that organizations must find ways to serve their employees rather than pontificate to employees that their purpose is to serve the organization.

What Is Culture?

The Funk and Wagnalls dictionary defines culture as "the sum total of the attainments and learned behavior patterns of a specific period or people." We would modify that definition a bit. Culture is a state-of-mind that gets translated into a set of actions, communications, and responses. It is a series of human signals that includes verbal, physical, and emotional signs. Culture therefore resides in our brains, which are frequently deciphering the signals we receive daily from others. *How* each of us responds to these, in effect, describes how effective the culture is for any specific group of individuals.

Culture is a human product. Humans decide what it should be. Humans use it. Humans enhance or poison it. Culture is still one aspect of every organization that remains in the hands and minds of humans. It involves developing and sharing a common set of beliefs, norms, attitudes, goals, and information. While culture can be consciously created, too often it develops unconsciously without a concerted effort or focused vision for what employees want the culture to become. That's why culture, like a fine-woven fabric, needs all the threads sewn tightly together. Humans are the threads that create a culture. The culture in turn integrates all individuals into the organization.

Culture is what you need to know to act so that other people within the organization will accept you and your actions. Just as every country may have traditions and cultural information that is shared, every work setting or organization has its own culture, too. According to James Spradley, a noted cultural anthropologist, culture is a shared set of rules, maps, and plans. "People learn rules for appropriate behavior. They acquire mental maps which enable them to interpret the behavior and events they observe." Norms and values within the organization are then developed, and this information is shared with cultural members. Spradley stresses in his book *Culture and Cognition*: "Culture consists of whatever it is one has to know or believe in order to operate in a manner acceptable to group members. Culture is not a material phenomenon. It is the forms of things that people have in mind, their models for perceiving, relating, and otherwise interpreting them."

We like this definition because it emphasizes that the culture of an organization is something that is carried around in the heads of employees. This is indeed why it is so difficult to change an organization's culture. The norms and values that exist in the workplace are the organization's cultural rules and beliefs. Specific norms and values—cultural information—are exchanged from one member to another by interaction in the group. The culture is passed on in this way. How does this happen?

Members of the group share their expectations, usually implicitly, about how to behave in relation to other members. They share their norms and values through their dialogue and actions. Erving Goffman, in *Presentation of Self in Everyday Life,* says that group members exchange information about the group's culture very naturally. Goffman likened interaction in organizations to being on stage, initially without a script. Group members have to learn what the play is all about after interacting for a time with the other actors. The script is not there to tell them what to say and do—they have to learn how to present themselves to the organization in everyday life. When they learn how to do this, they have formed "the edges" of the cultural boundaries. One very gradually becomes a member of the group and is socialized into the values and norms of the workplace. It takes time to learn the norms and values of a culture, just as it takes time to learn the script of a play.

Socialization happens over time. You begin to pick up some of the same word choices, facial gestures, presentation styles, and so forth, of fellow co-workers whom you respect, admire, and look up to. Without fully knowing it, you're using them as role models—trying to emulate their signs and signals.

This is why, in an organization where people like and respect one other, behaviors appear rather homogeneous. What's vitally important to recognize is that these individuals were not, in any way, forced to "conform," but rather consciously chose to emulate others out of a respect for and a desire to be "like them." In a values-ful culture, employees *are* more aware of, in touch with, and consciously able to integrate themselves into an organization. Without a clear-cut culture with defined values and norms, new employees, in particular, have to pick up—often unconsciously—the implied values and observable-only norms of the organization.

Kotter and Heskett (1991) reiterate this cognitive definition of corporate culture. They stress that culture is an invisible, powerful force that teaches its members a specific set of norms and values. Interdependency is a key concept when defining culture from a cognitive perspective.

According to Kotter and Heskett, "Culture is an interdependent set of beliefs, values and ways of behaving, and tools for living that are so common in a community that they tend to perpetuate themselves, sometimes over long periods of time. This continuity is the product of a variety of social forces that are frequently subtle, bordering on invisible, through which people learn a group's norms and values, are rewarded when they accept them and are ostracized when they do not."

Since culture is a human product, employees must take part in establishing their own interdependent cultural norms and values. We've established that culture is shared information that tells employees how to act (norms) and what is important to the group (values). We've explored the fact that it takes time to learn the organization's norms and values, especially since no script is given to the "actors" (employees). It's no surprise, then, that an organization's culture is a powerful, pervasive, yet extremely subtle force. With these key ideas in mind, let's now take a close-up look at how an organization can *create* cultural values and norms. Specifically, how can individual employees draw up their own guidelines for culture development? How can each individual take part in establishing cultural values and norms for the group and for its leadership?

Perpetuating Norms and Values

We asked managers and employees several questions on the topic of culture in order to explore what integrates the individual to the organization.

- How do you define your organization's culture?
- How has your culture changed during the past three years?
- What makes employees get personally involved with their work and find satisfaction in their job?
- How do employees effectively build teams and work well in cross-functional groups?
- What behaviors are accepted by group members?

- What is the impact of leaders on the culture, and what role do they play in shaping it?

As our "believers" research team explored these questions, it became increasingly clear to us that many of the cultural rules and behaviors in work organizations are acquired through participant observation, that is, by watching and observing others. In short, cultural norms self-perpetuate themselves because new employees and recent employees (e.g., less than two years with an organization) have nothing else to latch on to. By default, they resort to observing how others act, dress, behave, write, and speak. This is not to suggest that this process is necessarily bad, but it does indeed mean that cultures won't change unless the stated norms and values do.

In order to describe how employees learn about an organization's culture, become integrated into it, and to some extent, influence it, we will discuss two new terms—culturbation and cultural regenerative osmosis.

The first, culturbation, is the most commonly used, but least desirable approach for integrating employees into groups. When employees culturbate, they acquire and assume the norms and values of the organizations through repetition by merely going through the motions of learning what's accepted and what's not. The individual is not really integrated—just accepted in, if he or she behaves according to the "rules."

In contrast, the second concept, cultural regenerative osmosis, allows individual values to be accommodated in the integration process. The individual first learns the norms and values of the organization through osmosis and then provides a regenerative benefit to the organization by augmenting the culture with their own values.

Culturbation

Culturbation is the repetitive process of becoming assimilated into a culture by practicing the group's norms again and again so that eventually they become automatic and habitual behavior. It is the process through which nongroup members are converted and transformed into members. It enables the culture of the group to be perpetuated over time. In order for this to occur, nongroup members watch insightfully and listen intently to the unspoken and spoken signals and signs that group members use to communicate and interact with one another. Once they have observed the cultural "rituals" of the organization, they begin to culturbate. They imitate the group's observed actions without really thinking any longer of what they are saying or how they are behaving in the group. They are learning and adapting to a specific culture—with all of its uniqueness, particularities, and eccentricities. In the case of employees, the unique and particular culture to be learned is the specific culture of the workplace.

Culturbation is an efficient way of getting nongroup members (or new employees) to become integrated into a group. But it is in some respects a rather mindless, nonthinking approach. We've chosen the word "culturbation" as a deliberate illustration of one of the ways our business organizations today are actually contributing to pervasive employee disillusionment.

When people culturbate, they replicate what they see and hear without changing the culture, adding to it, enriching it, making it better, or improving upon it. They simply imitate. They mimic. Unfortunately, most organizations want employees only to culturbate. They want them to merely observe rather than acquire, filter, enrich, and interact with the cultural information received. But the sad part is that, under this scenario, the sparkling, unique, and creative beliefs, insights, and perspectives of new employees never have a chance of being developed and added to an existing organization's culture. Instead, employees mindlessly adopt the current norms, which are then self-perpetuated. They don't get a chance to try to leverage, enrich, and improve the culture.

The sad fact is that most of us have never learned to go beyond culturbation. Unfortunately, adult workers in organizations have learned to culturbate from their earliest years—in a school setting. Most educational systems expect and demand children to culturbate. Most "traditional" teachers want children to act and behave in ways that respond to the teacher's desired behavior. Children are asked daily to recall, imitate, and replicate words, facts, computations, and bits of information. They are often instructed to follow directions, play in a certain way, and produce a rote response to most every question. The culture of the classroom is determined and dictated by one person—the teacher at the top. And heaven forbid if a child wants to do something creative—to inject his or her own beliefs or motivations into a project or endeavor. He or she is discouraged from doing so. The child needs to "adhere" to the culture created by the teacher.

In the same way we need to change the way we work in organizations, we need to change this situation in our school environments. Why shouldn't children have a say in the norms and values that they believe should be inculcated and instilled in a classroom culture? Probably your first response is, "But, they're just children." Okay, but this is exactly where children *learn* that trying to change an organization's culture is usually a fruitless and ineffective endeavor.

The culture of a school should include the desired norms and values of its customers—the students. If you think this is way above the heads of children, ask a ten-year-old you know what his or her values are. You'll be shocked by the child's insights.

Certainly, by high school and college, students should most definitely be allowed to influence the culture that they are living in five days a week. But, no, in fact, it seems as if more regimentation, rules, policies, restrictions, and rigid codes of conduct are established in the higher grades of learning. How can we expect individuals to feel as if they can have control over and be able to shape and influence their work environments if for twelve to sixteen years they're taught just the opposite. They're taught to culturbate. They learn this lesson so well that they forget how to influence their organizations as adults.

In a work setting, you'll often hear questions from a new employee regarding, "Why is it done that way?" or "Why don't you include manufacturing people in that decision?" or "Why do people always argue with what the president suggests?" The response the person typically receives is usually the same: "That's just the way we do it around here." This is a vivid illustration of the negative aspects of culturbation.

Indeed, as we have stated, a part of culturbation *is* actually positive and healthy. People learn how to become an "accepted" participant and a member of a group. Their integration helps to convert nongroup members into full-fledged "lifetime" members. But, too much culturbation can literally prevent the group member from making an impact on the culture and from having it make an impact on the individual as well.

Cultural Regenerative Osmosis

We believe that culturbation can be directed effectively if an organization accepts and endorses what we define as cultural regenerative osmosis. This new term means employees learn the norms and values by participant observation and then integrate those observations into their *own* set of values. In turn, employees influence and impact the culture through new norms that they've developed in the process. This, of course, requires a mindset by managers and leaders that is very open to change, accepts alternative styles and behaviors, and evokes a belief in the value of all individuals. Easier said than done. The challenge is to truly believe that all employees deserve respect and equal treatment and have valid contributions to make to an organization's culture.

Cultural regenerative osmosis enables members of groups to acquire a strong sense of community. This process integrates their own personal values with the already established norms and values of the organization. What results is a common identity, common sense of purpose, and common norms and values. Over time, this sense of community builds each individual's self-confidence and self-worth and ultimately creates group solidarity.

By participating in work groups, task forces, and project teams, employees are exposed to the current culture and begin to learn the individual values and beliefs of fellow group members. They begin to pick up what others think and feel, in effect, through osmosis. This enables individuals to participate effectively in the social interaction of work groups. It enables them to better understand which behaviors and communication styles work and which ones don't work. By practicing these skills and learned behaviors, group members gradually take on roles that others expect them to play or perform. It is through this interactive process that group members learn the meaning of different roles that are adopted by other group members. This enables them to participate in the social order of the group.

Regeneration occurs when an individual, after having acquired the norms and values of a group through osmosis, integrates his or her own personal values into those learned, stirs the culture pot, and slightly alters, adds, or deletes some of the practiced norms of the group. This provides a regeneration of culture that includes, not excludes, all members of a group. It provides a rebirthing and growth of an organization's norms and values. It's the process approach that we recommend organizations endorse for developing a values-based culture.

To succeed in the actual job function, it is imperative that a genuine sense of cooperation be established with others in the workplace. Cooperation can't happen without acceptance or membership into the group. This is a very important tenet for cultural success. Employees must learn how to cooperate with each other. Cultural regenerative osmosis can help to foster this cooperation through shared knowledge and by facilitating new norms that can strengthen the cooperative spirit of a group.

Culture as Shared Knowledge

In our cognitive definition of culture, we have said that it is the knowledge employees must acquire in order to act appropriately in a given workplace. An employee must have this knowledge or cultural information in order to interact in an orderly and sensible way within their organization.

For example, as a member of the development department in a large private university, a new employee quickly learned that no one ever said anything negative at staff meetings. These were "show-off" sessions where staff members reported only positive news—how many proposals had been submitted to foundations—for how much money. The more positive information formally presented the better—the vice-president for development liked that. He did not want to have doubts expressed or entertain any creative brainstorming or tentative ideas. The culture of this particular workplace dictated that such behavior was inappropriate. Employees had to learn this fact—this cultural knowledge—in order to act correctly. This is an example of culturbation in action. Yet it also illustrates the potential for regenerative osmosis to occur and augment the culture. Through the process of regenerative osmosis, this new employee's style of expressing creative ideas, doubts, and pessimism at staff meetings could possibly cause the culture to evolve or regenerate in a new positive way. Unfortunately, this did not occur at this particular workplace. Turnover was frequent. Culturbation won out.

Interaction with others in everyday work life is constantly affected by our common exposure to one another's norms and values. It is through the everyday activities of the workplace that employees and leaders demonstrate and live their culture. Sharing knowledge or information enables individuals to become better integrated into the organization.

Small Groups Better Integrate Employees

Think about two different-sized parties you've been to—one with ten people in attendance and the other with 100 people. Did you behave differently at each? Did you feel more comfortable at the smaller party and a bit awkward at the larger one? A sizable portion of people find they are able to "socialize" more easily with a group of ten than with a group of 100. Why? Because in the process of getting to know new people in a very short time period, we accelerate the socialization process. We are trying to gain information quickly about another person: where they work; the size of their family; their avocations and sports, interests, and so forth. With a group of ten people, the process can work more effectively than with a large group, as enough time can be allocated to getting to know the other members of the party.

What happens to us at the 100-people party? We undergo socialization overdose. In effect, we go into an emotional coma: We freeze up and revert to a corner somewhere to talk to an even smaller group of three to four people we know. We virtually do no socializing; we choke and turn our social-interaction and dialogue engines off.

The same happens in a work setting. Most often, our frequent interactions with co-workers is limited, on average, to ten people or less. Sure, we're exposed to scores of different people in meet-ings, travel, and the like. But most of our socializing occurs in small groups. That's why task forces, work teams, quality circles, and project groups are usually far more effective than dropping an employee amidst the sea of 100 other divisional employees.

Small-group formation should be encouraged and activated in every organization—regardless of its size. Employees need to feel as if they are members of a group in order to feel integrated into an organization. They need to gain acceptance and become involved in sustained efforts to support, maintain, and build their small-group community. This community-building process per-mits members to acquire a common identification with other members through shared experiences, norms, values, traditions, sentiments, and other cultural information. As members learn this cultural information, they become part of the group. A collective orientation develops that enhances the solidarity of the workplace or community.

When the solidarity of the work organization is extended from a small task group to the large organization, then the small-er group acts to integrate its members. In this way, the communi-ty-building process serves to socialize by teaching employees how to become members of the larger work organization.

Therefore, a large part of the activities and experiences that can be observed or experienced in the workplace can help to regenerate organizational cultures. Each organization differs in how it encourages cultural regenerative osmosis to occur and how it helps to integrate its employees. Nevertheless, by performing an integrative function, and by participating in cultural regenerative osmosis, employees maintain a collective orientation and loyalty to the core norms and values of the workplace. In turn, work organizations provide for the transmission of norms and values. What is the conduit for this transmission? It is nothing more—or less—than a sense of community.

Emotional Glue—The Sense of Community

Cultural regenerative osmosis provides employees with a deeply fulfilling sense of belonging. They begin to feel that they really can make a difference. By integrating the organization's values with their own, disseminating a new value or norm, and watching the culture adopt it, employees are given a positive sense of personal power. They can actually "see" the impact of their own values contributions on the culture. It's through this self-gratification that anomie is reduced and that a sense of isolation can be abated.

In providing strong emotional ties among its members, the workplace serves an expressive function. But, there is also a strong sense of interdependence and identification with a set of mutual values and norms. In this way, the workplace serves a solidarity function. That is, it offers employees common experiences, giving them an identity to their workplace or community. A strong internal collective orientation exists among members of the workplace. Taken together, the expressive and solidarity functions describe the process of forming an organization culture. The development of a strong sense of community is manifested by a common identity, common experiences, and common values—all of which are distinct cultural characteristics. This culture—found within each workplace—is learned by its employees through small groups.

Rosabeth Moss Kanter notes in her book *Commitment and Community* that the clearer a definition of the group becomes to a member, the greater is the sense of commitment. She describes three types of commitment. The first is called instrumental commitment; it facilitates continuance and ongoing participation in the community. The second is called affective commitment; it facilitates cohesion or group solidarity, emphasizing relationships and gratification through emotional bonds. The third is called moral commitment; it facilitates control within the community, supporting the norms, values, and authority of the group. Commitment provides an internal drive that enables individuals to overcome major obstacles placed in their way. Commitment, of course, can be strengthened only over time, once a person feels a strong part of a group and can begin to see how his or her personal values are linked to the group.

In our interviews and research, we found that employees define and administer their own initiation rites for new employees. They clearly lead a process of "granting membership status" to these employees. Specifically, they bond with their cohorts and put the new employee through a process in which they must "gain acceptance" into the group.

Six Types of Integrative Norms

The cultural features of an organization are built from the norms shared among fellow employees. That is, a "regular" in the distinct culture of the organization shares a set of norms and values with other members. These norms and values act as guides to their behavior and activities, both individually and as a group. These implicit cultural norms are divided into six categories that can be used across all types of work organizations (e.g., corporate, non-profit, etc.). As an example of how a set of norms actually illustrates a culture, we have specified these norms within the workplace of our consulting company, Kuczmarski & Associates.

1. Define a range and kinds of acceptable topics of conversation.

This first category identifies what employees talk about, or don't talk about, within their organizational setting.

At Kuczmarski & Associates, employees talk about clients, report deadlines, data collected, selling new business, marketing themselves, mentoring situations, cash-flow challenges, personal problems, professional development needs, client problems, and creative solutions. The formal and informal chatter, or lack of it, at a staff meeting is a good place to identify the range of conversation topics acceptable within any culture. Hallway conversations also display a great deal of cultural depth; often more personalized conversations occur here.

2. Enable individuals to display their own identity.

This places emphasis on allowing different personal and professional identities to exist within a group. It focuses on the image given off to others in the workplace.

At Kuczmarski & Associates, employees display professional identity by engaging in a practice area, taking ownership for problems, engaging in selling activities, using creativity and flexibility to achieve results, never compromising ethical standards, always displaying high intellectual qualities, brainstorming ideas without fear of being laughed at, and rarely being afraid to make mistakes. Personally, it is appropriate to express emotion, sensitivity, consideration for others, respect for fellow employees, and a sense of caring.

3. Define clearly the job function of individual group members.

This third category clarifies what employees are expected to do in their job, work function, or team project—it identifies their normative role expectations or rules.

At Kuczmarski & Associates these include both internal and external norms. When interacting with clients, consultants are expected to take ownership of their problems, emphasize data-based solutions, and demonstrate intense caring about and knowledge of the client's situation. Internally, consultants are expected to take pride in their work, engage in "high-quality work," have a learning-ful attitude, exude entrepreneurial spirit, engage in a continuous personal evaluation process, offer personalized training, volunteer to help when help is needed, promote on merit, and recognize and reward excellence.

4. Develop group solidarity.

This fourth category emphasizes what members need to do to help build togetherness. Each workplace is marked by a distinct sharing system that acts to establish the solidarity of the members.

At Kuczmarski & Associates, emphasis is placed on sharing leadership, team work, consensus building, holding team members accountable, and maintaining and cultivating a team environment—particularly with respect to client work, administrative needs, and business operations.

5. Spend quality team-building time.

The fifth category describes what members do outside the work organization to foster team building.

At Kuczmarski & Associates, employees share in team-building activities: all firm-sponsored events and project/team events. Firm-sponsored events include the annual pub crawl, awards banquet, Christmas party, summer lunch cruise, week-long winter planning cruise, and tennis barbecue. The firm's project team events include team lunches, dinners, order-in pizzas, pub excursions, nonproject conversations and team celebrations!

6. Nurture strong relations with leadership.

The final category emphasizes how members interact with organizational leaders.

At Kuczmarski & Associates, leadership takes on a unique style—a shared leadership approach. That is, members of the firm are expected to take on champion roles and to assume accountability for these advocacy roles. They are also expected to become trainers or teachers. Specifically, consultants teach topics to others within the firm, including sessions on the following: What is consulting? What is data collection and analysis? How do I interview? How do I write a report? How does the consulting team work? What are some presentation tips? How do you measure quality? How do I sell business? How does the administrative team work? How do I market the firm? An organization "gets" a motivated and highly dedicated group of employees from having these norms.

Besides offering internal training, Kuczmarski & Associates also encourages taking outside professional development courses. It encourages personal development and training (subscribing to journals, going to conferences, taking night courses, working out). These encompass an individual's professional development objectives.

Mentoring as an Integration Tool

Mentoring is yet another tool for integrating an individual into an organization. A mentor is a supporter of the individual—someone who tries to help advance the individual's career and help resolve his or her professional problems. "I'm looking out for your best interests and I'm here to serve as a sounding board for you," is the mindset a good mentor should adopt. Mentors serve to bring employees into the culture of the workplace. But in order for a mentoring relationship to really work well, a mutually agreed-upon mentor-mentee partnership is essential. If a mentor is simply "assigned" to an employee, it usually won't work. A partnership that is based on mutual trust and respect of each other needs to evolve over time. Mentors, therefore, act as an:

advisor: "The things she [the client] looks for in a research consultant are energy, quality, and a great attitude."

trainer: "Let's spend time learning about interviewing."

friend: "Let's go get a cup of coffee."

counselor: "Marketing strategy seems like the best practice area for you."

sage: "If I were on that project with you, I would tackle the segmentation like this. . . ."

teacher: "The way I've done it in the past is . . ."

confidant: "Your self-appraisal looks great."

big sister/big brother: "I think sending him a thank-you card for that bonus is a smart idea."

When mentoring is done well and a true partnership is created between two individuals, effective integration of the employee into the organization is greatly facilitated. Mentoring can provide powerful advancement of an individual's personal and professional development. It also can help to build a stronger sense of community within the workplace. How? Mentors provide a support system. They focus on helping an individual join a group and remain a cooperative member of that group.

That mentoring programs *exist* within the workplace is critically important. But they should be designed to be as flexible as possible. Guidelines and a structure are discussed below, but the bulk of the relationship is up to the mentor and his or her mentee. And, almost unilaterally, those employees we interviewed stated the need for this relationship to be both personal and professional.

We suggest that every mentor-mentee relationship should start with a two-hour meeting to discuss what the goals and objectives of the relationship are and what the roles of each participant should be. A follow-up to this meeting should be a written note between the two individuals on what those goals and objectives are. This note should then be submitted to someone in the workplace who will serve as the mentor's leader—an interested individual who will guide the mentors.

The mentors' leader within every work organization should be given a one-page quarterly update on the relationship, including its progress and future needs. We call this mentor maintenance. The mentors' leader is also responsible for gathering together responses as to who would like to work together as mentor and mentee, and to actually formalize the relationships that evolve between two persons. The mentors' leader is a key individual in that he or she needs to train, motivate, and encourage mentors to keep their mentees top of mind. He or she must have considerable people skills and teaching sensitivities. At Kuczmarski & Associates, the mentor leader frequently checks in with all mentors to see how their relationships are going. A sample of a recent memo of his follows in Exhibit 11–1.

After this relationship starts, there are only a few "rules" each mentor-mentee should try to follow. These include:

* Schedule weekly get-togethers or chats to keep each other up-to-date.
* Schedule a monthly breakfast, lunch, dinner, or drink to discuss personal and professional issues out of the office.
* Finalize mentee's annual development plan, including training needs and potential courses to take; review this plan with the mentor leader, once completed.

This mentoring plan at Kuczmarski & Associates might include goals, objectives, and timing for professional development (e.g., analysis, writing), marketing (e.g., publish an article), selling (e.g., assist in selling two new projects), organization-wide development (e.g., recruiting), and personal growth (e.g., time management).

Recruiting—Opening the Door to the Workplace

The recruitment process is one of the critical areas that directly impacts whether an individual will eventually be successfully integrated into an organization. If the wrong decisions are made about *who* should enter the culture of the workplace, then, rather than integration occurring, disintegration will result. Instead of consen-

EXHIBIT 11-1

Mentor Prospecting Plans

One of the roles we should all look at as mentors is helping our mentees along with their individual prospecting efforts. Many of our mentees really do not know how to get their whole prospecting cycle started, and I think this is an area we can add a lot of mentoring-value.

1. Schedule a meeting introducing what you would like to accomplish (maybe over lunch).

2. Sit down and establish three-, six- and twelve-month goals. For example:

   * Three-month—develop my contact list
   * Six-month—have lunch with four contacts
   * Twelve-month—have a couple of inquiries

   Give as a homework assignment—creating your database of contacts using individual concentric circles as the model (i.e., hometown people, parent's friends, college and grad school contacts, personal friends, association networks, business people they may have crossed paths with).

3. Meet again, two weeks later, to go over the list and help your mentee segment their contacts into hot, warm, and cold segments, with a hot contact being someone we would consider to be a potentially strong prospect.

4. Meet again, two weeks later, to help with the letter, script out phone conversations, and finalize the monthly game plan.

   Set up one-hour monthly meetings *now* for the rest of the year to track against set goals.

5. Keep on top of your mentee's progress!

This is an initiative that we can't afford *not* to do. All of us are responsible, and each of us needs to take the initiative. Let me know how you are doing with your mentor-selling efforts. I will keep in touch. Thanks!

sus, there will be an unhealthy and often overwhelming lack of consensus. Instead of agreement, there will be negative confrontation and frequent disagreement.

At our firm, we refer to recruiting as the "adoption process." In effect, the organization needs to "adopt" a new employee candidate before a job offer is extended. This doesn't mean that all employees need to interview the candidate nor does it require that all interviewers are in unanimous agreement on everyone extended an offer. However, it does mean that any *one* interviewer does have veto power. If any current employee feels strongly that a candidate should *not* be hired, he or she won't receive a job offer.

Invitations to join our firm are difficult to obtain. A mutual fondness, respect, and trust have to emerge in the rather brief and often stiff interviewing process. Candidates will typically interview with five, six, or more members of our firm with multiple site visits being part of the recruiting methodology. People who find this process inefficient or too cumbersome obviously don't belong at our firm. Thus, the adoption process was coined—implying that the candidate and representatives of the organization have adopted each other.

Consequently, when a new employee begins, the transition period is greatly shortened. The new employee feels a member of the group from week one.

The best recruitment practice is to create an interview team that can spot the key characteristics and skills sought when meeting each candidate. Members of this group should represent key areas within the organization. For example, if an administrative person is needed, then the team should be composed of those individuals who will be working with this person. Additionally, recruiting team members need to use their intuition as well as objectively evaluate the candidate's professional skill base and academic criteria in making decisions. They need to use both their head and heart in evaluating prospective new-hires. They will need to trust the judgment of one another or learn about the judgment process of others. Additionally, the evaluation process should be completed within a given time frame. A definite decision should be reached. No "maybe" hire decisions are acceptable. Remember, decision making needs to be quick and heartfelt. Again, if we are truly seeking new members to a group, some personal, emotional feelings about the person are appropriate and need to be positive.

A social interview is also paramount. Having a drink or a cup of tea with a candidate and a friend or spouse, along with members of the interview team, is a critical learning opportunity. Interviewees must have the opportunity to express themselves in a nonoffice setting. It is truly remarkable what new information surfaces during this process, not to mention the clarity of this information. Specifically, the interview team can better see how well the candidate will integrate into the culture of the workplace. The cultural regenerative osmosis process will operate at its best when the candidates feel more part of the group even before they've joined it.

In short, individuals need to be integrated into organizations. The functions of culturbation and cultural regenerative osmosis help to explain the integration process. Small groups, socialization, mentoring, and recruiting are additional mechanisms that can be employed to more effectively weave individuals into the culture of organizations and explain how individuals are integrated into organizations. In turn, anomie is further eradicated, allowing a values-ful culture to burgeon.

Chapter 12

Creating a Values-Based Leadership Mindset

In order to eradicate anomie within an organization and create a values-ful culture, leaders need to set a values-based tone and attitude that establishes the right mindset. The underlying principle for developing a values-based mindset is relationship building. Leaders need to effectively relate to others in the organization, set the values-based example through words and actions, and achieve success in building meaningful relationships throughout the organization. This chapter will describe ten key initiatives that values-based leaders undertake and continually focus on improving.

Leaders Must Lead the Values

One leader within an organization can have a huge impact on the company's norms and values development. Lou Gerstner, at IBM, is a good example of a leader who demonstrates the values that he wants the organization to adopt. In a few months after coming to IBM from RJR Nabisco as CEO, he was making several blatant values statements by what he did—not by just what he said. In October 1993, Gerstner stated: "I want to manage by principle rather than procedure. It means when a situation arises, you don't go to a manual. You know in your heart and head what to do." This suggests Gerstner believes strongly in the innate and intrinsic talents embodied in every employee. Rather than turning to the employee policy manual, turn inward to yourself. Most employees have enough experience, intuition, and common sense to make good decisions. But, most organizations don't value that value.

On protocol, he states: "A corporate culture has to be built around expectations of performance, not rules of behavior . . . If in the IBM lab in Austin everybody decides they want to come to work in jeans and sandals, God bless 'em." Gerstner recognizes that agreed-upon *expectations* of behavior and resultant performance is what really matters—not a handbook of policies and procedures that are supposed to dictate, punish, or rule out behaviors.

Gerstner frequently meets with employees and customers to discuss their issues, wants, and problems. Perhaps without even knowing it, he's initiating the first step in identifying norms and values—asking others what's important to them. He also conveys a value that's aimed at serving customers, and he avoids lofty promises often found in strategic mission statements. In July 1993, Gerstner told the press: "There's been a lot of speculation as to when I'm going to deliver a vision. The last thing IBM needs right now is a vision. What IBM needs is a series of very tough-minded, market-driven, highly effective strategies in each of its businesses."

This example illustrates the impact that one individual leader can have on an organization. Indeed, there are hundreds of examples that demonstrate the impact that a leader can have on thousands of employees in a work setting. This suggests that leaders need to better understand, inculcate, and accept this huge responsibility. Everything they say, do, preach, or ask about is observed, discussed, and interpreted by employees within the organization. Leaders in an organization need to become far more aware of their *own impact* on others. This is a responsibility that cannot be shirked or given short shrift. It is absolutely essential that *all* leaders within organizations recognize this fact—not just the CEO or the president—and lead the values.

A values-ful school that we are well-acquainted with is the Chicago City Day School. Founded by Galeta Clayton more than a decade ago, she has created a school unlike any other that we've ever seen or been exposed to. Not only does she instill a strong sense of values in teachers and students, she has instituted a progressive curriculum that "teaches" values. Our fourth grader actually describes feelings and emotions as a class homework assignment and discusses the attributes he likes and dislikes most about himself. It's encouraging to see a school with such dedicated teachers and visionary leadership. They indeed are making a values impact on the young students who attend this elementary school.

The key for leaders is to inculcate a belief that an organization-wide value system must be built on the platform of individual credibility and cooperation. A focus on improving the total human environment is where leaders must turn. That's not to say that we should begin losing profits or market share to the sacrifice of improved employee satisfaction. Both can be achieved simultaneously. In fact, if the human condition is enhanced, the economic picture will brighten. It's the result of natural consequences.

But credibility is a tough thing to establish and even harder to hang on to. So what's a CEO, executive director, or school principal to do? First and foremost, each needs to model and exemplify in his or her daily behavior and communications the norms and values he or she wants others in the organization to espouse.

Developing Leadership

Leadership is a responsibility of a group. Without the group, there is no need for a leader. Because we work in groups, we all need leadership skills. Leadership is learned behavior. It is not inborn to a select few. Rather, it is developed through experience. Learning leadership is an ongoing process. Someone is not suddenly a leader. Nor does someone stop learning leadership skills. A university president or a top corporate executive should not think he or she can stop learning how to be an effective leader.

Educators have long known that the most effective way of learning is through doing. When a child works with the material, actually "plays" with it, especially in the case of learning certain behaviors, there is more learning and greater retention. The individual then must practice, actually perform, the behaviors associated with leadership.

But can values-based leadership really be learned? It can and must be taught in the workplace. The concept of the workplace as educator is a profound and powerful one. It is founded on the idea that leadership is the responsibility of all group members, not just of one designated person.

Leadership is learned when individuals interact with one another in a group—when personal relationships are built and trust is developed. But the group must be participative, be supportive, and must demonstrate trust consistently. To facilitate personal growth and leadership development, the work environment must be open and accepting. Autocratic settings do not teach leadership. To the contrary, they force members to do things that often reflect the self-vested interests of the leader rather than the interests of the group.

Building relationships is tough to do. Many leaders wrongfully believe that their primary job is to guide the strategic direction of the company or increase stock price or achieve the financial goals of the organization. Not so! The primary job of organizational leaders is to build relationships with co-workers, employees, managers, customers, shareholders, distribution suppliers, and so forth. There is nothing more important they can do. This relationship-building endeavor will help to instill norms and values internally, which will create motivated and dedicated employees. It will also strengthen how customers, shareholders, and other external constituencies involved with the company perceive the values of the organization.

Becoming an Effective Leader

To build effective relationships, leaders need to ultimately cultivate the following characteristics and attributes:

> **L**istens actively
> **E**mpathetic
> **A**ttitudes are positive and optimistic
> **D**elivers on promises and commitments
> **E**nergy level is high
> **R**ecognizes self-doubts and vulnerabilities
> **S**ensitivity to others' needs, values, and potential.

These attributes are the foundation for values-based leadership and for cultivating interpersonal relationships. They reflect a strong belief in and respect for each individual. The workplace should value more than bottom-line profits and future growth. It must become a pathway to personal growth for each and every employee.

Leadership needs to be practiced—again and again. Enhancing leadership is an ongoing and never-ending process. No leader has ever reached the point of perfection in leadership acumen and effectiveness. We propose ten initiatives (Exhibit 12–1) that should be developed by any values-based leader.

EXHIBIT 12-1

Values-Based Leadership Initiatives

1. Build personal relationships
2. Know the personal goals of each group member
3. Have a feel for group members
4. Allow for group conflicts
5. Manage learning
6. Share responsibility
7. Use teaming
8. Communicate two-ways
9. Link internal culture with external performance
10. Display passion and support diversity

---

1. Build personal relationships.

Men, in particular, are typically pretty bad at relationship building. Given the dominance of male leaders in our large organizations, it's no wonder that relationship building is often void and missing in our leaders. Relationship building takes work, time, and action. It doesn't—we repeat—it doesn't just happen. The first step calls for a desire to build a relationship with others; the second step requires a willingness to spend the requisite time to do so; and the third step involves undertaking a series of actions aimed at nurturing a relationship.

Yes, professionals need to develop personal relationships in the workplace. They need to know that genuine caring and interest in the other person is the underlying premise of the relationship. When people have developed a strong relationship, they work more effectively together, understand one another better, and can jointly be far more effective in their job efforts. Each step is further detailed below.

STEP 1. DESIRE—Desire has to be visible and felt by the other person. A leader who is always "too busy," "under a crunch," or "on the run" clearly conveys a lack of desire in developing a relationship. Most people have many fears in building a personal relationship with another employee. The number-one fear is, "Does this other person really want to develop a relationship with me?" Consequently, the effective leader conveys through words, actions, and emotions a genuine desire to get to know another person better. One of the easiest ways to accomplish this is to express this interest verbally, spend time with the other person, and ask him or her personal questions.

2. TIME—As we already mentioned, you can't develop a relationship in a two-hour time slot. It requires spending time with a person in three ways: (1) working together, (2) socializing further in a nonwork setting, and (3) interacting in these ways frequently and consistently.

By now, the ever-so-busy executive may throw up his or her hands and say, "This is ridiculous; I don't have time for that." And that's exactly the point, and a key reason why busy executives are often so poor at relationship-building. Make time! Or recognize and acknowledge that you just won't be able to cultivate meaningful relationships. Nor will you ever become an effective values-based leader. Take the time in a work setting to explain something more clearly; help another group member to think through a problem; spend time understanding why a group member continues to procrastinate; listen to another team member's goals for a project.

Moreover, some time also needs to be spent in a social, nonwork setting. Different dynamics are automatically established. The dialogue is usually more personal; the conversations are often more personally enriching or fulfilling than around a conference table. And above all, time needs to be spent with the other on a rather consistent basis. Obviously, the frequency of time spent will vary from one relationship to the other, but a dinner once a year, for sure, will not make a relationship.

STEP 3. ACTIONS—Several types of actions can be used to cultivate a relationship. These range from sending the other person a letter, note, or quick memo praising his or her performance, expressing verbal recognition, asking questions about the other person, or inviting him or her to join you somewhere. Actions do speak louder than words; relationships require interactive participation by two people—not just one. There's nothing worse than one person trying hard to develop a relationship with little response in return from the other person. Again, personal relationship building is the responsibility of all group members as well as the leaders. It's essential for values-based leadership.

2. Know the personal goals of each group member.

Each group or team member has a set of personal goals or objectives that he or she has developed or at least thought about for him or herself on most any project team, task force, or group. The leader, in particular, needs to uncover and understand these personal objectives in order to know how to help the individual achieve them.

Individual goals can be used as a platform upon which to build group goals. However, the needs and goals of a group are often changing. The leader must remain flexible and adaptive to these evolving group needs and goals. Creative leaders are sensitive to this dynamic. In addition, they *nurture* it! In turn, members have new demands and revised motives and interests. They are ready to take on more individual and collective responsibilities, if their new needs and demands have been recognized and addressed.

This is an engaging process. Leaders must understand their members' needs and help to satisfy them, and then they must define new needs and related group requirements. Effective leaders respond to the changing setting and address the interests of their group members. They encourage a structure for constructively sharing their interests. Thus, effective leaders are sensitive to the individual and collective needs and goals of their group members.

Leaders are responsible for coordinating and monitoring this dynamic process, for helping the group to satisfy the individual's personal needs and organizational requirements. Members are responsible for articulating their needs, helping in the process of satisfying them, and projecting their new needs onto the group. It is a highly personal and dynamic process. Leaders must know the personal goals of each group member.

3. Have a feel for group members.

The key to leadership effectiveness is having a *feel* for each group member who, in turn, has feelings toward the leader. Group members and leaders must know one another's strengths and weaknesses. They need to discover each member's "hot and cold" buttons to know how best to motivate each. Leaders must know when they disappoint others in the group. They must know how to successfully motivate group members. Most work settings do *not* have a format for sharing this information. They may value leadership, but end up avoiding discussion about it.

Every leader must focus on other individual's strengths and weaknesses. They need to determine how do I motivate and when do I disappoint group members?

Unless a leader is truly able to discern the innate and unique "gifts" and potential of each individual, the group's potential will never be maximized. Granted, this requires a time investment to acquaint "leaders" and group members with the needs and motivating characteristics of each.

In Chapter 7 we provided an exercise entitled, "Knowing the Needs and Characteristics of the Group." This is a good tool to use with a group to cultivate a feel for each member. It's vitally important for each group member to understand the needs and characteristics of the leader, too.

Another good exercise to employ is displayed in Exhibit 12–2: "Getting a Feel for Group Members." Each group member should pair up with another and share each other's responses. Then the group should meet and share all responses with one another. This helps to foster an open and candid discussion on what "turns on" and "turns off" all group members as well as provides greater insights on one another's perceived strengths and weaknesses.

EXHIBIT 12-2

Getting a Feel for Group Members

What is my greatest strength that can be brought to this group, and which weakness needs to be shored up?

Greatest strength

Greatest weakness

When do I disappoint members of the group?

When I . . . _____

_____

_____

_____

I can really motivate a group member . . .

When I . . . _____

_____

_____

_____

4. Allow group conflicts.

Leadership is acquired when individuals interact with one another in a group. Part of the natural course of any series of inter-actions is conflict. Conflict is a normal part of group interactions and personal relationships. The effective leader knows how to deal with conflict in a group. What's the best approach to take? Try to resolve the conflict—right? No, wrong. Leaders need to let groups experience conflict. The group must not have a formal mediator who steps in to resolve the conflict. In doing so, group members are robbed of learning how to deal with the conflict situation themselves. This suggests that families, schools, and corporations that halt conflict are not allowing for growth and development of the group. Now, this may be a difficult pill to swallow, allowing conflict to surface and heighten. The customary leaders of these three groups—parents, teachers, and managers—should not step in and try to immediately resolve the conflict themselves.

Conflict in a group can serve as a catalyst for a group member to step in and take responsibility for resolving the situation (see Exhibit 12–3). It changes a group member into a leader—one who takes responsibility for conflict resolution. If the leader mediates, this opportunity won't occur.

Leadership is a result of getting people to do things through the group. It requires that direction be given to the group effort and that the commitment be made by the group members themselves.

Specifically, the group must be participative, supportive, and have an informal supervisory style. It must be relatively small in size to facilitate a sense of ownership and to demonstrate trust in others while building group identity. The process of identification with the group members serves a developmental function by enhancing the individual member's self-esteem. Informality in the group structure allows members to experience conflict. Accordingly, members engage in or practice leadership behaviors, particularly responsibility-taking and decision-making, to resolve their own conflict. No formalized mediator, such as a dominating supervisor or operating executive, can constantly step in to resolve the conflict. The extent to which these characteristics exist or not determines the degree to which leadership is learned and the group is maintained.

Leaders learn how to instill and nurture conflict into a particular work setting, since it is a critical ingredient. When the workplace appears intensely disorganized, conflict needs to be resolved. Leadership behaviors can be practiced. At the same time, group members also attempt to maintain the group and build

EXHIBIT 12-3

Characteristics of Group

- Participative
- Supportive
- Informal supervisory style
- Small size
- Informality in group structure
- No formalized mediator

Experience Conflict

Consequences of Learning Setting

Maintaining the Group/ Building Community

- Shared values
- Ownership
- Pursuit of common goals
- Trust in others
- Identification with members (gives meaning)
- Enhance individual member's self-esteem

Learn Leadership Behaviors
(Resolve Conflict)

- Communicate
- Take responsibility
- Nurture/accept criticism
- Teach others
- Share leadership
- Know resources of the group
- Use descriptive praise

a sense of community. They are motivated to lead, not just to ame-
liorate their conflict, but to maintain and continue their group.
Group membership brings them a strong sense of community:
shared values, ownership, common goals, identity, self-esteem,
and opportunities to pursue a goal larger than the self.

Group maintenance efforts teach members to be concerned
with the continuation and perpetuation of the group, building its
potential for continued growth and prosperity. Activities within
the workplace function to intensify the sense of community,
whether experiencing a three-day annual meeting or sharing the
numerous activities involved with planning and running an internal or client-related seminar. These experiences serve a unifying
function, thereby intensifying the sense of community.

5. Manage learning.

As previously discussed, leaders need to serve as socratic
teachers. They need to develop a learning environment or a learning organization, as Motorola describes its company.

The managing-learning process calls for drawing information
from the participating learners, keeping them involved and
engaged in the learning, and recognizing their progress when they
have learned. The emphasis is on what the learner learns. The
learner is the most important person in the process—not the
teacher or leader. The leader assists the learner in acquiring skills,
knowledge, and techniques, and helps the learner integrate this
information into a real-world application. The three stages of managing-learning are:

1. **Discovery**—finding out what a person already knows before
   giving information or trying to "teach" him or her something.
   If the learner already knows the material or has acquired the
   skill, then the plans need to be adjusted accordingly so that
   the learning is relevant to the learner.
2. **Teaching**—new material is "presented" to the learner and
   customized according to which mode of learning is best
   received by the learner. Modes to choose from include hearing, seeing, experiencing, writing, and doing.
3. **Application**—gives learners a chance to try out or use the
   new knowledge or skill, and informs the leader if learning has

occurred. Learners find out for themselves what they have learned correctly and evaluate their own level of learning achievement. In the managing learning process, the learners assume responsibility for their own learning. The onus is on them—not on the teacher.

6. Share responsibility.

When organizations begin to develop a values-ful culture, employee performance will become a shared responsibility and not simply a matter of individual success or failure. In order to share responsibilities, organizations need to realize the benefit of changing leadership styles. The work force must shift to one that is no longer responsible to top-down directives. Employees now want, if not demand, to participate in decision making in their workplaces. They want to be empowered. They want to take collective responsibility for establishing values and norms, defining their culture, and learning how to be leaders.

7. Use teaming.

There is a strong trend toward teaming in many organizations, especially self-directed teams. These teams or groups can be viewed as one means of addressing the changing work-force dynamics. They can allow for conflict to occur. They can provide opportunities for individuals to practice their leadership skills and behaviors—and do leadership. They can help maintain and build a sense of community or group culture by establishing shared values. We have stressed that employee satisfaction and commitment to the organization depend on whether or not shared values exist within the culture.

8. Communicate two ways.

Two-way communication versus one-way monologues is a key to establishing a values-based culture and implementing cultural change. Employers must communicate to their employees and ask for their input. Together, they must establish a vision and develop values that will facilitate accomplishing that vision. Good communication is essential for this process to occur. This means that constant employee involvement, input, and feedback is paramount.

Most important, leadership and employees need to communicate support for their cultures by sending consistent messages to one another. The individuals that we interviewed stressed this point all too often. Unfortunately, mixed messages or lack of an agreement often circled back and forth. If communication is inconsistent, then norms and values are extremely difficult to establish within the culture of the workplace.

9. Link internal culture with external performance.

Satisfaction with the internal culture affects the external performance of an organization. Often, organizations fail to see this link. If organizations have established and focused on norms and values internally, then their employees will feel greater pride in, and more positive about, their organization. Their individual performance will improve, yielding greater overall organizational performance.

10. Display passion and support diversity.

Values-based leaders are secure within themselves and feel comfortable expressing emotion. This means communicating your true feelings—being open enough with an employee so that positive praise, neutral dialogue, or constructive criticism can be conveyed openly. Expressing emotion is the first ingredient of passion. The second is a clear demonstration of belief in or conviction to something. Leaders who display passion tend to throw off a charisma that excites and motivates others around them.

Passion also includes recognition of individuals—as they are and who they are. A strong belief in diversity and support of pluralism provides a leadership that legitimizes the value and respect for all individuals within the organization.

The Dynamic Process of Group Satisfaction

Leaders must motivate their employees to get involved and stay involved in the group. Let's take a close-up look at this process of involvement. Employees first elect to get involved in their workplace because it proposes to satisfy their individual needs. Specifically, these may range from providing financial or psychic rewards, to learning certain skills, to playing a key role on their project. Second, the workplace satisfies an individual's social need. It offers opportunities for members to participate in a community setting. When the group no longer satisfies these needs—individual and social—the nature of the group must change, or members will leave it.

The Impact of Norms and Values

Having a strong set of norms and values can be beneficial in that it can act to replace bureaucratic rules and regulations in a company. If employees know what the goals and objectives of the organization are and are motivated to work toward those goals, there don't need to be so many rules. Employees will do what they are supposed to do because they want to, not because they are told to.

This can then be a bridge to the leadership styles of participatory management and shared leadership. Since employees are self-motivated to work toward achieving the organization's goals, they can become more valuable as decision-making resources, instead of merely being "mechanical workers."

As soon as workers are "pointed in the right direction" by establishing a clear system of norms and values, and as soon as they are given clearly communicated organization goals and objectives to pursue, they can begin actively working to promote the organization's stated mission and objectives. At this point their values as corporate resource will go through the roof. Values-based leadership recognizes the impact of a strong set of norms and values and guides this process. Values-based leadership knows that group norms and values must be created, identified, and nurtured within the workplace.

How Does Values-Based Leadership Occur?

No one learns how to play the piano just by sitting back and looking at it. Nor does one learn how to play baseball by watching—the skills of catching, batting, and throwing can't be acquired through observation. Rather, the pianist and baseball player have to practice their respective skills over and over again, until playing a song or hitting a ball have been accomplished. There is always room for continued improvement, too. Most skills, regardless of the "sport," are learned by doing. This is true with leadership skills as well.

By *doing* leadership, we mean practicing the ten initiatives discussed in this chapter. Now these aren't your typical set of leadership initiatives. They are different because they reflect back to the importance of the culture in the workplace. These leadership initiatives allow the leader to recognize and address the needs and interests of group members. They allow for group-established values and norms to be pursued and cultivated.

If the stage has been set—shared responsibility, teaming, two-way communication, and so forth—the dynamic nature of group satisfaction can be established. The workplace must value differences. In doing so, the workplace gives employees a reason to believe that their differences *are* valuable. Moreover, leaders in the workplace must design a personalized learning program based on how their employees learn best.

Diversity as a Value

In the past, employees have been expected to fit into the mold. The workplace wanted only certain types, kinds, and colors of employees. It is imperative that the workplace of the future place greater value on diversity. If this is to be accomplished, then leaders must have capacious minds, versatile attitudes, unquestioned integrity, and must be promoters of diversity. If we don't value diversity, then the internal potential of our employees will be lost. And, the external performance of our organizations will be affected. Instead of trying to make individuals conform, leaders need to focus on what each employee can bring to the workplace. Each individual employee has different gifts. Encouraging the expression of a diverse range of gifts is necessary. Leaders can begin by valuing diversity. If diversity is encouraged, then the workplace will grow and flourish.

Leaders must constantly expand their own minds, perspectives, and points of view. It is a prerequisite to establishing diversity. Second, developing versatile attitudes is another critical component of leader-ful minds. Organizations have not nurtured the development of versatile attitudes. Differences in attitude within the group can enrich the workplace. They can give energy to the organization. Third, leaders must adhere to the cultural norms and values of the workplace. This is called having unquestioned integrity. It is critical if a values adoption process and norms action plan are to be established. And, finally, leaders themselves must be overall promoters of diversity. Most leaders promote similarity within their organizations. They look for clones or persons just like them. But when differences are promoted within the group or organization, synergistic energy occurs.

The values-based leader acts like an artist who is completely absorbed in creative activity. Composing, painting, or writing becomes a process of discovery where the artist's music, art work, or book unfolds. Its form is revealed in the process of doing. After dedicated involvement, where the artist gets totally absorbed in the activity itself, the art form is made visible. The pages or canvas unfolds as words and brush strokes come forward. Similarly, the leader helps unfold the creativity of the group by serving as the catalyst for its energy. A values-based leader engages the group in this process of creative discovery.

Chapter 13

Leading
from the Inside Out

Leadership is one of the most sought-after and revered human characteristics. Yet it is a barely understood and rarely practiced phenomenon. Leadership is learned behavior. Employees of all ages and in all types of organizations can learn how to be leaders. Leadership should be viewed as a collection of behaviors and skills that are necessary for a group to survive and reach its goals. Put differently, leadership facilitates the development of a group and the accomplishment of group tasks. Individuals need to acquire leader-ful skills.

Leadership skills can be developed by any group member, regardless of their formal designated position in the group. They can be displayed by one or more members of the same group simultaneously. Leadership is not a mantle that is passed on, nor a baton relayed from one member to another in a sequential fashion. What is important is that leadership cannot be studied in isolation; it involves the interaction between group members. It requires an involvement with a group whose ongoing activities, informal and formal, give group members opportunities to practice their leadership skills.

Taking Time to Learn

Leaders who lead from the inside out encourage employees to develop and maximize their own inner potential. Employees also need to learn leadership skills and be able to practice them. We'll propose later in this chapter seven leadership "tools" that can be used to foster learning innovatively. Rather than the old, learning by imitating, employees can participate in learning by doing.

Most organizations do not make time for leadership building activities, especially during the work day, when profits "should be" generated. This is unfortunate. We believe that in the long run, greater profits will be made, organizational goals achieved, and personal objectives reached if equal attention is paid to the personalized learning of employees and the development of their groups. At all times, learning should be the goal of work organizations. We call this participative learning. It is far more effective than passive learning. We are all natural learners. We learn by listening and watching. We need to see things done well. We can teach ourselves. Our accomplishments need to be recognized. We deserve courtesy. We can be extremely good at learning, but the workplace must give us time to learn. Effective leaders acknowledge this and focus on nurturing employees' "insides." Leading from the inside out means:

- Tapping into individual and group feelings.
- Helping employees experience and achieve personal success.
- Using descriptive praise to motivate and facilitate personal growth.
- Facilitating learning, open communication, and self-awareness.

Tapping into Individual and Group Feelings

What do you really believe in? What is important to you? What are your inner needs, drives, and passions? These can be translated into a personal values statement. It addresses personal questions, emphatically important ones. Your norms and values shape and influence your inside feelings.

Each person carries these "insides" into the workplace. This should be no surprise. The differences between past work settings and current ones are major. In the past, the "insides" were not viewed as important. An employee was expected to become a "corporate soldier." We are declaring that now the "insides" help to define individuals and their entire work group—its needs, values, norms, and attitudes. This personal information facilitates leading from the inside out. The need for employees to express emotions and feelings requires a new kind of leadership. It is the leader's role to help employees look inward at themselves.

Groups can have an intrinsic developmental and nurturing component to them. The key to values-based leadership effectiveness is intuitively tapping into the feelings of group members in order to gain insight and perspective. Members must demonstrate trust in one another. They must maintain and build the group by creating a caring community. They must become more keenly aware of the role norms and values play within the workplace. It is the leader's role to help each individual and the group become more aware of its insides.

Every person must know, at the deepest personal level, what is important in his or her life. Carl Rogers, a noted educational psychologist, writes "unless one has true convictions as to how his values are arrived at, what sort of an individual he hopes will emerge, and what kind of relationship he is striving to build with others, he will have failed not only his profession, but his culture."

As a contributing employee within your workplace, you must determine where your values lie. First, you will find it necessary to identify the primary elements within your personal value system. Then, highlight from this value-set those values you would most want to pass on to the employees with whom you work. For example, perhaps you value knowledge of subject matter, affective expression or communication of feelings, open thinking, creative problem solving, or exploratory discussions. Write these values down and attempt to identify how you acquired them. Also, try to examine how your primary values have changed over time and why. This becomes your personal values statement. Communicate this with yourself. Don't write it for your boss, your colleagues, or for someone else. Try to understand yourself. Give yourself the freedom to do so.

As leader, or as someone performing a leadership role in the workplace, it is critical that you also identify these inside values, examine their sources, and encourage such "work" by other employees. As leader, you are not evaluating them. Rather, you are encouraging the evaluation to take place internally by each individual.

Values-based leadership requires group members to look inside and develop norms and values to guide individual and group behavior. Members provide norms or shared expectations for the group and establish a set of agreed-upon behaviors for individuals to follow. In effect, each individual within the group takes on a leadership role in some dimension.

Helping Employees Experience and Achieve Personal Success

When people feel good about themselves because of experiencing a success within their workplace, this positive feeling will spill over into other areas. These individuals will start to perform better and seek out *more* responsibility and accomplish more in their workplace. Because of continued successes, they are more apt to take a risk. That is, they will try to do things that are more difficult for them because they have experienced earlier success. Risk taking causes learning to occur. If adults would take more risks, there would be greater learning in their lives.

By identifying employees' greatest strengths and matching those with responsibilities and tasks that draw upon their strengths, leaders will increase the chances of employee success. It's important to "rig" small successes to some extent. It does no good to put employees into situations, roles, groups, or task activities where there is a good chance of failure. Continuous failure breeds only one thing—more failures. It becomes a self-fulfilling prophecy. Self-confidence is weakened, and it is more and more difficult for the individual to achieve success.

Managing and "staging" a few small wins for employees increases their "inside" value and self-worth. This, in turn, improves their self-esteem and fortifies their own skill base. This begins to feed positively on itself and brings more successes to individuals.

Leaders who lead from the inside out make sure that successes *do* happen. They help employees experience success and they recognize them when employees achieve it. Over time, employees inculcate this successfulness into their ongoing behavior. Success becomes expected by the individuals themselves and tends to be self-perpetuated.

Using Descriptive Praise to Motivate and Facilitate Personal Growth

The leader can facilitate the development of his or her employees —thus causing success "spillover" to occur—by using descriptive praise. This is a technique that is very useful with children! Authors Adele Faber and Elaine Mazlish, in their book *Liberated Parents Liberated Children* find that words that evaluate tend to hinder a child; words that describe set the child free. If a child has done something well, rather than saying, "you did a great job," it is much better to describe what you saw and felt when the child did it. Describing the child's work in detail adds a whole new dimension to the child's view of himself or herself. It creates a motivated learner.

For example, if a child built a bird house and showed it to her teacher or parent, one response might be "Good work!" But this is merely global praise. It is not a bad response. But specific, descriptive praise would be much better because the child would learn more about herself. Accordingly, the parent could respond by saying something like: "How warm the birds will be when they live in it . . . the color you painted it will help to camouflage the birds . . . it reminds me of one I saw in the pet store recently that housed bluebirds." The child's view of herself has added a new dimension. The child has built a place to house birds from the elements and intruders, and since bluebirds live in similarly built structures, they could possibly inhabit this birdhouse. Isn't this child more motivated to learn than the one who was told "Good work?" Descriptive praise is more motivating than global praise.

Similarly, descriptive comments can be used, instead of damaging insults. Words should be used to describe what has occurred or how the parent feels about the situation. For example, if a child has left a big mess, rather than say "You're messy!" the parent could describe what the sight of it does to her, or describe how it makes her feel. "It makes me want to throw out everything because I have to spend so much of my time stepping over it and picking it up." In this case, the parent is providing descriptive information to the child that helps him begin to learn why it is so frustrating to encounter such messes.

Name calling does nothing to improve a bad situation. Identifying something that was left unorganized within the messy room and emphasizing or building from that is always a better choice of direction. Similarly, picking out something that an employee has done particularly well and building from that is also a much better course of action than saying the employee's work was bad.

Telling an employee that she has done a "good job" is not good enough. This response *limits* learning and growth from the inside. It would be better to point out a number of things that never would have occurred to the employee on her own. For example, if she gave a presentation, she could be told that it helped teach some especially important information using a very effective style of presenting material; or that it was done in such a way as to make the audience enjoy themselves; or that her style left everyone feeling very unified and hopeful that change would occur. This descriptive praise adds a whole new dimension to the employee's view of herself. Now the workplace has a motivated employee.

Leaders also need to be able to provide employees who warrant constructive criticism with proactive advice on how to improve. This advice should be descriptive too. It must specifically describe what an employee can do to shore up a development need. Leaders must identify what should be done to correct a weakness area. They can translate constructive feedback into an action plan for the employee. For example, if an employee has been told he is not a good writer or presenter, then the leader may recommend a specific public speaking class for him to take. If an employee's marketing plans are not creative, then the leader can suggest ways to weave more innovative thinking into her future planning activities. If an accountant is told that her projections don't include the needs of the new product department, then the leader can suggest ways to work with this group to build their needs and estimates into the overall budget picture. The leader learns that when there is a problem, rather than saying, "This person has a problem," it is better to say, "This person requires a different response." The leader focuses *not* on the faults of employees, but on what needs to be done to improve their performance.

At the same time, leaders, just like parents, can help build and strengthen a self-image, using present and past behavior and experiences. The parent knows the child's past achievements and can share this information to provide encouragement and comfort. Similarly, the leader of the workplace should also have a well-stocked warehouse of information—past achievements where the employee has done something particularly well. These might include knowledge of how he managed to share information with the client just at the right time or recall critical findings during the presentation or sell a follow-up job to help implement the findings. Drawing on past information to fortify the employee's self-esteem is an important role of the leader. It is called leading from the inside out.

Ultimately, if employees have heard over and over again that they have special abilities and positive qualities and that these are recognized, then the leader is helping them to believe in their own strengths and better understand who they are. The effective leader should be actively involved in this positive reinforcement endeavor with all employees. This provides employees with self-knowledge and reinforcement recognition by telling them again and again what their special qualities are, using illustrative words and descriptive-action steps.

Values-ful people carry this self-knowledge within themselves. Self-evaluation can be achieved because of the information they have about themselves. In contrast, people who have been confronted with constant negative feedback will be unlikely to acquire this inner self-knowledge. These people are *dependent* on others to tell them how well they are doing, who they are, and what they can do well and not do well. When people truly understand their unique qualities and know themselves, this provides a source of strength. It is a leader's role to help them look in, using descriptive praise as well as descriptive advice. When the leader accomplishes this process, there is leading from the inside out.

Facilitating Learning, Open Communication, and Self-Awareness

The leader also needs to:

1. *Help persons learn,* and guide them toward maximum self-realization. The leader must have insights into how each individual can best learn. Everyone has different hot and cold buttons. Consequently, learning needs to be tailored and customized differently for each employee. The leader must promote greater understanding of the learner, the learning process, and the learning situations present in the workplace, as they come together in dynamic interaction within the setting of work. Work must be viewed as an educational setting—the leader as teacher or facilitator of learning.

2. *Develop each employee's communication skills and allow for and support open dialogue.* Employees usually have acquired the ability to absorb knowledge and play it back, but are inept at listening, integrating new information, and making themselves clear. A lack of clarity in communication not only interferes with goals but also affects their relationships with other employees. The leader must focus on designing ways to help each employee become a more effective communicator, verbally and nonverbally, and a more active listener.

3. *Make individual employees more aware of themselves:* their values, needs, goals, and potential, their need to take responsibility for their own learning, and their need to develop enriching relationships with other employees to better relate to them as persons.

To do this, the effective leader has to make learning fun and interesting. This is not easy to accomplish. There should be numerous opportunities provided in the workplace where learning can take place. The trick is providing a stimulating and innovative learning environment both in content and learning style. The learning tools next described do just that. These learning methods will make individuals more aware of their values and potential—

their "insides." Moreover, it will facilitate employees taking responsibility for their learning through self-discovery.

Employee as Immersed Learner

It is assumed that as a person you do have an interest in learning. If you did not, you would never grow or advance. In the past, the workplace was designed in such a way as to replicate the traditional classroom: a lecture-examination format. You had a boss who supplied you with information and supervised your work— just as old-fashioned classrooms had strict teachers who imparted their knowledge, expecting students to learn best just by imitating. Well, this isn't how a person learns. It might be a surprise to some of you because so many people carry around this false notion of how we learn.

Work settings have tended to use only one of the ways in which people learn—absorbing information, recalling it, and reciting it. Now, organizations must offer all employees an experience that maximizes their personal learning. Tools that can help to facilitate learning include interactive discussion groups, debates, briefs or white papers, simulation games, experiential groups, and self-evaluation. These tools provide ample opportunity for personal exchange and active involvement in the learning-ful organization.

Learning and Applying Leadership Tools

The tools next discussed provide a multitude of learning options. Taken together, they offer the employee—the learner—a variety of ways to learn. They are based on the notion from Carl Rogers that the "most significant learning is acquired through doing." The leader can set up these seven learning tools and make them available to employees.

1. Team discussions on readings

One way to learn is to focus a team or group discussion on a specific topic area. By providing the team with reading materials a couple of weeks prior to the discussion, all the participants could prepare general real-world applications of the topic area in their own job. At our own consulting firm, we readily order copies of books and hand them out to employees when we feel the content would provide helpful information and individual learning. For example, we bought copies of *Yes or No?* when we felt our decision making needed improvement. We handed out copies of *Maximum Achievement* to all employees when we felt it offered ways to enhance team building in the workplace as well as personal learning. The key, though, is having employees discuss the readings in the ways they are relevant to their own job and the organization. Without this key step, learning will not take place because reading materials will just remain on shelves or be tucked away in file folders. When leadership takes the responsibility for learning, then employees will do so too as they come across something that is helpful or appropriate. This passing around of books and articles by everyone in the workplace suggests interest and enthusiasm for growth and learning. There is a sharing of responsibility for personal and professional development. Sharing knowledge also facilitates communication, increases personal learning, and helps provide employees with a competitive edge.

2. Small-group discussions

When ideas, issues, or problems surface, it may be beneficial to meet in a small group to discuss them informally. We like to select an employee as group moderator and another employee as the recorder. Everyone over a period of time should have the opportunity to play these roles. All other group members are participants. However, participants don't sit back and remain passive. Instead, their role is to thoroughly understand the topic; that is, they should be able to describe the issue and take a particular point of view of it and apply it to a specific situation.

The moderator is responsible for directing the discussion on the proposed topic. The moderator should encourage the group to follow techniques that create a positive discussion climate: Listen carefully to what each person says, acknowledge one another's ideas, and avoid individual monopolization of the discussion. The moderator should encourage participants to respond to one another's ideas by agreeing or disagreeing with them, by asking one another to clarify their ideas, and by asking for supportive information (from readings, research, personal experience, etc.). In addition, other useful participative techniques for the moderator include:

1. Use supportive silence—it will facilitate more interaction.
2. Set forth the right of each person to express his or her own opinions without fear of criticism.
3. State the issue at the beginning, and restate it, when necessary, to keep the discussion focused.
4. Paraphrase and summarize occasionally each participant's ideas and opinions.
5. Summarize key areas of agreement and disagreement.
6. Urge participants to clarify and give more information.
7. Call on silent participants.
8. Try to increase the range of thoughts or opinions on an issue.
9. Provide a comfortable, informal setting.
10. Nurture a friendly, fun atmosphere, *always* knowing and using the names of participants.

Moderators should have fun with this discussion group. Remember, participative learning is far more effective than is passive learning. A moderator self-evaluation form (see Exhibit 13–1) can be used to self-discover learning areas for the moderator.

3. Debates

Whenever an organization is thinking about entertaining a new idea, making a change, adding a new service or product, it is useful to first explore the option internally. One fun way to do this, which also serves as a good learning tool, is through debates. A selected employee or team of employees can formally present material to the larger group, with several scenarios or possibilities mapped out by opposing individuals or teams. Debates can be an enjoyable, lively way to accomplish and practice these skills internally within the group. At the same time, they can generate alter-

EXHIBIT 13-1

Moderator Self-Evaluation Form

Check those areas below that you observed while acting as the group moderator. Leave blank those that were not accomplished.

____ Group members address me as informally as they do others.

____ Members frequently show real feelings.

____ Members usually address remarks to one another instead of me as leader.

____ At times, members have openly disagreed with me.

____ The group is reluctant to quit discussing the subject when time is up.

____ Members speak up without asking my permission.

____ Bright ideas seem to come from almost all members of group.

____ Members don't wait for me to deal with "problem" members.

____ Different members seem to lead the group's thinking.

____ Members seem to be listening to one another without interrupting.

____ Disagreements arise, but members try to deal with them objectively.

____ Members seem to be making use of one another's insight and information.

____ Members try to draw reluctant or shy members into participation.

As group moderator, how well did you do? How do you think you could improve? In what way is this skill important for you in the future? How are your communication skills improving?

native ideas and scenarios and be used to facilitate decision making or to reshape future directional changes.

Employees have not learned how to communicate well just because they dress the part. Work organizations are excellent settings to practice and improve upon members' formal communication skills. How to present material is taught by numerous communication seminars on the outside, or techniques can be taught internally by those colleagues who are good at presenting material. Peer teaching can be very effective. That is, colleagues who have mastered the art and skills of formally presenting material can also be available for teaching and follow-up tutoring and questions. The key is to have debates be viewed as a learning experience—there should be no perceived winners or losers—only active participants.

4. Briefs or white papers

If an employee has an idea that she would like to further develop, it can be written up in a brief statement called a white paper. It requires the employee to familiarize themselves with the idea, describe the relevant issues, and take a particular side on it. After the employee has taken a position on the idea or issue through this written document, he or she can share it, initiating the idea-exchange process. Both verbal and written reaction can occur. Most important, this involvement and exchange of ideas can accelerate learning by the group, its individuals, and the entire organization. Knowledge is acquired, personal learning is facilitated, and participants have a greater sense of value in themselves.

A member of a consulting firm developed the following "white paper" on his professional principles, which was shared with his leadership group. It is an excellent example of leading from the inside out, since it communicates deep-down personal learning.

Example of a "White Paper"

The purpose of this "white paper" is to clarify several key principles of mine and how I apply them in everyday life. Three of the many core principles I try to live my life by are:

(1) Confidentiality of information someone shares with me;

(2) The keeping of promises I make to another person;

(3) Not talking disparagingly about another person when they are not present.

These principles run deep into my soul. While I'm human and will sometimes fall short, I always feel terrible when I realize that I have violated these principles—so I do not intentionally or willfully go counter to them.

I also recognize and honor my responsibilities as a member of the leadership group. Depending on the norms and values we choose to follow as a management team and firm, there may be times when these personal principles conflict with the group's. In the more obvious extreme situations of either a personal issue or a potentially detrimental issue to our firm, I would take appropriate action. If, however, I feel someone has put me in a compromising position between my responsibilities as a leader of the firm and my principles, I will attempt to convince the individual to agree to let me discuss the situation with other appropriate "advisors."

In the end, we cannot control all possible people situations and reactions. I hope that this helps to better clarify who I am. I also hope that, in time, you will be able to trust me, the *person*, and me, the responsible *leadership group member*, to understand the individual needs of the firm's members and react accordingly for the good of the firm.

This "white paper" led others in the firm's leadership group to react and to reply back, also in the form of "white papers." Personal growth, learning, communication, and self-awareness had been facilitated. Leading from the inside out had occurred.

5. Simulations versus the "real thing"

At our children's school, every year a student gets to be the principal for a day. You can bet that this individual learns a great deal about the personal decision making and demands of this role. Simulations ask the learner to look within, use his or her existing resources, and to experience a role or job firsthand. Learning occurs very quickly. In effect, "what-if" scenarios are generated for specific problems, strategies, or issues.

This method of teaching is not used enough in corporations or other organizations. In fact, it is rarely used in most work settings. This is because it requires the leader to take a certain degree of risk. Simulations give the group freedom by presenting them with the opportunity and task of addressing their own needs and solving their own problems. Participants have to take action. They also learn critical thinking and decision making. They require knowledge of the organization. Participants must face the consequences of their actions.

Simulations can be a good way to let employees see the reasoning behind a change in strategic direction, according to Roger Martin in "Changing the Mind of the Corporation" (*HBR* Nov.-Dec. l993). He notes that the most exciting way to generate and develop strategic dialogue "is computer-generated, competitive simulations—war games, as it were—in which managers model the competitive battle field and practice a kind of company doctrine with one another."

Employees can engage in an open dialogue on the future of their company or organization. Futuristic simulations ask employees to figure out which direction their organizations should take, define key questions, collect information, investigate alternatives, question findings, and evaluate the learning process. Simulations facilitate important futuristic thinking and learning. They can also anticipate future moves by competitors. Most important, they encourage strategic dialogue. It is Martin's view that this "strategic dialogue" should be an ongoing and permanent part of the organization—in fact, it should be a routine part of every organization.

In our own firm, we are looking at expanding into new practice areas and adding a new strategic area. How would we look five years from now, ten years from now, if we added these areas to our business? And, important, how will these strategic changes, if initiated, influence the culture of the organization? These questions—this simulation experience—must be examined by the employees through ongoing strategic dialogue. If the employees are involved in this dialogue, then any changes will better address future organizational needs and resources.

6. Experiential groups

Experiential groups offer opportunities for individuals to spend blocks of time with others and go through an intensive personalized learning experience together. These groups usually exist for an extended period of time (i.e., several days or more). Two examples are next discussed, including a leadership training course and an Outward Bound program.

The experiential group surfaces and discusses issues of trust, participation, risk-taking, affective expression of feelings, sensitivity, and individual strengths and weaknesses. Experiential groups greatly facilitate interpersonal knowledge and involvement. When developing leaders from the inside out, these are critical ingredients and key developmental areas indeed.

When a group of individuals gets together and they drop their own defenses, at least temporarily, intensive personal learning can occur. The participating individuals try to understand how an experience seems and feels to the other person. They state their own uncertainties and get closer to the meaning that the experience had for them and the others in the group.

The primary purpose of these experiential groups is to improve interpersonal communication and to grow and develop as persons, as leaders. By exploring the feelings and attitudes that exist among individuals, members of the group become more aware of themselves and the impact they have on others. Everyone has greater awareness of his or her strengths and weaknesses.

Carl Rogers said that "self-initiated learning which involves the whole person or learner—feelings as well as intellect—is the most lasting and pervasive." Week-long leadership training courses can offer this type of impact through their experiential group. An *Industry Week* magazine editor recorded her personal impressions of a leadership course taken at Utah's Covey Leadership Center in her daily journal. (*Industry Week,* June 1, 1992):

> I never got so close to people I didn't know as I did with my nine teammates. When we made it across after several tries, the achievement, appreciation, and fraternity was overwhelming.

I was astonished, inspired, and moved by the deep level of listening—empathetic and analytical. Questions were so pointed and on-target that they caused, at times, real discomfort. The keys in this process were: trust, rapport, synergy, openness, support, and a genuine interest in learning. Diversity became the foundation for mutual respect, inquiry, and learning.

Susan Kuczmarski went through a personal experiential group in a nineteen-day Outward Bound program close to twenty-five years ago. She writes in her own diary:

. . . Larry is unequivocally slow, three-quarters of a mile behind the others. How does the group motivate him to speed up? The expedition of ten has two days to reach the Santa Bell pass. Brian didn't skirt the issue; he dealt with this conflict situation directly. Some members felt Brian was too abrupt, was too honest! Others would have been more polite or nice—after all, Larry was learning, hopefully expanding, his limits, both physical and mental.

Yet, it was a shared experience. The other team members were frustrated; his pace was jeopardizing their goal: to join the larger group at an agreed-upon campsite that night. The instructor would not give the answers; he kept pushing "be honest" in a very confident tone. But, this "directive" increased the conflict among the ten. Coming from multiple temperaments, communication styles, and ages, each had different ideas as to what degree of honesty should be exercised.

Both examples reveal individual observations, interpersonal learning, possible solutions, uncertainties, discomforts, yet continual attempts to synthesize discoveries about themselves, the other group members, and their environment. Experiential groups personalize learning, opening the door to leading from the inside out.

7. Self-evaluation—the learning contract

What does evaluation mean? As leaders, you will evaluate your employees by their ability to perform their job and interact within their work groups. Why not involve your employees in this process? Have them evaluate their *own* performance and how well they work with others in the group. Two steps should be followed in the process of learning through self-evaluation:

- Employees should draw up their own *learning contract* by:
  - establishing their *criteria* of evaluation and
  - deciding which *goals* they want to achieve.
- Employees need to develop a written evaluation on how well they achieved each of these goals and met the criteria.

In so doing, the employees have chosen to take responsibility for their own learning, first defining what they want to learn and then evaluating the achievement of these goals.

Fifteen Leadership Learning Tips

The concept of leading from the inside out is a powerful one. Leaders need to know what they can do to help employees look inside and personalize their learning within the workplace. The following fifteen learning tips are by no means exhaustive, but are intended to help guide the values-ful leader of the future (see Exhibit 13–2).

To lead from the inside out, leaders can tap into individual and group feelings, help employees experience success, motivate growth through descriptive praise, and advise and facilitate communication and self-awareness. They must engage in a fostering, nurturing, and cultivating process. They must *personalize learning*. They must facilitate attitudes that encourage a quest for more learning. In fact, they must encourage learning all the time. They must actively seek creative answers to problems. They must create multiple learning settings—formal and informal—to help group members learn. When group members have engaged in this learning process, they, too, can lead from the inside out. And when they lead from their insides, employees will gain job satisfaction and personal meaning in the workplace.

EXHIBIT 13-2

Leader's Learning Tips

1. Do I trust and respect the group's capacity to develop the potential that exists in the group?
2. Am I sensitive and empathetic to individual needs?
3. Do I communicate openly by expressing my own feelings and emotions?
4. Do I take risks, if it facilitates more personal learning?
5. Do I suggest to the group ideas that I believe might promote the achievement of the group's goals?
6. Do I actively listen?
7. Do I help employees experience success?
8. Do I frequently use descriptive praise and descriptive advice?
9. Do I show my more human side through greater interpersonal involvement, sharing my weaknesses as well as my strengths?
10. Do I ask for feedback on how well I am communicating and interacting with each group member?
11. Do I stimulate self-initiated growth and personalized learning?
12. Do I give sufficient freedom to learn?
13. Do I frequently use humor?
14. Do I ask group members how I could improve?
15. Do I stimulate creative and intuitive thinking?

Chapter 14

Igniting New
Leadership Skills

The Power of Learning Leadership

The concept of learning leadership is one that perfectly captures the mood in our organizations and corporations, and it's one that will capture the interest of employees. It capitalizes on the growing dissatisfaction with work environments that have failed to develop and educate their workers. It suggests opportunities for liaisons with more traditional learning organizations (e.g., training seminars or schools). It provides workers with an alternative to boring and meaningless work settings that can be both fun and learning-ful.

The workplace has the power to teach one of the most important concepts for the twenty-first century. As we get closer to this juncture—only five years away—we must think through these timely ideas. The workplace is the key *educator* for teaching leadership in the coming age. Leaders need to adopt norms that foster values-based leadership throughout organizations.

We have generated four new leadership norms that we feel are important for creating a values-ful workplace. There is a critical need for leaders who can: (1) make quicker, more heartfelt decisions, (2) actively listen, (3) use the collective knowledge of the group, and (4) engage the group in consensus building and ownership taking.

1. Make quicker, more heartfelt decisions.

Speed is critical in business today. All types of organizations—from schools to law firms—need their employees, from leader to group member, to act more quickly than in the past. Decision making, especially difficult decisions, must be executed with greater speed. Fortunately, decision making is a skill that can be learned and greatly improved upon.

Given the numerous decisions that one has to make every day in the workplace, we all need to improve our decision-making ability. In the past, we have developed a habit of using just our heads to make our decisions, especially at work. Thinking and identifying options—employing our heads—are indeed an important part of making a decision. And these, of course, cannot be overlooked. We are stressing the importance of also employing our hearts! The "business" of adopting values and defining norms will require our hearts to be involved in the process of making decisions. We will have to ask ourselves personal questions, use our intuition, and trust our hearts.

The key point we want to make is that the skill of decision making requires that we practice it. We must practice using both our heads and our hearts. Making more heartfelt decisions requires listening to ourselves and others. Active heartfelt listening is a prerequisite for sharing norms and values and establishing a values-ful, caring culture. If the work group is to activate a values-adoption process and a norms-action plan, then the members of that group have to practice a new type of heartfelt decision making. What is important is that there is less risk of pain if the decision turns out badly. Acting with the heart gives us a fundamental permission to accept potential failure. "Head" decisions, on the other hand, offer no such "mercy" if we choose the wrong direction, person, or action step.

2. Actively listen.

Active listening can also be practiced inside our work groups. The bottom line is we must listen to one another better. Active listening is a prerequisite for sharing norms and values and for establishing a values-ful, caring culture. All members of every group have to practice active listening. It is a skill. It is a prerequisite for making better, quicker, and more heartfelt decisions. We can all improve our listening skills. There are continuous opportunities to practice them in work settings. Stephen Bloom's courses in communication have greatly influenced us. This discussion of "roles of speaker and listener" are adapted from his excellent course. We use it in our own classrooms and work groups.

In teaching active listening skills to groups, we first emphasize the roles of both the speaker and the listener. They both must be there, alive, awake, and on time. They both must be aware that the other is there. The speaker must observe the listener attentively, looking for indicators as to whether she is listening. The listener must observe the speaker attentively, expressing intention. Intention is expressing feeling: warmth, physical contact, smiling—and enthusiasm. While it is the role of the speaker to communicate, it is the role of the listener to listen to the meaning of words. The speaker has a specific message, which he or she has prepared. The listener's role is to learn, understand, and retain that message and acknowledge that this has been accomplished through the use of the indicators in Exhibit 14–1.

If there are no indicators, then the speaker should make an adjustment. The speaker must observe for indicators all the time. This is not easy to do. If there are no questions and eye contact is poor (looking out the window is common), then these are clear indicators to the speaker that two-way communication has not been accomplished. Poor indicators include asking questions just for the sake of it—patronizing the speaker—and looking at the speaker, but not listening.

It is important to remember that, as a listener, your main task is to understand what your speaker is trying to say and to let him or her know that you understand. Your attitude is more important than what you say. Nonverbal responses are sometimes more meaningful than words. As a listener, you must ask yourself if you: (1) actively listened, (2) accepted the speaker and the situation, (3) clarified and understood, (4) saw your views change, (5) encouraged, and (6) let your listening guide you.

EXHIBIT 14-1

Active Listening Indicators

1. Whether listener is looking at you or not
2. Nod of head (non-verbal)
3. Smile or facial expressions
4. Note taking
5. Questions—conversations
6. Acknowledgment verbally
7. Attentive posture
8. Adds information
9. Leans in—closer distance between you
10. Stays there listening!
11. Eliminates outside disturbances (e.g., shuts door, closes window)
12. Asks others to join into group
13. Listener—moves from general to specific, i.e., wants to apply the information heard
14. Listener is on time and prepared—communicates degree of desire
15. Warmth—part of communicating intent
16. Eyes clear and alert

— Stephen Bloom, Communication Seminars

Active listening is indeed a key skill to have in the workplace. We actively listened when we were children. This is how we learned as infants, then as toddlers and young children. Unfortunately, when we became adults, most of us lost this essential skill. We focused in on talking about ourselves or our ideas instead—neither listening nor asking questions. Courses in communication and active listening skills such as Stephen Bloom's serve to jump start us into recovering these lost skills. There are an infinite number of communication courses offered to employees, usually outside the work organization. Take one! Begin to reacquire this skill.

3. Use the collective knowledge of the group.

Leaders must use the collective knowledge of the group. They must involve the entire group in problem solving and idea generation. This "group-think" process is a prerequisite for sharing norms and values and guiding the values-driven change process.

The group has an incredible knowledge base. Most leaders do not take advantage of this power source. Have you ever thrown out a difficult question that has been troubling you, seeking the input of other individuals within the workplace? What comes back can be phenomenal! This group-think process surfaces ideas of all types. Brainstorming together is a powerful tool. When a group of caring individuals get involved, the idea of one member generates an idea from another. Wow! The group continues discussing the question or problem and something occurs. A super-consciousness state is reached. Ideas are generated that no individual would have thought of alone. When members share their thoughts and ideas with one another, they build together, creating a masterpiece.

Using the collective knowledge of the group is a skill. Most leaders never engage in group-think. Instead, they hide out in their office. They are afraid to admit that they don't know the answer to a question. Wouldn't this make them appear weak and unknowledgeable to their employees? These leaders don't want to say, "I don't know the answer!" Aren't leaders supposed to have all the solutions? To the contrary, we contend that the collective knowledge of the group is a super-power source. If leaders will open their doors, express their vulnerabilities, and say to their group, "Let's solve this difficult problem together!" then they will receive greater respect and warmth from their employees.

Group members will, then, feel part of the problem and the solution. They will feel better about themselves, because they have been told their ideas and input are important and valuable. When a group's members are happier and more participative, they will be more confident. They know their ideas are key to the group's success.

4. Engage the group in consensus building and ownership taking.

Consensus building and ownership taking can be encouraged by leaders within the workplace. If group members are encouraged to participate, if the collective knowledge of its members has been sought, then the leader must focus on building consensus and ownership. The workplace must become *their* workplace, *their* problems, and *their* solutions. How does a leader build consensus and encourage ownership?

Consensus building must be the ultimate goal of the group when it engages in problem solving. But the group or team wants to do more than investigate solutions. The group is seeking action. It wants to implement the ideas that are generated. The very act of engaging in the process of seeking a group solution produces a type of consensus. Unfortunately, most workplaces do not ask for group members to get involved in the process. With the emphasis now on "teaming" in the workplace, fortunately, this is becoming more prevalent. When the leader says "we want your ideas—let's find a solution," then the door is left open for consensus building per se to occur. We are not simply suggesting that the invitation itself produces consensus, but it certainly makes it a possibility.

For consensus to be assured, the leader must communicate the value of their inputs and ideas back to the employees. Positive feedback is critical. So is a type of "consensus-building talk." Leaders need to become extremely skilled at this type of "talk." It takes the following form:

> I like that thought—it helps me understand one piece of the puzzle. Does anyone else have a related thought? What other ideas do you have that can help us understand this problem from a different dimension? What is your reaction to that idea? Do you think it sheds some light on this aspect of the solution? Should we try to define an action plan, putting some of your ideas and suggested solutions into effect? What should be our next steps? Does everyone in the group agree? If not, should we incorporate other ideas into our solution?

If leaders engage in this consensus-building talk, then employees will take ownership. Of course, this talk must be backed by supportive action. If the mindset encourages consensus in its talk, but doesn't back it up with the opportunity to carry out the group-derived action plan, then the leader has failed. Leaders must seek out the ideas—build consensus—and then act to execute the ideas and plan arrived at by the group. This is "carrying out the talk." Ownership would not be possible if a leader did not "activate the talk."

Just as a young person practices the bow and arrow until the arrow hits the center of the target, a leader must acquire dexterity or artistry with leadership. The young learner of the bow and arrow must develop the ability to pull the string back, hold the bow in place, and let the arrow loose just at the right time and angle. The leader must also mix the right amounts of our four norms or guidelines for interaction just at the right times. Decision making must be heartfelt, intuitive, and timely. Active listening must permeate the entire culture. The collective knowledge of the group must be tapped—it is powerful. Building consensus and taking ownership are keys to hitting the target and, ultimately, getting a bull's-eye.

Learning Leadership Skills

If one observes how a child learns to master isolated skills—sitting up, crawling, or coming down the stairs—it is quickly evident that this learning process involves practicing the behavioral approximations associated with each skill, until sitting or crawling per se is finally achieved. Similarly, it is helpful to think of learning leadership skills in terms of practicing behaviors. The extent of practice time required to acquire each skill, as in the time and effort mandated by a child, cannot be understated. Most groups are short-lived, not offering settings where continued practice over time is acceptable. Work settings are ideally suited to this task. Participation in a workplace provides a wealth of learning opportunities over an extended period of time.

Besides learning how to become a member of a culture or group, employees can practice the behaviors associated with the role of leader. The process of practicing these roles, of learning the behavior of leaders, is called learning leadership. If learning how to be a leader involves practicing the behaviors associated with that role, then work organizations should give numerous and frequent opportunities to employees to play the role of simulated leader.

What skills constitute leadership? Or, what skills best allow the leader to recognize and address the needs and interests of group members? Since group members must also become leaders, what behaviors must they learn within the group to best address their immediate and future needs? Six key skill areas include:

I. A leader must communicate, both emotionally and professionally, with group members.

The art of communicating involves displaying and expressing emotions, or showing an involvement with the feelings or emotions of others in the group. When a leader communicates excitement, recognition, integrity, and compassion, the followers perceive trust, fair play, and genuine interest in them. Communicating also requires, when the situation mandates it, displaying professional expertise—knowledge, competencies, discipline, and organization; followers then perceive an understanding of business-related events and relationships and the ability to handle or manage them.

2. A leader must take responsibility for selected tasks.

Each activity in a group requires individual members to take responsibility for assigned tasks. One member may be in charge of contacting group members, another with providing information, and still another with finding and organizing the materials to be used in the planning activity.

The leader is specifically responsible for delegating these tasks, foreseeing problems and needs with respect to the overall activity situation, and breaking the "logjams" that may occur. Activities such as these, both spontaneous and planned, pervade the work setting and provide frequent opportunities for members to practice responsibility-taking behaviors.

3. A leader knows how to nurture and to accept criticism.

Successful informal communication within the group requires learning how to attract, get along with, and receive support and respect from group members. A successful leader allows the conflict to be processed by the members themselves. At the same time, a leader must have adequate confidence in his or her own leadership style and communication skills to be able to accept criticism and not be threatened by it. Leaders with personal security and self-acceptance tend to trust others, let them make decisions, and take responsibility for their own activities.

4. A leader knows how to teach others.

Group members engage in both informal and formal teaching. Informally, members may tell others how to handle certain parts of a job, or offer instruction on how to solve a problem. Within the context of a discussion group, informal teaching frequently occurs when one member makes a point or shares his or her personal thinking on an issue. Our observational data in a variety of group settings across all types of organizations revealed a high frequency of these teaching activities or experiences, which go largely unnoticed by others. Of course, formal teaching opportunities also exist in groups. These occur when group members with specific expertise and competencies are given opportunities to share their abilities and knowledge with others. Presentations, internal training sessions, and demonstrations on selected topics are examples of more formal teaching. It's important that a leader knows how to seek out these teaching opportunities and to arrange and present material so learning takes place.

5. A leader knows how to share leadership.

The behavior of collaborating on joint enterprises or taking collective responsibility—sharing leadership—requires working together toward a common goal and demands the cooperation of each member, whether follower or leader.

A sense of collective responsibility is crucial to the group; if members do not contribute, the group will not succeed. As a result, members exhibit a strong group-maintenance feeling. As expressed by one group member: "If members do not participate, then the group will lose; it's our responsibility." Involvement in committee work, for example, directly contributes to the group maintenance task. Participation through committee activity channels allows managers to organize and plan, thereby sharing the leadership for events.

6. A leader knows and uses the resources of the group.

Because leaders often emerge from a group through the leadership process, they are cognizant of group member's skills and needs. Leadership effectiveness requires not only knowing the specific skills and resources of each group member, but calling upon members and their skills in appropriate situations or activities.

Furthermore, the leader should have a feel for the developmental needs of each group member. Information in these areas is not easily obtained. Yet, the leader must be able to answer the question, "What are your needs?" with the same familiarity that the individual group member would. If the leader's answer matches that of the individual's, then the group will most likely satisfy the individual. Learning about each group member and his or her needs offers personal growth activities.

EXHIBIT 14-2

Diagnose Your Work Environment for Leader-fulness

Measure your own workplace's leader-fulness. Evaluate it using the following twenty descriptive characteristics. Score five points if the characteristic exists within your work organization or group, two and one half points if it is only partially present or zero points if it doesn't exist at all. Then add your scores, and refer to the scoreboard below.

(Score 5 points if 100%; 2.5 if 50%; 0 if 0)

1. Everyone in my workplace is encouraged to talk informally about new ideas and ways of organizing or thinking about a topic (plan, product, or process).

2. At meetings or other formal gatherings, employees are encouraged to talk about issues, express ideas and thoughts with every person, and get a chance to speak and listen.

3. We encourage good communication skills and try to teach new ways to communicate more effectively.

4. Everyone in our organization is encouraged to talk about his or her feelings with one or more group members and share his or her emotional thoughts.

5. Group members are praised for showing an involvement with the emotions of others in the group and for communicating compassion and genuine interest.

6. Everyone in my work group has responsibilities or tasks that are well understood by all group members.

7. A manager or a more seasoned employee is specifically responsible for delegating these tasks and for coordinating other tasks.

8. Everyone in my group is encouraged to take on more responsibilities, both spontaneous and planned.

9. I praise my group members for attracting, getting along with, and receiving support from other members and for accepting criticism when things don't go well.

10. I encourage my group members to offer instruction on how to solve a problem, make a point, or share their personal thinking about a topic.

11. I encourage my group members to work together or to take collective responsibility in planning an event by getting the group and materials thoroughly organized.

12. Our group goes on fun events and activities that help build a togetherness feeling and provide an opportunity for team building.

13. Everyone in my group knows each member's skills, resources, strengths, and weaknesses.

14. I praise my group members for calling upon other members to use their skills in appropriate situations or activities.

15. As a group member, I have a feel for the developmental needs of each member in the group and can answer, "What are your needs?" the same way that the member would.

16. I encourage my other team members to learn about each group member and their needs.

17. I talk to my group members about their own individual goals now and in the future, and about the importance of being aware of these goals.
18. I try to create a work environment that invites good listening and question asking.
19. I recognize the importance of group rituals by establishing daily time together, weekly gatherings, and monthly or annual events.
20. I encourage risk taking and accept that group members will make mistakes.

SCOREBOARD

60+	Strong environment. However, values-based leadership will further leverage the already strong work setting that exists.
40-60	Problems exist. Values-based leadership will greatly help, but group leaders need to take a very active teaching role.
Below 40	Stop! Take a deep breath. Begin developing a plan that will address practicing each leadership behavior.

A Flexible Scorecard

Take your test results as a helpful, but by no means permanent, scorecard of how your workplace is doing in teaching leadership. Remember that your score can easily change. You can increase the learning within your organization by igniting these and new leadership skills in your employees. Encourage them to communicate, emotionally and professionally, with other group members, take responsibility for selected tasks, learn how to accept criticism, teach others, share leadership, and use the resources of the group. The workplace *is* the educator for teaching these leadership skills. They will facilitate and guide the values-driven change process.

Chapter 15

Building
a Values-Ful Culture

To take the wrong stream at this period of the season, two months of the traveling season having now elapsed, and to ascend such stream to the Rocky Mountains or perhaps much further before we could inform ourselves whether it did approach the Columbia or not, and then be obliged to turn and take the other stream would not only lose us the whole of this season but would probably so dishearten the party that it might defeat the expedition altogether.

Lewis, June 3, 1805
Lewis & Clark Expedition

What would happen to the group of explorers on the Lewis and Clark expedition if they did take the wrong turn? Would they survive their strategic error—that is, complete their journey on the Oregon Trail and reach the Pacific Ocean? Or, would they become so discouraged as to end their exploration outright, forcing them to pack up their covered wagons and remaining supplies and navigate back to the East Coast?

The answer depends on whether or not the group had created a values-ful culture. A values-ful culture creates a sense of belonging among group members. It gives them an identity. It brings them together and enables them to do far more than they could as individuals. There is an internal togetherness that is communicated outward. It turns the group into a cohesive energy source and helps them fit externally with their environment. A values-ful culture serves as the compass to guide explorers on their expedition. If a values-ful culture has been built, maintained, and perpetuated, then Lewis and Clark will counteract, deal with, and survive their difficulties to reach the Columbia River. The expedition did succeed, and the group made it. The goal for the journey was achieved. The group's leaders fostered a values-ful culture. They encouraged equal participation in decision making, supported risk taking, confronted change, developed a sense of community, conveyed passion and a strong emotional conviction, and instilled values that generated self-confidence and a belief in the purpose of the expedition.

Values are enduring beliefs. If values are in place, it is likely that the "expedition," or task at hand, will endure hardships of any kind. If a group has established and clearly identified what it highly regards, cherishes, and believes in—its values—then it will be able to handle the disheartening and challenging ups and downs that happen along any journey. Similarly, if a work organization has a values-ful culture, it, too, will be able to survive the bumps along its road.

There are two characteristics of values that are critically important to highlight. First, values influence the decisions that we make and impact the courses of action that we take. If a group has commonly agreed-upon values in place, then the group's decisions and actions will be influenced by them. The group will be able to handle "mistaken turns" during their own organization's journey. Second, maintaining our values requires both commitment and risk taking. A values-ful organization is made up of a group of people who have identified a core set of values that are important to them. They have prioritized these enduring beliefs. They have organized them into a value system. Holding onto their values requires a commitment to them. And when they are in place—and commitment is strong—then greater risk taking is possible. If your work organization has a values system in place, then commitment to ideas, actions, decisions, directions, and turns in the road is going to be intense. Greater comfort with risk taking will also occur because the group has a reason to believe.

Equality Is Paramount

The workplace must nurture the value of equality. Each person is important. Each person has equal significance within the organization. This does not assume that all members have the same skills or equal "gifts." There are major differences between one another's strengths. However, it does mean that each person in the workplace has unique talents that contribute to the group's power base.

The workplace should be viewed as a democratic community. A community, though, is very different from a family. In a real community, the members that comprise it share an equality in their stature, roles, and relationships with each other. In contrast, families tend to be patriarchal and hierarchical. In fact, to describe the workplace as a family is fallacious, since most families are not democratic and do not treat their members as equals. Most family settings end up having unequal participants—the father and mother are the authoritative figures or "leaders."

We believe that families should be considerably more democratic and should replicate a community to a much greater extent. But most are not. Many organizations then take on the characteristics of the autocratic family far more than those of a democratic community. Rudolf Dreikurs, M.D., in his book *Children: The Challenge* provides a valuable list of characteristics for both as depicted in Exhibit 15–1. Perhaps you'll recognize some of them as descriptive of your own family or organizational workplace.

Autocratic families or organizations do not promote the concept of equality. For a values-ful culture to exist, equality must be established. But how do we build and maintain a values-ful culture? The answer obviously lies in the democratic community.

Democratic community building, stresses Dreikurs, requires a knowledgeable leader who recommends that action be taken by the entire group when it is necessary for the group. There is no authority figure who stresses, "You do it because I said you had to." This type of power and pressure would be inappropriate and

EXHIBIT 15-1

Autocratic versus Democratic Characteristics

Autocratic	Democratic
• Authority figure	• Knowledgeable leader
• Power	• Influence
• Pressure	• Stimulation
• Demanding	• Winning cooperation
• Punishment	• Logical consequences
• Coercion	• Encouragement
• Imposition	• Permit self-determination
• Domination	• Guidance
• You do it because I said to	• Listen! Respect one
• Prestige-centered	another
	• Situation-centered

ineffective. It dominates and imposes the demands of one over the others. Instead, the leader listens and respects the other group members, encourages independence, and offers guidance in the spirit of cooperation. Rather than punishment, there are logical consequences that "teach"—a person is allowed to experience the consequences of his or her actions, providing an honest and real-world learning situation. Encouragement is given to create a sense of accomplishment and self-respect. Encouragement nurtures the self-concept.

The leader of this type of community is much like an educator. Dreikurs states: "A good leader inspires and stimulates his followers into action that suits the situation. So it must be with parents. Our children need our guidance. They will accept it if they know we respect them as equal human beings with equal rights to decide what they will do. . . . We can create an atmosphere of mutual self-respect and consideration and provide an opportunity for the child to learn how to live comfortably and happily with others. We need to arrange learning situations without showing a lack of respect for the child or for ourselves."

In his foreword to *Children: The Challenge*, Dreikurs stresses that "parents have to learn how to become a match for their children, wise to their ways, and capable of guiding them without letting them run wild or stifling them." We propose that leaders in the workplace take a similar posture. Consequently, we have adapted Dreikurs' thirty-four ways to help children grow to the principles of democratic community building in organizations, as depicted in Exhibit 15–2.

EXHIBIT 15-2

Principles of Democratic Community Building in Organizations

1. Encourage the employee.
2. Avoid punishment.
3. Use natural and logical consequences.
4. Be firm without dominating.
5. Respect the employee.
6. Induce respect for order.
7. Induce respect for the rights of others.
8. Eliminate criticism and minimize mistakes.
9. Maintain routine.
10. Take time for training.
11. Win cooperation.
12. Avoid giving undue attention.
13. Sidestep the struggle for power.
14. Withdraw from the conflict.
15. Action! Not words!
16. Don't shoo flies or nag—give it your full attention until there is change in behavior.
17. Use care in pleasing—have the courage to say "no!"
18. Avoid that first impulse—do the unexpected.
19. Refrain from overprotection.
20. Stimulate independence.
21. Stay out of fights.

22. Be unimpressed by fears.
23. Mind your own business.
24. Avoid the pitfalls of pity.
25. Make requests reasonable and sparse.
26. Follow through—be consistent.
27. Put them all in the same boat—treat all employees equally.
28. Listen!
29. Watch your tone of voice.
30. Take it easy.
31. Downgrade "bad" habits.
32. Have fun together!!!!
33. Talk with them, not to them.
34. Establish a Community Council.

The "family council," as Dreikurs calls it, or Community Council as we have adapted it to our workplace, could offer a means of resolving problems in the workplace. It is a group elected by members of the organization to discuss problems and generate solutions. It meets at the same time every week or month with everyone expected to be in attendance. If participants are not able to come, then they must abide by the decision of the group. Remember that it is important that each member can bring any problem up to the group. As a unified group, a solution is reached with the course of action decided upon by the entire group—consensus is the operable norm. The key to success, notes Dreikurs, is the "willingness of all members of the community to approach a problem as being a community problem. This approach develops mutual respect, mutual responsibility, and promotes equality." Equal participation in decision making is critical to the group's success. It helps build a values-ful culture.

Total Participation in the Organization

People invest their lives in their work organizations. There must be greater respect for them as individuals. They want a sense of involvement and participation. They want to participate in the organization's culture, share its values, and experience a psychological and emotional attachment. To what extent and in what way they participate tells us how much they are respected. Are they involved in decision making, stock ownership, and profit sharing? Peter O'Toole suggests a mix of these types of participation.

> ...An organization needs to offer both participation in decision making and participation in profits. If you only have participation in profits but not in decision making, people will not see any way of influencing the returns that come to them. If there's participation in decision making but not in profits, they will feel it is illegitimate, because all the gains go to the organization. ("Values Added" by Peter O'Toole. *INC.*, January 1986.)

If employees actively participate, then it is less likely that they will job-hop. Corporate America is filled with job-hoppers! Everywhere you look, people stay for relatively short periods of time—from three months to one and one-half years, sometimes two years! They are not receiving respect within their workplace; they are not being asked to participate in decision making and in profits. And they are not having fun. Yes, the workplace should be fun, too. Fun helps build a values-ful culture.

Fun! Work Can Be Play!

Children learn through play. Jean Piaget's well-known cognitive stages of development are based on the theory of learning through play. Adults can learn through play, too. Isn't it funny that the workplace is supposed to be so very serious. It must go back to the type of leaders, autocratic and regimented supervisors, that existed in factories and now in hierarchical, bureaucratic workplaces. The leader was supposed to watch over and hand down directives "from above." The "leader" was uninspiring, to say the least. These leaders said "no play" because with play it meant to them that no work was taking place.

These "no play" organizations still exist. No, they haven't become dinosaurs. In fact, they outnumber the more democratic playful work settings. Let's take a look at two work organizations where play is encouraged—yes, they say it's okay to have fun while working. We think it is, too! Play helps build a values-ful culture.

Sun Microsystems

Sun Microsystems is eleven years old. Its sales approach $4 billion annually. They are computer innovation leaders within two major trends in the computer industry. John Tortorice in the April l993 issue of *Hemispheres* notes that they are at the forefront of "open computing (nonproprietary systems that are compatible with products from other companies), and the move to distributed computing (decentralized networks to computers)." Tortorice also chronicles that they "lead the way in good old-fashioned fun—under the dictum that all pranks are done on personal time!" Listen to this.

The engineering division does frequent prankstering on the top corporate executives. Tortorice reports the following: The engineers tore apart and put back together a Volkswagen beetle inside the office of the chief software exec, sending him keys to the car at his home. He found out what the keys were for when he arrived at work. . . . The engineers built a platform submerged under water and put the co-founder's new Ferrari on it. Upon arrival at work, they gave him paddles and a rubber raft. . . . The engineers relocated the vice president's office at the bottom of the shark tank at San Francisco's Steinhart Aquarium. He wore scuba gear and shared the tank with a safe tiger shark.

While these anecdotes may be a bit extreme, they certainly illustrate our point.

Southwest Airlines

Southwest specializes in low-cost "short-haul" flights—most are only about an hour long—to twenty-seven cities in thirteen states, making it the ninth largest airline carrier. The airline has three core values, according to James Quick in "Crafting an Organizational Culture: Herb's Hand at Southwest Airlines." These are:

Value 1: Work should be fun—it can be play—enjoy it.

Value 2: Work is important—don't spoil it with seriousness.

Value 3: People are important—each one makes a difference.

Quick simplifies these to values of humor and altruism, and also adds the value of "luv." These three beliefs or values are practiced and reinforced by the airline's founder, Herb Kelleher. He told his "people department" or personnel department, as it is known in other organizations, that he wanted to hire people with a sense of humor. He qualified humor in this way:

"Humor never excludes people, nor does it create joy at the expense of others. Using a sense of humor as one of the hiring criteria at Southwest is at the core of the organization's culture. Kelleher looks for people with a certain attitude (an approach to life, a way of living, or a set of values) that is not narrow, rigid, tightly defined, or restrictive . . . tolerance for human beings, their peculiarities or eccentricities, and their differences is very important." This point of view best demonstrates our fundamental belief in endorsing diversity in any workplace culture.

Besides humor, Quick documents the unusual presence of caring for one another as another important component of Southwest's culture. When an employee's young son had leukemia, 3,000 employees individually sent him cards on their own. (There were only 5,000 employees at the time.) The employees have established a catastrophe fund; they contribute on a regular basis to help those people in the firm who have sudden financial needs.

The Most Important Challenge

The critical challenge to leadership in the workplace is to build, maintain, and perpetuate its culture. It can do this through establishing a set of values. This values system acts as the steering wheel for the entire organization. It enables the leaders to hold the organization in place, creating positive outcomes. Quick continues:

Work is transformed into play; challenge leads to achievement; environmental threats become opportunities; and individual strengths are transformed into collective power . . . We cannot think of organizational culture as a substitute for responsible, problem-solving behavior on the part of leadership. Culture becomes the vehicle through which problems and challenges become addressed, defined, reframed, and ultimately solved. When cultural values do not work in this fashion, they must be modified or jettisoned. The culture is not the end or goal but rather the means.

Leaders must focus on building a values-ful culture. If the goal for their journey is to be achieved, then fun, humor, play, and caring are critical ingredients indeed to this culture.

Supporting Change and Confrontation

To perpetuate their culture, leaders must confront change head-on. Confronting change offers unlimited possibilities to individuals. Change can give individuals a renewed sense of dignity or importance within the organization because it gives them new opportunities to participate and take charge. They can play a key role while working together on teams. A values-ful culture must seek out leaders that encourage varying points of view on the team, even to the point of encouraging confrontational discussions. Disagree! Take others on! Talk openly with one another. No politics. Do things with your heart. Make hard decisions. Don't be afraid of conflict. Take risks to reshape the organization. Be courageous. Make bold changes to transform the work setting. This mindset will perpetuate a values-ful culture. When organizations give individuals the power to change their own culture, they give employees a reason to believe.

The values-ful culture in the workplace must also communicate that it's all right for leaders to be vulnerable. They need to be on the front line—to be seen as real people by others. They need to get employees excited about their core values, help them celebrate their successes, and learn from their mistakes. In so doing, they make change possible. And they make the workplace a more rewarding and meaningful environment. This mindset will help to perpetuate a values-ful culture.

Insecure and defensive leaders are the worst possible kind. They create an impossible backdrop for change. They slow down the change process, particularly if they don't delegate well. The best employees to have around you in the change process are ones that are highly motivated, that is, when there is something inside the person that desires change. When such internal motivation exists, unlimited energy is released. The possibilities are endless.

Dealing with the Change Process

Reluctance to change can cause major problems within an organizational setting. Change should be viewed as a positive characteristic of organizations. The world outside one's place of work is in a constant state of change. Consequently, change does not suddenly end when a project is completed or a product developed. It is an ongoing process—more change will come! And then, more! An organization *needs* change in order to survive and avoid stagnation. Change offers positive opportunities for perpetuating the culture. Within a state of constant change, the values hold the organization together.

Within a workplace, change is not something to be hammered out or experienced only by the leaders. Rather, employees need to be continually brought into this process. In order to reduce resistance to change, they need to be told all the facts and be given the opportunity to work through problems and new challenges and issues as a group. This is called sharing reality. The team or work group lays the information out on the table, then works on the problem together. They decide what to do, share their objectives and plans, and take responsibility for launching them. Most important, their shared values guide their decision making. Thus, the change process must be driven by the organization's core values.

Emotional Depth and Leadership

In the workplace of the past, leaders had to convey financial and strategic depth. Now, and in the future, leaders will need to communicate emotional depth. Leaders must build and guide a values-driven change process. Emotional depth will help them accomplish this goal.

The old management paradigm was to roll with the punches—don't express yourself emotionally because it meant you were weak. Distance yourself—be arrogant! But now, leaders need to be engaging, self-effacing, unpretentious, endearing, and charismatic. Yes, these are all attributes that can be learned, developed, and practiced by leaders. The new leadership paradigm asks you to contribute your total self, express yourself emotionally, show enthusiasm, excitement, and concern about others—to express you *really* care. Add texture to your relationships so that employees and managers link and bond. Show personal warmth, pulling others in by being a good listener and asking questions. This type of emotional communication builds cultural values within the organization. If leadership has this emotional depth, then work organizations can perpetuate a values-ful culture.

A cultural transformation has occurred in the workplace. We used to have employees who gladly obeyed their managers. These managers resisted change. Why wouldn't they? Change threatened their position within the autocratic hierarchical ladder. But, employees have different demands now. They want to participate and be treated as equals. They want to help build the work community, and perpetuate its values. The culture of the workplace is defined by them, too—by their values, beliefs, and norms. They want a reason to believe. They're going to go for it. They aren't going simply to obey anymore. They want to participate in the change process. Values-ful leaders must encourage them to communicate their emotions and interests.

Professional Passion

If the workplace can build a values-based culture and express values leadership, then a major cultural transformation will occur within our work settings. Something will then happen of such monumental, unprecedented significance that it could completely change the complexion of the work force. Employees will be able to express their professional passion.

Professional passion is the opportunity to engage in something we truly love to do in the workplace. It requires that a cultural environment be built that nurtures this freedom. Imagine this. After considerable soul searching, a person finds what he or she wants to do within an organization but learns that the culture of that workplace says "no." That is, the norms and values say you can't express your interests, enthusiasms, even knowledge. You can't engage your creative fire. This restrictive culture is found in nearly every work setting.

However, if professional passion exists, a different mandate is presented. Employees experience the freedom to pursue their professional desires, interests, and skills, applying them to numerous opportunities and problems encountered within the workplace. Work becomes an act of creative professional expression. A professional purity exists because the culture is not prohibitive. Professional passion today is rare. Anomie has replaced it.

An autocratic and normless workplace destroys professional passion. But the lack of this passion will eventually cause the work organization to lose—across all dimensions, from profits to people. The increasing number of people starting their own businesses support the desire for employees to pursue their own professional passion. Entrepreneurs are doing just that. Their professional passion is pervasive. If an organization can build a values-ful culture and nurture values-based leadership, then the workplace will flourish with professional passion.

Building a values-ful culture will take time, effort, stamina, and endurance. But future leaders won't be wondering whether or not to make their "investment." Their employees will mandate that they do so. Our work organization continues its revolutionary evolution.

Part IV
The Future

Chapter 16

Applauding Pluralistic Diversity

The one value that almost all organizations will adopt by 2020 is a belief in and respect for individuals and their personal values. Individuality will be in. Prejudicial discrimination will be out. In organizations, as in society, we will increase our tolerance for the differences among individuals along with their corresponding diverse values. Without a greater and unconditional acceptance of individuals, for who they are, anomie will not be eradicated.

The good news is that we believe a diversity revolution is already under way within our country. While its existence today may still be masked by a buildup over time of discriminatory attitudes and behaviors, the revolution for diversity is alive and well and gaining momentum. However, we still need the next twenty-five years to bring pluralism to fruition, enabling it to reach the stature it deserves in organizations and society. But, it will take some time yet to change the mindsets of many Americans today who remain relatively myopic, prejudicial and narrow-minded about their acceptance of the differences in individuals.

A profound endorsement of pluralism and belief in diversity will set the tone and serve as the foundation for the core values structure of organizations in the future. Pluralistic diversity will eventually be celebrated by future values-based leaders and acknowledged as the one value that must underscore all others. Employees will passionately applaud it, endorse it, and establish norms to reinforce it.

Therefore, the future scenario for organizations becomes crystal clear. Leaders by 2020 will holistically support the need to elevate individuality to the forefront of organizational values. In so doing, support for diversity and acceptance of pluralism will flourish. In turn, employees will become stronger, more self-confident, more dedicated and loyal and more self-fulfilled and satisfied. Increased productivity and enhanced performance will result, thereby energizing organizations and making them a nonanomic entity. While other values will also be decidedly important, it is our belief that pluralistic diversity will be the values cornerstone for the 2020s.

Peter Thorp, the headmaster of the Cate School, a private residential secondary school in Southern California, sums it up well in a letter he sent to all staff members. He takes a bold visionary stand on the urgent need to create a diversity mindset throughout organizations in the twenty-first century. He notes:

> I am committed to making the School a place where many peoples are brought together—where students can learn from each other. For me, diversity is a means to an end, not an end in itself. Let us be a diverse community, and let us recognize the very challenge that term carries with it. In fact, I think that if we are able to bring together people from a wide range of backgrounds and to create a community which enables all its citizens to subscribe to common values while not sacrificing their personal integrity, we all have accomplished something really important, especially given that we live in a world where both nationally and internationally we are witnessing the breakdown of widely-held community values as people are "balkanizing" their outlook on life . . . Let Cate be a place where students learn to respect differences while they are learning that only through common effort will the world be able to solve the great environmental (just to mention one) problem it faces in the future. Our "political correctness" will be the expectation that all people are treated with respect, that no student will be made to feel that his or her background is considered of less worth than any other, and that when we have differences, we will resolve them effectively

because we have worked to establish trust and mutual respect. Our challenge, then, is to work to establish that which is common from that which is different. I think that is a wonderful challenge! As we go about creating the Cate School of the twenty-first century, let us be sure that we enjoy each other's company, that when we disagree, we come to resolution based on mutual respect, that when we have differences we address them directly and forthrightly, and that we never forget why we are here—to provide an extraordinary group of young men and women the chance to make this world a better place. I cannot think of a greater job in the whole world, and I cannot think of a place where I would rather be doing it.

His insights on diversity are eloquently written. In particular, his challenge statement captures the essence of what we must do to make pluralistic diversity really work: "Our challenge, then, is to work to establish that which is common from that which is different." In order to better understand how we can achieve pluralistic diversity, we first need to assess our current state of pluralistic ignorance. By determining our level of nonpluralistic understanding, we can use that as a starting point to determine how far we have to go to reach a pluralistic mindset.

What Is Pluralism?

Now tell the truth. Do you know what pluralism means? Probably not—but don't feel bad. We frequently hear definitions of pluralism that range from: "Isn't that engraved on the back of a silver dollar?" or "It's the process of making a word plural," to "a new form of socialism." Chances are you've heard the term pluralism bantered about, and you may even have used the word to impress your friends socially.

Pluralism means having an openness and nonjudgmental view toward the differences in individuals. It means you believe in equality for all human beings. Period! It requires that you don't discriminate or label people according to their beliefs, attributes, or externally perceived common characteristics. Pluralism means that we don't judge or characterize someone based on attributes they *can't* change, such as gender, age, skin color, or sexual orientation, nor attributes they believe in such as religious affiliation or ethnic rituals.

But belief in pluralism is sorely missing in our society today. Most people don't have the foggiest notion of what pluralism is all about. Even more disturbing, few understand the debilitating impact of pluralistic ignorance. In fact, it may well represent the most serious disease that has pervaded our social fabric beyond anomie. When you have pluralistic ignorance, you "sticker" people and discriminate against them. Unfortunately, this process of discrimination is rampant.

Certain stereotypes come to mind at this point. Yet have you ever asked yourself, "Do I really have the information to judge a group of individuals who appear only to have an alleged set of common characteristics?" Worse than any criminal offense or deadly epidemic, pluralistic ignorance relentlessly eats away at people's self-worth and self-esteem. It's like a spider web. Misperceptions are woven into self-entangling patterns and perspectives. Over time, these patterns begin to shape people's thinking and views on certain types of people. Pluralistic ignorance has a way of trapping you into believing that you really do "know" certain things about "female executives," "over-forty men," "militant blacks," "gay men," and "the Generation X twenty year olds." But the fact is we don't. Misperceptions, biases, and second-guessing conjure up discriminating images of people.

Fear, suspicion, dislike, and negative opinions about all sorts of "minority" groups is driven by two key factors: (1) our own ignorance by not understanding the needs and characteristics of minority groups and (2) our own insecurities about ourselves.

The key point is that one very effective way of building ourselves up and making us feel more secure about ourselves is by putting other people down. By downgrading others, individuals in effect make a statement about how great they are. Nonpluralistic values set up a mindset that ultimately can devastate a community of people. Simply put, people can pigeonhole and categorize individuals based on things they have no control over—that is, skin color, ethnicity, sexual orientation, age, and gender. Individuals cannot stop the aging process or willfully shift their gender or recolor their skin, change their origin of birth, or press a button to shift sexual orientation.

Individuals need to feel part of a group and have a sense of belonging. We say to ourselves, "We don't want to be associated with *them*" because we fear others will reject us.

By maligning people, we weave a threadbare security blanket revealing our own insecurities. This personal insecurity and lack of self-confidence then appears in our workplaces, where it breeds an even greater fear of being rejected.

But bigots, as individuals, demonstrate their pluralistic ignorance and insecurities within themselves. They perpetuate a mindset that continues to break down the core values of our country. Let's not get into a moral debate over homosexuality, race, or gender. It's appropriate to leave these issues in the personal belief category. However, what must stop is our nonpluralistic values system.

Why Do We Have Pluralistic Ignorance?

How could a country that was founded on a belief in diversity and passion for justice and equality for all evolve backwards toward massive pluralistic ignorance? Why do Americans tend to discriminate so quickly?

Even one of the most well-respected management consulting firms, McKinsey, faces the challenge of creating a pluralistic organization. According to *Business Week,* McKinsey has 422 white male directors out of 443 in total. I guess that means 5 percent women and 95 percent men. That certainly does not convey a balanced or even remotely diverse pluralistic values structure. Future clients will mandate greater diversity. It will become an essential ingredient for business success.

In our personal lives, we encounter pluralistic ignorance every day. It's amazing that virtually every time we are introduced as Dr. and Mr. Kuczmarski, the new acquaintance turns to Tom and refers to him as Dr. Kuczmarski. They automatically and unconsciously assume that the Dr. in the family isn't Susan—but rather the man. To take another example, just last week, we overheard a woman say, "I couldn't possibly go out with him; why, he's a _____." Go ahead, fill in the blank. Do you think she completed the phrase with "serial killer" or "rapist"? Or, more accurately, do you think her pluralistically ignorant response was more like: "Hispanic," "Jew," "gay," or "old person"?

In our daily professional life, we run across a lot of good, well-meaning people. But when we canvass the corporate landscape, we don't see many signs of real support for diversity or pluralism at work. Instead, the reign and terror of pluralistic ignorance pervades. In a recent dinner conversation, a colleague shared with us that, "he hired some cheap Polacks to do his construction work." Did it slip his mind that our last name was Kuczmarski? Was he trying to tell us in a nice way that we were cheap? Was he casting aspersions about people born in Eastern Europe? Or was he just pluralistically ignorant? We once heard a female consultant give a great response to a male client who asked her: "Why did your firm send a woman to manage this project?" Her response: "Because the firm couldn't afford to send three men." While that quickly shut him up, his discriminatory thinking remained.

When Will Discrimination End?

Our biases and prejudices must stop. If, as a country, we don't start adopting a values system based on a belief in pluralism, we're destined for continued deterioration and degradation of our work organizations, social communities, and family structures. We need to adopt pluralistic values that accept people unconditionally for who they are. Granted, behaviors of individuals should be evaluated and judged, but not attributes that individuals have no control over or can't change.

In short, our workplace must support and endorse a values system based on mutual respect of co-workers, managers, and executives. Mutual respect is an essential and nonnegotiable value for an organization's future economic or survival success. It's an imperative—not an option.

Examples of discrimination such as the following one are plentiful. In late 1993, a three-judge panel of the U.S. Court of Appeals in the District of Columbia said the U.S. Navy had violated the equal-protection rights of an officer by forcing him to resign from the Naval Academy after he told a superior that he was a homosexual. The court ordered the Navy to give the man his diploma and that he be commissioned as a naval officer.

While the end result of this issue was positive, the incident as a whole is a frightening and terrifying reminder that there is a values erosion pervading our society. We have moved backwards, not forwards. The idea of discharging a naval officer based on his homosexual thoughts and desires is irrational and dangerous. While we fully support discharging someone for behaviors such as engaging in blatant or disruptive homosexual conduct in the military, it is wrong to do so based on *who* someone *is,* how that person feels, and what that person thinks.

A brilliant editorial written by Barbara Ehrenreich in *Time* magazine, May 10, 1993, writes about the gap between gays and straights. She describes the unspoken assumption about human sexuality that seems to pervade our society today. "The human race consists of two types of people: heterosexuals, and on the other side of a great sexual dividing line—homosexuals. Heterosexuals are assumed to be the majority, while gays and lesbians are thought to be a 'minority.' " And yet, many studies have recently shown that homosexuality is genetically based.

The dividing line appears to be getting wider, when in actuality the line is gray. This graying of sexuality suggests that sexuality lies on a continuum with bisexuality, somewhere in the middle. The continuum does not have a right or a wrong end, just different ones. Herein lies the myopic perception of far too many Americans: They think homosexuality is bad. Unfortunately, AIDS has been linked to homosexuals and therefore through this association has "made" them the culprits of this dreaded disease. Not true.

Barbara Ehrenreich concludes, "Quite apart from sex, all men would sure be better off in a world where simple acts of affection between men occasioned no great commentary or suspicion, where a hug would be a hug and not a 'statement.' "

And as Vernon Jarrett, a columnist for *The Chicago Sun-Times,* wrote in a recent column: "Gays were never declared three-fifths human by the Constitution." We agree.

Belief in Pluralism and Diversity

What about the role of pluralism within a company or workplace? One essential value that must be adopted by all organizations is pluralism. Without this essential belief, both workers and management alike ultimately focus on the games of "political correctness" and minority quotas. Both of these seemingly equality-oriented initiatives are in fact the opposite. They support the premise that our organizations indeed *do* discriminate against people. Consequently, needing to be politically correct and adopting equal opportunity hiring practices is a demonstration of our inherent biases. We apparently need rules to force us to accept a wide mix of different types of people rather than having that acceptance be an intrinsic value that guides our daily thinking and behavior.

The point is that when we try to pigeonhole people according to apparently similar characteristics, we don't come out with a smoothly blended, homogenous mixture. Rather, we still end up with a group of different individuals. We wrongfully try to piece together a string of misperceptions and then call it a chain link fence. It's actually chicken wire.

Avoid the word "them." You can't tag a human being or collectively refer to certain types of people as "them." The "them" word is infuriating. "Well, you know, if you let *them* into the military," or "You should hire some of *them* to do some odd jobs around the house." Our key question is: "Who is *them*?" We need to start accepting people for who they are—unique and superbly individualistic. Let's stop trying to judge and change "them" or wish away some aspect of their individuality. The time has come to stop misrepresenting the innate character differences of individual human beings. We need to cease the casual labeling that is applied to people. Putting "bumper stickers" on certain groups is childish and socially irresponsible. These stickers display the driver's own ignorance and insecurity. This, in turn, causes greater "avoidance" of people that don't fit the "acceptable norm." And as a result, organizational hierarchies soon take hold, further perpetuating the "haves" and the "have-nots."

The way to dispel pluralistic ignorance and eradicate the cancerous cells of this social disease is to: (1) actively listen and better understand "them," (2) stop forming preconceived misperceptions about "them," (3) apply only one label to human beings—individuals, and (4) undertake discussions with different "types" of people to overcome the fear and misinformation that are often the roots of pluralistic ignorance. The type casting must be redirected. A new curtain needs to rise, and a new play in America needs to begin—"Pluralistic Appreciation."

Here's an example of what we mean. We can start to overcome homophobia and discrimination against gays by simply changing the jargon. We should eliminate the words homosexual, heterosexual, gay, and lesbian from our lexicon. All people should be referred to as sexuals. Sexuality lies on a continuum rather than at two polarized ends of a spectrum. Rather than trying to pinpoint exactly where an individual falls on this continuum, let's eliminate the spectrum and define everyone's sexual orientation as being just sexual.

Pluralism and the Diversity Revolution

Not since the turn of the last century during the Industrial Revolution has our society ever stood so closely at the edge of a values void. Doomsday talk does not really help this point. But the values void *can* be filled. To move our society to that point we must undergo a revolutionary change greater than any social changes experienced in the past century. Unlike previous societal upheavals, this revolution will alter the face of every societal organization in America. We call it the diversity revolution.

Never again will we experience such a powerful societal movement. It will leave its mark on every organization, large and small. By the year 2020, the diversity revolution will have made a pronounced and positive impact—virtually creating a pluralistically balanced work environment. Powerlessness and alienation will not exist. We will actually have eliminated anomie. This is what makes the diversity revolution so exciting. It is already underway, and it serves as a partial solution to our anomic state.

Organizational diversity will have a very different complexion from the configuration of our white, male-dominated business organizations of today. We will have once again established values that people can believe in. We will have opened up communications so that two men can actually say that they love and respect each other without being brand-named as something derogatory. With the diversity revolution a success, the number of female, black, gay, Jewish, and Hispanic leaders will at worst be equal to the remaining number of white men still in leadership positions.

Even though it started about twenty-five years ago, we are about midway into or halfway through the diversity revolution. During the past twenty years, our society has supported and cultivated several pronounced social causes. These include the Vietnam War, the Equal Rights Amendment, antiracism, pro-gays, pro-choice and pro-life, and AIDS research. The reason why the diversity revolution is in and of itself just now establishing a momentum of its own is because these past and current social causes are finally flowing together, establishing horrific strength and overwhelming power. With 50 years behind it, the Diversity Revolution will have built enough momentum to unleash itself in a permanent and pervasive manner.

The cumulative power of these social and values causes is driving the momentum and the energy to fuel the diversity revolution. In part, anomie is driving this revolution. The rancorous breath of anomie lingers in most all organizations, breaking down their norms and values and causing rootlessness and uncertainty. This negative anomic force, matched with the positive, pro-active momentum of several different causes, will further activate pluralism and diversity in the workplace.

In effect, anomie is ultimately the force that will destroy itself. The awareness-building efforts of women, blacks, gays, elderly, Hispanics, and other groups will finally pay off. Their hard work over the past twenty to fifty years—to have people accept them as individuals—will be realized. We believe the diversity revolution will continue to pick up speed during the next few decades and will eventually impact cultural change within our country.

After the diversity revolution, organizations will look, act, and feel completely different from the way they do now. Beyond having more then 50 percent of the Fortune 500 corporations led by nonmale Caucasians, a shared leadership approach must further support and perpetuate the continuation of diversity. Moreover, pluralism will have become a fundamental value that is no longer questioned, discussed, or argued. Pluralism will just exist. People will no longer be discriminated against because of their age, gender, sexual orientation, place of birth, ethnicity, or religion. People in 2020 organizations will be searching for and evaluating others based on *performance* attributes rather than on prejudicial ones.

Diversity Mindset in a Global Society

We believe it is essential for pluralism to be totally calcified into the marrow of our society and our organizations. As Delores P. Aldridge, founding director of Black Studies at Emory University wrote: "Diversity is a global reality. America's status as a world leader, and its ability to compete in the next century could well turn on its response to the challenge of diversity. Contrary to the melting pot mythology, and popular belief, American culture and institutions do not manage diversity well. Preparing leaders for the global society means putting diversity first."

This astute commentary succinctly supports our premise. That is, our global society must mandate that diversity is accepted and pluralism is applauded. We Americans must move beyond our provincial, parochial, and prejudicial blinders and see the world as it is—a diverse mix of different people from different cultures, countries, and backgrounds. As global companies have already recognized the need to develop and market their products and services differently to one country and the next, so too must leaders recognize the need to accept and support diversity within their management ranks and pluralism in their hiring practices.

The diversity revolution is already showing signs of making headway. Notwithstanding specific company situations, white men are slowly becoming less than one half of the work force. From 1983 to 1993, the percentage of white male professionals and managers dropped from 55 percent to 47 percent. This phenomenon is confirmed in a January 1994 *Business Week* article, "As companies hire and promote more women and minorities, white males are feeling frustrated, resentful, and most of all, afraid. For many white males, the issue is the question of merit—in a rush for a more diverse workplace, they will lose out to more qualified workers."

We believe this concern is unfounded. The fact is that diversity is already alive and well and breathing throughout the world. While many U.S. leaders may still not understand that a global society *has* arrived, future effective leaders will instill a diversity mindset in their workplaces because they will recognize its benefit as a competitive advantage. Yes, leveraging a diverse work force will enable companies to compete more successfully in the global marketplace. In short, winning organizations will deemphasize their focus on gender, white males, race, and ethnicities and will instead recognize the uniquely diverse talents of individuals.

The Self-Perpetuating Diversity Revolution

At some point, possibly in about fifty years from now, we will have an Earth Leader. That's right, a global leader whose job it is to manage and take care of the earth. While the United Nations and the UN ambassador leading the UN can be considered a great step forward in endorsing diversity and pluralism, the UN actually receives little recognition. Americans myopically focus on their own domestic issues, rarely worrying about others elsewhere.

There's one big problem with this type of nationalistic, sovereignty-oriented thinking. There are no geographic boundaries, no air currents, no oceans that are off limits. Eventually, we will all have to recognize that there's only one boundary—gravity. All other boundaries—countries, territories, or states—are superficial. By the time 2030 arrives (see earlier discussion), we predict Americans will have to be speaking more than two languages, reaching out to peoples of all types of ethnic groups and religions. Heterogeneity will exist, and homogeneous groups will be extinct.

Organizations of the future will reflect the need to mix foreign nationals and Americans together, and to have gay and straight men talking to one another in business meetings, not focusing on the sexual orientation of the other. Organizations with a black

CEO will not be referred to as a minority or black company. "Black-owned and managed company" is prejudicial and discriminatory.

Acceptance of our differences and celebration of the power of pluralism and diversity will be the pervasive value by 2030. Anomie will become a word to describe a problem that organizations used to have—a problem of the past.

Chapter 17

Marketing Values
to Consumers

Consumers wrestle with the same lack of norms and values as employees do. Consumers experience social anomie and instinctively search for values to provide meaning to their lives. They seek proxies and substitutes that can fill their values void. Consequently, more and more, consumers are beginning to buy products and services that offer values they can relate to. While price, quality, reliability, and performance will continue to serve as primary purchase determinants when consumers go shopping, the values conveyed by the products, and the companies that make them will become ever more important in our valueless society. Simply put, consumers are trying to buy products and services that convey the values they are seeking.

Admit it. "Values" buying has happened to you and me. Just ask yourself if you've ever felt that inexplicable "pull" of your values when you go shopping. What happens when you're faced with a shelf full of, let's say, dishwasher detergent? A sea of brand names floats before your eyes. They all claim to be new and improved. They're all priced within pennies of one another. Some even have similar color patterns on the box. You're busy, and you don't have time to compare the minute differences between each type of dishwasher detergent. But wait . . . there's the brand that your mother used for years—and swore was the best—as you were growing up. You let the feeling of certainty creep into your mind. You actually feel a vague sense of comfort about this product. You pluck it off the shelves and wheel on down the supermarket aisle. It's another victory for values marketing.

At a time when traditional values are missing from our daily lives, familiar products can become surrogates to help fill the gap.

For example, when Ben & Jerry's launched Cookie Dough Ice Cream, they were capitalizing on the feelings of nostalgia that are associated with the concept. Cookie dough is something many of us ate as children when mother was trying to bake. Or take Kellogg's marketing approach on its old standby, Sugar Frosted Flakes—its key message is to enjoy the cereal you once loved as a kid.

Values marketing helps to explain the popularity of other vintage products such as Pop-Tarts, Ivory Soap, and graham crackers. Baby boomers who have happy after-school memories of devouring graham crackers and milk are now feeding them to their own kids. And they are still eating graham crackers themselves. Keebler Grahams, the number-two brand in the category in 1992 grew 39 percent while sales of Nabisco Honey Maid, the top brand, grew 13 percent,. And the successful introduction of Teddy Grahams in 1988 helped get consumers thinking again about the old-fashioned traditional product.

What are these marketers trying to do—tap into consumers' state of rootlessness or lack of shared norms and values. While at first this may appear manipulative or exploitative, it actually fills a void in consumers that our institutional society has generated.

Consumers for sure have recognized the need to start taking care of our environment. This is a cause that has stamina and endurance. "Green" products grew to $121 billion in sales in 1993 and are expected to exceed $150 billion by 1997. Environmental consciousness in the United States has established a strong and growing presence. In its fourth annual "Green Gauge" report, Roper Starch Worldwide, Inc., a research organization, finds that "fifty-five percent of Americans polled consider themselves environmentally active, up from less than half in 1990."

But values marketing is about much more than nostalgia. At times, the product itself conveys a value, such as SnackWells cookies by Nabisco, which communicate healthiness and implicitly suggest "good-for-you." The value of taking care of ourselves is instilled in this product. At other times the package or the box conveys the value, as with Celestial Seasonings teas. The printed words on the box provide a treatise on the evils of government debt. This is certainly a value most taxpayers can relate to. And often the values are communicated and created through advertising. Volvo clearly advertises the value of safety. Their television ads showing a Volvo crashing into a wall make a stunning visual impact and, at the same time, a memorable values statement. Who doesn't want a safe car for the family?

Other products appeal to "family" values and may substitute for a lack of family values in the mind of a consumer. Products such as Quaker Oatmeal or Campbell's Soup may be purchased as a reinforcement of or substitute for the family values of an anomic consumer.

Values marketing communicates to consumers so as to pull on their heartstrings, invade their inner sense of values, and make them feel good about themselves in buying the product. People ultimately buy the values of a company and its products. Consumers are heading in this direction. Manufacturers and service providers need to catch up. While we have moved beyond demographics to better understand psychographic characteristics of consumers, we have yet to reach one further stage of consumer understanding that will be critical for successful marketing in the future—valuegraphics. This will become the new cornerstone for market researchers to uncover—the underlying values of consumers in various segments. This will enable values segmentation to be the basis for developing new products and targeting values-marketing spending initiatives. Valuegraphics will provide marketers with an understanding of the consumer values that influence decision making and purchase intent of products and services.

Consumers will buy more and more in the future based on a desire to satisfy their values satisfaction needs. And values marketing makes good business sense: It provides a solid platform for competitive differentiation and strengthens and reinforces employee commitment and loyalty to organizations. Values marketing works. Companies have already demonstrated its potential to drive success. Many *other* companies will, too, in the future.

Why Do Values Marketing?

It is becoming more and more difficult to differentiate "commodi-
ty" products and services. One way that many companies are
keeping from becoming just another me-too product on the shelf
is by creating a "value-image" association with their product or
service. By creating a link in consumers' minds between particular values and a specific product or service offering, the customer
can become "drawn" to that particular product based on the values it conveys as opposed to choosing one of the alternatives that
is not differentiated by implied values.

For example, if people make an association with a product
such as Pepsi and with youthfulness as a value, they may be more
apt to choose it than to buy Coke, especially if they are trying to
feel younger again.

But values marketing also embraces a concept commonly
known as cause marketing. We believe that this approach is in
actuality a subset—or early incarnation—of values marketing.

Cause marketers recognize the power of tapping into the
social responsibilities of their consumers, and they strategically
pursue the development of programs and products that capitalize
on those commitments.

A few years ago, when you read about companies such as
Ryka, The Body Shop, or Ben & Jerry's, the typical manager
response was: "It's nice that some companies are recognizing the
importance of values." Cause marketing represents a major new
trend that has already begun to restructure the fundamental way
marketers try to sell their "wares" to consumers. These examples,
as well as an increasing number of other companies, are boldly
proclaiming their involvement with social causes such as hunger,
the environment, and human rights.

What does this mean? Cause marketing recognizes that the
purchase of almost any product or service can carry with it a host
of personal value differences. Cause marketers understand that
social causes can be used to influence consumer decision-making.
What's more, purchase intent can be directly linked to an individual's set of norms and values.

In today's anomic society, where people feel isolated, alienated, and, in short, normless, customers are searching for a proxy or

substitute approach to building roots or norms back into their lives. Cause marketing aims to do just that.

How to Undertake Values Marketing

Can higher prices, margins, and profits be realized by companies that undertake values marketing? You bet they can. Not because anyone is exploiting consumers, but rather because a real need is being met—a values need. One of the ways to embark on a values marketing campaign is through the medium of advertising and communications. In early 1994, General Motors launched a most impressive values marketing advertising print campaign. Full-page newspaper ads did not talk about the luxury features, speed, or four-wheel-drive benefits of their cars. Rather, they advertised values—hard-core values that penetrate more deeply into the values fabric of potential purchasers than any functional performance benefits could. The following advertising copy from two sample ads clearly conveys strong values. While the obvious intention of the ads is to sell more cars, they illustrate a clear picture of the company's internal culture by showing employees making their own values statements. Not surprisingly, these values statements mirror GM's intended values memorably.

Liz Wetzel, a member of the Cadillac Design Team at General Motors, spends a fair amount of time listening to consumers react to her ideas. This is not always fun. Human nature being what it is, most people instinctively want to discount views that don't square with their own. Sometimes responding to customer input means scrapping a beloved notion. It can mean a costly retooling or a delay in production. So be it. These days at General Motors, the customer isn't just somebody with an opinion. The customer is a colleague with a whole lot of clout.

This ad would have consumers believe that General Motors takes them seriously—that they really do count. GM wants consumers to feel as if they are partners with them, as if they are part of the group or a member of the family. Whether or not the campaign sells more cars remains to be seen. But, given how personal a car is for many people, it makes a lot of sense to tap into consumers' emotions and provide a values statement on the quality and care that goes into a GM car. One other example of a GM values-based ad was:

> What if you ran a division of General Motors and were due to debut an important flagship model . . . and it wasn't quite ready? Just a few glitches that meant not every car coming off the line was just right. What would you do? Here's what Chevrolet's Jim Perkins and his team did; they pulled the plug on the introduction and said, "When we know we've got it right, we'll bring out the car." That night, Jim Perkins did what people who do the right thing always do. He got a good night's sleep.

This ad speaks for itself. It's personal and real. It's a classic case of values-based marketers identifying the values that will provide meaning to their consumers, and then matching those in the products being made and messages being conveyed. Of course, the major challenge in values marketing is *delivering* on the values conveyed. Once consumers feel as if they've been duped or deceived (in that the values communicated don't match or aren't supported by how the product performs or how reliable is the service provided) they won't be back to buy again.

One of the most superb examples of values marketing is Anita Roddick's offbeat The Body Shop. While her retail chain of skin and hair care products has been growing by leaps and bounds, as profits soar, The Body Shop is unlike the local cosmetics shop around the corner. The Body Shop markets *values*—not products. They market community care, human rights, environmental protection, social change, and belief in the individual. The uniqueness of The Body Shop is almost staggering compared to more typical retailers. This chain does no advertising. Salespersons are trained to *educate* consumers who shop there rather than going for the sale. Employees are highly motivated—they feel good about their work. They feel as if they belong to a group that enhances consumers' passions and feelings about themselves. They have a spirit that conveys care, responsibility, and a sense of community. They provide values to consumers. The Body Shop gives employees *and* customers a reason to believe. The Body Shop exudes passion.

Anita Roddick relates to Frances Lear in an August 1993 interview, "Passion persuades. More than intellectual debate, more than reasoning, more than strategy plans. It all makes sense if your passion is in service to something other than yourself." Roddick, a strong advocate of social change, believes that profitability does *not* have to be the primary and utmost objective of businesses. In Harlem, The Body Shop contributes 50 percent of its profits to local community projects. Its "Trade Not Aid" program encourages Third World countries to grow ingredients or produce finished goods in exchange for employment by The Body Shop. And Roddick herself feels strongly that "companies have a responsibility to give something back—not only to shareholders but to their communities as well."

Wow! Do you have any doubt that this is a wonderful example of a values-based leader who does values marketing from a values-ful culture? She states, "When you're not obsessed with profits, the imagination soars. We're trying to use our products as emissaries of social change. We bring political and human rights issues into the workplace because we don't know how to separate trading from humanity." This woman does represent the values-based leader who will become the norm by 2020. But we have a couple of long decades in front of us until the idea reaches the majority of organizations. The Body Shop Organization Pledge is a wonderful example of a values-ful culture, but because they print it on product information that goes to consumers, it's used, too, as values marketing. The four core values of respect to customers, environment, community, and life are profoundly described in their values statement as depicted in Exhibit 17–1.

So The Body Shop is at least one great example of the 2020 values marketing company that has already arrived—twenty-five years ahead of time.

Values Marketing Is Here to Stay

In March 1994, *Fortune* magazine cited a poll by Roper Starch Worldwide taken on social responsibility. "Customers like companies that support good causes. When choosing between products of equal price and quality, 78 percent of the respondents said they

EXHIBIT 17-1

The Body Shop Values Statement

We *respect* our customers by offering them a range of sizes and keeping packaging to a minimum. So you pay only for as much—or as little—as you want. And instead of expensive advertising campaigns, we have opted for a non-exploitive approach that emphasizes health and well-being.

We *respect* the environment by doing all we can, at every stage of our operations, to avoid any environmental damage. We incorporate naturally-based, close to source ingredients as much as we can. We recycle waste whenever possible. And in most countries we offer a refill service to our shop customers on selected bottle products: this is waste conscious and cost effective.

We *respect* the community, at both the local and the international levels, in which we function. The Body Shop believes that principles must work hand in hand with profits to improve living and working conditions around the world for all people in need.

Most fundamentally, we *respect* life. The Body Shop is against animal testing for cosmetic purposes; we believe it is both cruel and unnecessary. We choose to use alternative non-animal safety tests and extensive research with human volunteers. Besides, many of our ingredients have been used safely by human beings for thousands of years.

The Body Shop has an ongoing commitment to bringing you effective products based on caring policies. If you'd like to know more about us, ask in your local branch of The Body Shop or drop us a line—we want to hear your suggestions.

---

would buy the one made by a company that contributes to medical research, education, and the like. Two-thirds of respondents said they would *switch* brands to a manufacturer that began to support a cause they deemed worthy." These statistics provide staggering support for values marketing. Consumers *are* becoming far more values conscious. To a great extent, the increased need intensity for values is a result of the ever-increasing and pervasive anomie that encroaches our society. The point is: (1) consumers are indeed getting much smarter and more sophisticated in their purchase decision process; (2) values are being sought by consumers, and if they perceive values satisfaction in buying a specific product or service, it will influence their purchase selection; and (3) consumers' decision-making process in purchasing goods and services will be increasingly shaped by a company's values, the values embodied in its products and services and the values messages communicated.

The 1994 *Fortune* article continued: "One-third of those surveyed said they were more influenced by a company's social activism than by its advertising." Now that's another remarkable finding that substantially supports values marketing. Many consumers would much rather have millions of corporate advertising dollars be used to help society, improve communities, counteract crime, or enhance the environment than spend the money on TV-viewed dancing grapes or talking animals. Television advertising is a waste of money given what's being advertised today. Coca-Cola and Pepsi spend well over $100 million annually in media advertising. What if, just what if, all that money were spent on advertising and programs that truly were aimed at communicating values to help improve humankind and our American society? Can you imagine the impact $100 million would have on increasing societal awareness of the need to replace anomie with values and norms? Just two companies could significantly influence the values structure of our society. Many people are subconsciously aware of the values void problem, but we need many more people to become cognizant of it. Focusing advertising dollars on the cause of values may very well pay dividends in the future to the companies that choose values marketing over product marketing.

By marketing values to consumers, four key benefits will accrue to future values-based marketers: (1) products and services can be further differentiated from competitive offerings based on the intrinsic or perceived values communicated; (2) consumers are more apt to purchase products they can relate to, especially when it stimulates emotional satisfaction; (3) increased loyalty for the product or company will develop as consumers receive the continuous benefit of values fulfillment; and (4) employees will be more motivated and feel good about making and selling values-based products that consumers feel good about.

From a company perspective, our research suggests three methodological approaches that can be taken to activate values marketing. The three approaches are: (1) invest in and promote causes and social awareness and action programs; (2) design and communicate values into products and services; and (3) convey values that consumers can relate to and identify with by stimulating an emotional attachment to or provide a sense of belonging to a values-ful group. This last approach spans two different types of values sets. One set is values that relate to childhood, young family values and experiences, growing up, nostalgia, school values, and the like. The other set relates to values that bolster an individual's self-identity, self-confidence, and self-esteem. In effect these values enable the consumer to feel part of a values-ful group.

Values-based products, services, and communications programs will help provide consumers with values that are missing in their routine lives. Moreover, it will provide employees with a new sense of meaning and self-satisfaction. It's just as important to identify the external values an organization wants to convey as are the internal values for motivating employees. A values-ful culture bridges the internal values of the organization to the products and services it offers externally. This is a vitally important part of values-based leadership. Keeping the values at the office is not enough. They need to be translated into the products and services that the company makes and sells. Can you remember buying a "lemon" of a car sometime in your past? You probably never bought another car made by the same manufacturer again. Companies can tout values all they want. But they really aren't meaningful until they are linked to the products made or services offered by an organization.

There is a groundswell developing that will make values marketing the right *business* decision in the coming decade. Values marketing will indeed *sell* products and services because consumers will recognize, appreciate, and buy products from values-ful companies. Consumers who see companies spending their dollars for causes, beliefs, and values will develop loyalty and commitment to the company's products.

It's going to be smart business for marketers to become social advocates rather than product hawkers. Consumers acknowledge goodwill initiatives and cause support that will benefit minority groups, education, research, and environmental and social programs. Companies can become values-ful and provide values satisfaction to consumers. In turn, consumers will respond favorably to their efforts and purchase their products and services over the competitor who thinks values marketing is a fruitless and useless endeavor. Values marketing will become the future cornerstone for success.

Chapter 18

Looking Toward the 2020 Organization

We must always change, renew, rejuvenate ourselves; other-wise we harden.

— Goethe

Be not afraid of growing slowly; be afraid only of standing still.

— Chinese Proverb

. . . and change we must. During the next twenty-five years, our organizations and society itself must undergo revolutionary change. The degree of change will be multifaceted and deeply penetrating. It could dramatically shift the way most individuals feel about themselves. Most people could again believe in their own potential, revel in a feeling of self-worth, and be robustly motivated. Employees could once again be excited about going to work in the morning. All of them could find a reason to believe—in themselves and in others.

If organizations recognize the harmful effects of anomie and strive to reinstill norms and values into our work lives, the year

2020—twenty-five years from now—will be a healthier, more productive era. The anomie of the past will have been pushed aside and a new feeling of being attached will pervade the workplace. Individual values will be back. Relationships will be in style. Society will have a renewed sense of right and wrong. People will be happier and more self-confident.

Throughout this book, we have emphasized the threat of anomie that confronts organizations and individuals. The underpinnings of anomie recognized in 1895 have once again surfaced to the forefront in 1995. If organizations effectively reduce anomie, they may have the potential to become highly successful values-based organizations where individuals thrive and grow. These will be the organizations of 2020.

But organizations will need to undergo dramatic change, set aggressive goals, and ensure that norms and values are in place before reaching a values-based state.

Anomie Revisited—1895–2020

In 2020, approximately 125 years will have passed since Emile Durkheim coined the term anomie. Increasingly isolated by their highly specialized work, employees had lost a sense of community in the late nineteenth century. The feelings of dependence and stimulation from membership in a common group did not exist. Individuals became separated. In 1895, the separation took different forms. It was present personally within each individual; socially, given the fragmentation of social relationships; and organizationally, through the isolation by specialized work tasks.

Personal separation can occur when the group's needs and concerns do not match the individual's. Durkheim identified two consciences in each of us—describing the duality of human nature. The first conscience involves our individual needs and concerns. When we act out of self-interest, our actions and conduct address personal requirements. The second conscience involves our membership in a larger group. When we act out of concern for a larger group, we act in the interest of its members.

Social separation also occurred in 1895 because social relationships were fragmented. There was a sense of isolation. It was more difficult for individuals to interact with one another and become integrated into the community. There were no shared norms to guide their behavior. The anomic person was socially detached, alienated, and cut off from the mainstream of society.

Durkheim also identified what he called anomic division of labor. Individuals, who were increasingly isolated by their specialized tasks, lost all sense of being integral parts of a larger whole. When the organizational parts become separated, preventing norms to be established by the group, anomie occurred.

Group norms are the foundation for social glue within an organization. Norms serve as guidelines to think, feel, and act in a particular way. If they are shared by individuals throughout the entire group, then they are group norms based on shared expectations or group agreements.

Today, our places of work do not have this glue. Business and other organizational leaders need to understand these forces and apply new effort within the workplace to combat anomie. An absence of clear norms is causing feelings of alienation. If there are very few norms to guide personal behavior, then the organization will break down. The state of normlessness will impact the emotional condition of the individual employee. If norms are not shared with others, or if they are ambiguous and inconsistent within the workplace, or if shared values are not in place, then there are widespread problems. This is where we are now. In the year 1995, there are widespread troubles indeed in the workplace.

One-Hundred Years Later—1995

In 1995, U.S. organizations lack clear-cut norms and values to guide the conduct and aspirations of employees. Society and its organizations are characterized by anomie. Today—one hundred years later—we use the concept of anomie to explain our current condition within organizations, whether they be small, nonprofit groups, small entrepreneurial companies, large corporations, governmental agencies, or schools. Anomie has helped us understand the personal disorientation of employees in the workplace. Individuals lack a sense of belonging to any cohesive group or community. Again, a century later, most feel an overpowering sense of *separation*—in their personal, social, and work groups.

They need norms and values that they can relate to and build upon.

If we jump ahead to the year 2020, we may see an employee such as Michael Thomason, an administrative assistant who works with Worthington Jones, the executive director of a not-for-profit organization. Michael has been associated with "his boss" for six years now, since 2014, and they have developed a warm, caring, and enriching professional relationship with each other. Michael has an intuitive sense and bond with Worthington that often enables him to anticipate Worthington's requests and virtually finish sentences and thoughts before Worthington completes them.

Michael and Worthington trust each other. They work together well. They have two fundamental principles in place: Always be open and honest with each other, and respect each other's individuality. Somehow, this simple "norm and value statement" between them has provided a strong relationship—bonding them together. This has enabled the two of them to flourish. Worthington has been on a "fast track," and Michael has really helped to further accelerate Worthington's career. Michael gets personal satisfaction from that.

Even though Michael plays a "behind-the-scenes" job function, he has always felt great about his job—because of Worthington. That's because Worthington has consistently made Michael feel an integral part of the team. Michael has become his trusted adviser and confidant as well as his professional friend.

Michael would describe his job to other friends in this way: "For as long as I can remember, Worthington has always treated me with kindness, respect, and consideration. He expresses appreciation almost daily for my initiatives and gives me praise often. He makes me feel good about myself. Just being near him provides me with an inner sense of self-confidence. It's hard to explain—Worthington just really knows me and understands me."

The Leaders of the 2020 Organization

The 2020 organization will enjoy a new *vision* for the workplace. Our vision sees organizational values in place, that are based on individual values, stemming from the personal beliefs of the employees. Similarly, group agreements or norms exist, originating from individual attitudes. Bold changes have occurred in the workplace. The platform for these fundamental changes will be the recognition of and appreciation for individual values and norms.

The Values Adoption Process (VAP©) and Norms Action Plan (NAP) will be employed to collectively develop the organization's values and norms. Organization and People Pledges will become tangible signs of these efforts. Employees will be integrated into their workplace through regenerative osmosis, small group work, socialization, mentoring, and careful recruiting. Each of these integrative mechanisms will weave individuals into the culture of their workplace. A sense of community or emotional glue will be created to alleviate anomie. Furthermore, the workplace will become a pathway to personal growth and self-satisfaction.

Leaders will lead the values in the 2020 organization. Leaders will be effective at building personal relationships, knowing the personal goals of each group member, having a feel for group members, allowing group conflict to occur, managing learning, sharing responsibility, communicating effectively, linking internal culture with external performance, displaying passion, and supporting diversity. Diversity will be a key value that gives energy to the 2020 organization. Leaders will promote diversity to keep organizations creative and innovative. Leading from the inside out, leaders will tap into the feelings of each group, help employees experience success, focus on developing communication skills, and facilitate personal growth and self-awareness. In addition, leaders will make quicker, more heartfelt decisions, actively listen, use the collective knowledge of the group, and involve the group in ownership-taking.

Leaders who recognize and address the needs of the group will have mastered six skills. Specifically, leaders will communicate emotionally and passionately with group members, take responsibilities for selected tasks, share leadership, know how to nurture and accept criticism, know how to teach others, and know and use the resources of the group.

Furthermore, a values-ful culture will have been created—a culture that promotes equality and encourages participation within the organization. Humor and fun will also prevail. Employees will express their professional passion. While these characteristics will exist internally within the 2020 culture, our values-based 2020 organization will communicate values externally as well. Values will guide customers and impact the marketing strategies of values-driven 2020 organizations.

A Day in the Life of a Leader—2020

John Howard is worried about his presentation to the Shared Leadership Team this afternoon because he's requesting $15 million in incremental capital to fund his project. Of course, he knows he shouldn't be nervous. Since he joined the company in 2015, he has truly enjoyed working for this $500 million services business. As marketing leader, he has been concentrating on building market share and margins and he has been achieving his goals.

John knows that the two key reports have already been completed and reviewed by each member of the Shared Leadership Team: the *PCC* report (Personal Conviction and Commitment) as well as the *BAR* (Business Analysis Report). Both reports had been completed for senior leadership to review. The PCC includes a detailed description of John's personal commitment to this project, why he believes in its value, and the benefits it will provide to consumers. Moreover, the report encompasses the intrinsic values to be conveyed in the new service, John's vision for how best to grow the new service into a profitable venture, ideas on values marketing themes, and John's perspective on how this new service will have a positive impact on society. The PCC report had been developed and reviewed, of course, by all members of John's cross-functional project team. They, too, were rooting for a "yes" on the project's funding.

The project team has already developed their project values and group norms. John continues to be impressed with how well these project teams work together once the norms have been agreed upon by the group. These norms really do facilitate group interaction and overall effectiveness—very different from his previous company. Although the previous company did have Organization and People Pledges that had been worked up from the employee base, their leaders did not reinforce small-group norms as well as his current company does.

The *BAR* report (Business Analysis Report) clearly shows a positive return on investment, few competitive barriers, and a high-need intensity for this new service by customers. The key service values, defined in the PCC, will be used as the cornerstone for the advertising campaign, which is primarily targeted to Vacation Learning Centers. These VLCs are at luxury sun spots where fascinating speakers, interactive learning exercises, and personal self-discovery complement the learning experience. Smart marketers know people are more open and receptive to services advertising messages at VLCs than through their "3DI-tele-visions" (three-dimensional and interactive televisions attached to computers to provide interactive response capabilities to many programs).

John's automated administrative assistant beeps John's watch and informs him that the conference discussion is scheduled for 1:00 P.M.—in fifteen minutes. John goes over to his home Full-Experience Conference Room, sits down at the table, and turns on the seven floor-to-ceiling video screens, which totally surround him. As he "tunes" into the SLT Conference room, he is able to smell the Italian coffee brewing there that the SLT likes to drink. Within minutes the Shared Leadership Team members walk in, enthusiastically welcoming John to the meeting. Each member asks John a question about some specific issue or project, and a couple of them give John some descriptive praise. John begins the meeting, proposing to discuss the PCC report first. They do, and John can sense that the team has already emotionally bought into his project. His intuitive sense, of course, was right. After twenty minutes of discussing the BAR, the team gives John full approval to pursue the project.

Within seconds, John conference-calls each of his team members with the good news and proposes a date to schedule dinner to celebrate their good news. Work life *is* fun in 2020.

The 2020 Organization

Managers, as we know them today, will disappear. One major shift that will occur having monumental impact on our organizations is the activation of shared leadership and the gradual elimination of managers. Manager suggests one person is superior, the other subordinate. This archaic organizational approach will cease as employees and leaders learn to work side by side as equal partners—together toward achieving an organization's goals.

Establishing group values or beliefs and norms or guidelines for interaction helps "attach" individuals to organizations. Managers, as we see and define them today, do not foster attachment and integrate individuals to their places of work. Frankly, managers are currently the "bad guys" in our typical work organizations. They have *no* inner, emotionally charged, intuitive energy. When they act, they tend to pit themselves against employees in a managers-versus-employees game. When this happens, managers do not view employee values as important. We need organizational leaders who will instill intuitive energy, fresh perspective, and creativity into the workplace. Managers need to become leaders who are full of intuition, feelings, and sensing capabilities. If they lack these critical skills, they should become extinct by the year 2020. We need values-based leaders who have vision, belief, and focus.

Energy, insight, and spirit will become infused into the places where we work. To accomplish this, organizations will undergo deep-tissue or endogenous growth. As molecules must be attached to their cell wall, employees must become attached to their organizations to grow.

What must happen in the workplace so employees will thrive and grow?

Employees must become attached to an available and responsive leader and also to their organizations. Employees need to know that a leader cares for them and is there for them—just as children need to know this from their parents. This basic secure relationship between leader and employee will be in place by 2020.

Employees who are not attached to a leader, or are insecurely attached, will become a personal and financial drain to the organization. They will leave the organization without feeling good about themselves or trusting others within their group.

As a leader, being available and responsive is the most important job. Child psychologists use the phrase "good enough parent."

It means that a parent does not have to be brilliant, funny, good in sports, rich, or blessed with many talents. Rather, a parent needs to *be there*—emotionally and physically, so that the child experiences his or her love. Then, this is a "good enough parent." Similarly, a "good enough leader" is emotionally and physically available, not distant, but responsive.

When an employee becomes attached to a leader, that employee is a stronger, more participative member of the workplace. Ironically, "becoming attached" creates employees who are more secure, independent, and liberated thinkers. Unattached employees spend their time trying to play politics, haunted by insecurities of organizational hierarchy. The year 2020 needs to find employees who have strong social ties and positive relationships. These are the benefits of becoming attached. Values-based leadership is the key to achieving our 2020 organization.

As we enter the year 2020, organizations must begin to take on a spiritual dimension. The workplace must help individuals use their personal resources to define their spiritual lives. At the turn of this century we must refocus on why we are alive and what is going on within ourselves spiritually. The workplace can help us do this. For too long, people have used work to achieve only materialism and economic wealth. The places where we work must next take a quantum leap into a completely new arena—spiritual growth and advancement.

Advanced technology will need to be used to help integrate employees to their organizations. Telecommuting and teleconferencing, however, could make matters temporarily worse. Telecommuting means sending employees home to do their work, while equipping them with all the latest technological equipment. They work several days a week or full time out of their homes, fortified by their home computers, fax machines, modems, voice mail, CD ROMs, and, eventually, full-experience video communication (which enables one to experience the meeting as if one were actually there in person). Employees will be able to see and "feel" the person they are interacting with located miles away.

But can video contact with colleagues overcome employee isolation? Being away from the workplace does not facilitate employee contact or interaction on a regular basis. Rather, what we could have is an uncanny replay of Durkheim's 1895 scenario, repeated due to the popularization of telecommunications hardware. If individuals become isolated, norms to guide their behavior and values to identify their beliefs may not be adopted. Anomie could resurface and worsen, with individuals becoming detached again.

To maintain attachment to their organizations, employees must continue to interact with co-workers, although technological advances make it possible to work alone. There are many valuesful mechanisms that can make all employees feel attached. If the home office set-up is to work, then there must be opportunities to socialize with fellow employees on a regular basis. Regular newsletters or electronic mail that provides personal information will also be important, filled with stories about individual employees, arrival of babies—the personal communications that used to be exchanged around the office coffee pot.

The "information superhighway" will facilitate this personal communication. In the twenty-first century, it will flood information into our workplace, not to mention our living rooms! Instead of carrying cars and trucks, the superhighway will carry information using movies, sound, and pictures. This new electronic network is currently being built. Just like a few cars traveling along the old road systems, communications used to entail only phones and cable TVs. In the future, the old copper wires or two-lane roads will be replaced with optical fiber that can carry hundreds of signals simultaneously to create an information superhighway. The workplace of the future will use this superhighway network to reduce isolation and enhance the quality of interpersonal communication.

Besides strategies for ridding the workplace of this potential technological-induced isolation, managers will have to add another expertise area. They will have to lead and manage employees who aren't physically present within the workplace. This will indeed be a challenge. It can be accomplished if a Norms Action Plan and a Values Adoption Process has been developed. We must focus on building norms, values, and new leadership skills—these will provide a way to link all employees, regardless of their geographic locations—around a common purpose.

Goals for 2020 Organizations

Work doesn't have to be the way it was in the past. It can be different. These 2020 goals should reflect and guide the desired changes for all organizations.

Our first goal for the year 2020 is to pluralize the workplace. Everyone is different and the culture within the workplace must encourage and nurture these differences.

Our second goal is to have leaders serve as values brokers and advocates for employees. This means that leaders will help employees find roles where they feel good about what they are doing, express their individual values, and help create a values-ful culture.

Our third goal is to have leaders serve as learning facilitators or socratic teachers. Leaders need to encourage employees to set up their personalized learning goals, offer descriptive praise, and have success "spillover" into other areas in the workplace.

Our fourth goal is to have leaders focus on building employees' self-confidence, self-satisfaction, and security.

Our fifth goal is to have leaders link employees by providing a common mission, values, commitment, and focus.

So, we have our vision of the 2020 organization. Now, we must focus on it. If we focus, continue to focus, and then discipline our focus even more, it will happen. We have to believe. Employees and leaders together have to believe. Miracles can happen! Make a commitment to the vision. And then focus, focus, focus on it! Focus away from anomic-ridden organizations and toward values-based leadership. The infinite power of focus cannot be overstated.

As Bob Howe, the IBM executive who virtually single-handedly created and led a $300 million consulting business for IBM within a three-year period states: "Leaders need vision, discipline, and focus. They need to believe in themselves. They need to believe in their mission. They need to believe they can win!" Indeed vision, true sense of belief, and inner conviction, matched with discipline and focus, *can provide* a powerful fuel to drive any organization toward success.

A Forecast: The Workplace in the Year 2020

By the year 2020 "values-based leadership" will be rooted in the workplace. Ten conditions will signal the end of anomie.

1. There is no disparity between the values of management and the values of employees within the same organization. Rather, there is agreement, with both having the same set of values.

2. The norms and values that have been nurtured and developed within organizations are positive. They reduce stress and tension in the workplace. They create a sense of bedrock beliefs, community, equality, and participation.

3. Leadership does a good job letting employees know how they are performing and acknowledging the contributions of each employee through feedback, descriptive praise, and performance-based monetary recognition.

4. Values-based leadership within the workplace will drive the Norms Action Plan and Values Adoption Process.

5. Individuals will be given more respect, increased responsibility, and freedom. Consequently, they will become happier, more loyal, and cooperative members of the workplace.

6. Leaders will personalize learning in the workplace. They will create learning communities and lead from the inside out.

7. Mentoring will be encouraged to transmit knowledge about norms and values and to increase feedback and job satisfaction.

8. Values will be reviewed and updated as collective individual values evolve over time.

9. Employees will tie their personal goals to the workplace and will nurture long-term relationships by creating "caring communities."

10. Employees will grow professionally, will be encouraged to develop their own talents, and will be able to express their professional passion.

These ten conditions are clearly not present in today's workplace. Rather, most work environments take little or no interest in the individual development of their employees. The personal and professional growth of employees is simply not a high organizational priority today. Nor are norms and values crafted by the employees. A sense of community is difficult to find.

We are optimistic, however, that the current state of anomie can be turned around. We have stressed that if employees share control, then the norms and values of the workplace can be crafted to become highly personal ones. In the next twenty-five years, we must establish values-based leadership within our work organizations. It is essential to bring shared norms and values back to the workplace, along with a new type of leader, who, as facilitator of learning, leads from the inside out. Mentoring is a key tool for integrating the employee into the work organization. *Values-Based Leadership* tells us how to begin. We are believers. We will have to bring new vision, belief, and focus to the workplace. Let's get to "work"!

Index